PRESIDENTIAL LANDMARKS

by

DAVID KRUH and LOUIS KRUH

HIPPOCRENE BOOKS, INC.

Presidential Landmarks
by David Kruh and Louis Kruh

Copyright © 1992 by David Kruh and Louis Kruh
All rights reserved.

For information, address the publisher:
     HIPPOCRENE BOOKS, INC.
     171 Madison Avenue
     New York, NY 10016

ISBN 0-7818-0027-7

First Edition
Printed in the United States of America

Table of Contents

INTRODUCTION

United States Presidents are larger-than-life figures for Americans and people all over the world. As a result, almost everyone is deeply interested in the lives of the Presidents and how they were able to rise to the leadership of the most powerful nation on earth. This fascination with United States Presidents has, in part, been responsible for them being commemorated by hundreds of sites ranging from birthplaces to burial sites. In between, there are a variety of places they have lived, visited, or touched in some manner which imbues them with a sense of history. These include museums, libraries, offices, courtrooms, battlefields, monuments, parks, assassination sites, and more.

The interest in Presidential sites is evident by their drawing power. George Washington's Mount Vernon, for example, attracts more than a million visitors a year. The relatively remote Calvin Coolidge Homestead in Plymouth Notch, Vermont, open only as a summer attraction, draws some 35,000 visitors during the season. In New York, the Franklin D. Roosevelt Library, with about 200,000 visitors a year, is the State's third most popular tourist attraction, "outdone only by the Empire State Building and Niagara Falls," according to the New York Times.

Reasons for visiting these sites vary. Living on Long Island near New York City, our family was fortunate to have many historical sites nearby. Sagamore Hill, the home of Theodore Roosevelt for many years, was a popular place to visit. But each trip was always more than just a chance to gawk at the beautiful home that our twenty-sixth President had built in Oyster Bay. It was also a chance for us to reflect on what had been accomplished by this man. A scion of a rich family, he took up the cause of the poor. A sickly youth, he became one of our country's greatest proponents of physical fitness and the outdoor life. Born in a city, he championed our nation's wildlife. All around this home are reminders of a man who could have spent his life enjoying the fruits of his family's labors, but chose instead to serve his countrymen, ultimately becoming the man who helped define twentieth century America.

This is why, for many, visiting sites related to the Presidents enforces the notion that America was destined to be unique. Unlike the monarchy from which it had revolted, this country was designed to receive its leaders not from a predetermined line of aristocrats, but from the very people that were to be governed. And although our first six choices for President of the United States seem to indicate a lingering predisposition towards an elite class, (all were either gentlemen farmers or lawyers), by the 1820s the electorate began exercising its franchise with a more populist theme, placing men of more modest and simple roots into our nation's highest office.

That is another reason for these sites' popularity. The log cabin is no myth, for by the time of the Centennial several of this nation's leaders had come from what were popularly described as humble beginnings, and in one or two cases could honestly have been described as wretched. Perhaps nothing in our national persona better catches the imagination and stirs the hopes of people than the concept that every young boy, no matter how modest his original station in life, can grow up to be President. To stand within the walls of what was once nothing more than a sharecropper's shack, but is now the site of a presidential birthplace seems to validate Thomas Jefferson's words in the Declaration of Independence that this is a nation where "all men are created equal."

This book was written to provide the first comprehensive guide to virtually all tourist attractions related to United States Presidents. It is also designed to make it easier to plan visits to presidential places of interest which may be nearby or across the country. To make the book as complete as possible it includes a few sites which are the homes of private owners and visiting is not permitted. Please respect their privacy and be satisfied with a view of the property from the outside.

The book is arranged chronologically, and there is a chapter for each president. A biography introduces each chapter and provides some background to the presidential sites surrounding his life. Places of interest which relate to more than one president such as the White House and Mount Rushmore are included in a separate chapter. All sites are fully described and information regarding visiting times, admission charges, if any, and travel directions are provided. Where available, telephone numbers are included and, because changes are inevitable, before starting a trip it is always wise to call ahead to check visiting details.

Writing a guidebook requires the assistance of many people and organizations to supply the myriad of details needed to make the book useful and accurate. It is always a pleasurable and refreshing experience to find strangers willing to extend themselves when writers appeal for help with information and photographs. For their assistance we are deeply grateful to the following individuals and organizations. Any errors or omissions are our own and we would appreciate having them brought to our attention for the next edition.

J. Richard Abell, Public Library of Cincinnati and Hamilton County (Ohio); Abraham Lincoln Tourism Bureau of Logan County (Illinois); Alexandria Convention and Visitors Bureau (Virginia); Joanna Angle, Olde English District Commission (South Carolina); Maria Balsano, Westchester Convention & Visitors Bureau (New York); Bruce Baraniak, Mason Neck State Park (Virginia); Charles G. Barnes, Little White House Historic Site

(Georgia); Bruce S. Bazelon, Pennsylvania Bureau of Historic Sites and Museums; Donna Bedwell, Montpelier; Cynthia J. Beeman, Texas Historical Commission; Mary Bell, Buffalo and Eire County Historical Society; Katheleen Betts, Society of the Cincinnati; Cynthia D. Bittinger, Calvin Coolidge Memorial Foundation; Nancy Blankenhorn, New Jersey Historical Society; Bruce S. Bleiman, The "Beeches"; Leonce Bonnecaze, Pierce Brigade; Lulu Brailsford, Richland County Historic Preservation Commission (South Carolina); Mrs. R.M. Breton; Roger D. Bridges, Rutherford B. Hayes Presidential Center; Diane Brockman, City of Independence Tourism Coordinator (Missouri); David Brook, North Carolina State Historic Preservation Office; Chris Brown, Hall of Presidents Living Wax Studio; Katherine L. Brown, Woodrow Wilson Birthplace and Museum; Mrs. Lawrence J. Brown, Episcopal Churches of King George County (Virginia); Debbie Browning, President Benjamin Harrison Memorial Home; Bruce Brumley, Rough Riders, Inc; Sally S. Cahalan, James Buchanan Foundation; William J. Butvick, New York City Mayor's Office; Thomas A. Campbell, Jr., Galena State Historic Sites (Illinois); Mrs. Floyd B. Case, Millard Fillmore House; Phillip M. Cavanaugh, U.S. Army Quartermaster Museum; Susan Ciccotti, The Octagon; Susan Cohen, Pennsylvania Historical & Museum Commission; Kevin Cartwright, Richard Nixon Library & Birthplace; Muriel J. Case, Aurora Historical Society (New York); Colleen Cearly, Dwight D. Eisenhower Library; Charlottesville/Albemarle Convention & Visitors Bureau (Virginia); Craig R. Channell, Maret School (Washington, D.C); City of Vancouver, Washington; Mary L. Clarke, Mordeci Historic Park (North Carolina); George Cleveland, Grover Cleveland Home in Tamworth, NH; Mrs. Christopher C. Colenda, Jr., College of William and Mary in Virginia; Margaret Conner, Valley Forge Historical Society (Pennsylvania); Robert S. Conte, The Greenbrier; William Copeley, New Hampshire Historical Society; Marygael Cullen, Springfield Convention & Visitors Bureau (Illinois); Cumberland Parks & Recreation Department (Maryland); Margaret Dannecker, Johnson City Chamber of Commerce (Texas); Emma-Jo L. Davis, Fort Jackson Museum (South Carolina); Decatur Area Convention and Visitors Bureau (Illinois); Ruth Deskins, Harrisonburg-Rockingham Convention & Visitors Bureau (Virginia); Jim E. Detlefsen, Herbert Hoover Library; Sally Donze, McKinley Museum of History, Science and Industry; Adrienne Dorfman; John P. Dumville, Vermont State Historic Sites; Walter S. Dunn, Jr., Buffalo and Erie County Historical Society (New York); Terri E. Edwards, New Hampshire Division of Parks and Recreation; Martin Elzy, Assisatnt Director of the Jimmy Carter Library (Atlanta); Rita Embry, Missouri Department of Natural Resources; Stan Fast, Missouri Division of Parks, Recreation and Historic Preservation; Mary A. Finch, Office of Presidential Libraries, National Archives; Katherine W. Fischer, Colonial Williamsburg Foundation; William B. Fishback, Jr., University of Virginia; Foothills Travel Association of Virginia; Forest Lawn

Cemetery and Garden Mausoleums (New York); Libby Fosso, Monticello; Fredericksburg Visitor Center (Virginia); Galena/Jo Daviess County Convention & Visitors Bureau (Illinois); Garden Club of Virginia; Kristin L. Gibbons, New York State Office of Parks, Recreation & Historic Preservation; Betty Gist and Dr. William C. Gist, Jr.; Glenn Godwin, Plains Nursing Center; Jeanette Graff; Greater Dallas Chamber (Texas); Kellee Green, Gerald R. Ford Library and Museum; Shirley M. Green, White House; Shawna Grinnell, Cortland County Convention & Visitors Bureau (New York); Ann Grube, Western Reserve Historical Society (Ohio); Kenneth G. Hafeli, Gerald R. Ford Library and Museum; Roberta Hallahan, Virginia Division of Tourism; Lorethea Hamke, Grouseland; Peggy D. Hanford, St. Albans Area Chamber of Commerce (Vermont); Herbert L. Harper, Tennessee Historical Commission; Barbara Henckel, White House; Elbert R. Hilliard, Mississippi Department of Archives and History; Hillsborough Historical Society (New Hampshire); Historic Gettysburg-Adams County; John Holtzapple, James K. Polk Memorial Association; Rennie Honeycutt, Mordeci Historic Park; Hoover Institution, Stanford University; Angela G. Horton, White House; Fabian Howard, Abraham Lincoln's Boyhood Home (Kentucky); Thomas Huges, Friends of the Ulysses S. Grant Cottage; Edwin L. Huntley, Macon County Historical Society (Illinois); Melinda Huntley, Erie County Convention & Visitors Bureau (Ohio); Hyde Park Chamber of Commerce; Illinois Department of Conservation; John E. Ingalls, Jefferson County Museum (West Virginia); Jackson County Parks and Recreation (Missouri); Squire Jaros, Michigan Bureau of History; Charles H. Jelloian, Ronald Reagan Presidential Foundation; William W. Jenney, Vermont Division for Historic Preservation; Eileen Jette, Hoover-Minthorn House Museum; Linda H. Jones, Virginia Historical Society; Peter L. Jones, Cayuga Museum (New York); Frances Killpatrick, Old Presbyterian Meeting House (Virginia); Terrie Korpita, Historic Northampton (Massachusetts); James R. Kratsas, Gerald R. Ford Library and Museum; Lake County Visitors Bureau (Ohio); Patricia G. LaLand, National Trust for Historic Preservation; Lee Langston-Harrison, James Monroe Museum and Memorial Library; Laramie Area Chamber of Commerce (Wyoming); Raymond G. Larson, Mercersburg Academy; Arthur E. La Salle, Historic Springfield Foundation (Mississippi); Florence Leon, Friends of the Hermitage (New Jersey); Loundon County Chamber of Commerce (Virginia); Loundon County Office of Tourism (Virginia); Dennis Lumpee, The Presidential Museum; Clarence F. Lyons, Jr., Nixon Presidential Materials Staff, National Archives; Madison County Chamber of Commerce (Virginia); Olivia Mahoney, Chicago Historical Society (Illinois); John Manguso, Fort Sam Houston Museum; Marion Area Convention & Visitors Bureau (Ohio); James A. Marvin, Hillsborough Historical Society; Beth Mason, Lake View Cemetery Association (Ohio); Judy Matheson, Augusta-Richmond County Convention & Visitors Bureau (Georgia);

Introduction

Eunice A. May, President Garfield National Historic Site; Nancy Maze, La Salle County Historical Society (Illinois); Carolyn McArthur, National Trust for Historic Preservation; George E. McCarley, U.S. Grant Homestead Association (Ohio); Joanna McCrary, Lincoln Memorial Association (California); Dennis K. McDaniel, Brandywine Battlefield Park Commission (Pennsylvania); Kimberly McKeough, Association for the Preservation of Virginia Antiquities; Bernard R. Meyer, White House Historical Association; Michigan State Fair; Marcia M. Miller, Maryland Historical Trust; Rich Mills, Council Bluffs Convention & Visitors Bureau (Iowa); Nancy Mirshah, Gerald R. Ford Library and Museum; Donna Misner, Ronald Reagan Home Preservation Foundation; Tania Moore, Greater Omaha Convention and Visitors Bureau (Nebraska); Linda Moorman, Sherwood Forest Plantation; Marsha Mullin, The Hermitage; Sylvia M. Naguib, Jimmy Carter Library; Elizabeth Newland, Little White House (Florida); Arthur Nordby, Fillmore Glen State Park (New York); North Carolina Department of Cultural Resources; Northern Neck Planning District Commission (Virginia); Ohio Historical Society; Sade Olatunji, Massachusetts Historical Commission; Barbara Olsen, Passaic County Parks Department (New Jersey); Francis P. O'Neill, Maryland Historical Society; Orange County Visitors Bureau (Virginia); Judy Osbourne, Abraham Lincoln's Boyhood Home (Kentucky); Palisades Interstate Park Commission (New York & New Jersey); Patricia Palmer, American Institute of Architects Foundation; Mette R. Parker, American Institute of Architects Foundation; Starr Pearson-Floyd, Washington National Cathedral; Pennsylvania Avenue Development Corporation (Washington, D.C.); Pennsylvania Bureau of Historic Preservation; Margarete T. Peters, Virgina Department of Historic Resources; Petersburg Visitors Center (Virginia); Philadelphia Society for the Preservation of Landmarks (Pennsylvania); Susan R. Phillips, Corporation for Jefferson's Poplar Forest; Martha Place, Decatur Area Convention & Visitors Bureau (Illinois); Mrs. Joseph Prendergast, Oak Hill (Virginia); Princeton University; Quincy Historical Society (Massachusetts); Quincy Tourism Association; Laurie N. Rabe, National Trust for Historic Preservation; Judith F. Ramsden, James Madison Museum; Ed Rauh, Jackson County Historical Society (West Virginia); Ann M. Rauscher, Mount Vernon Ladies' Association; Richland County Historic Preservation Commission (South Carolina); Frank Rigg, John F. Kennedy Library; Mary Ann Riordan, Parade of Presidents Wax Museum; Roanoke Valley Convention & Visitors Bureau (Virginia); Rebecca M. Rogers, United States Capitol Historical Society; Paul Rohrbaugh, McKinley Memorial Library (Ohio); Theodore Roosevelt IV; T. Cay Rowe, Southwest Texas State University; Judy Ruthven, U.S. Grant House (Ohio); Sandusky County Convention & Visitors Bureau (Ohio); Saratoga Historical Society (New York); Gregory W. Sassaman, Cowans Gap State Park (Pennsylvania); Richard Schachtsiek, Illinois Historic Preservation Agency; Mel Schroeder, George Fox College; E. Philip Scott,

13

Lyndon Baines Johnson Library; Sarah S. Shaffer, National Trust for Historic Preservation; Michael T. Sheehan, National Trust for Historic Preservation; Virginia W. Sherman, Westmoreland County Historic Preservation Officer (Virginia); Russell D. Sibert, Hiram College; Richard N. Smith, Herbert Hoover Library; Springfield/Washington County Chamber of Commerce (Kentucky); Stanford University; Henry W. Stevens, Roosevelt Campobello International Park Commission; Phillip C. Stone, Harrisonburg-Rockingham Convention & Visitors Bureau (Virginia); James Taylor, Andrew Jackson State Park; Paul J. Taylor, New Jersey Division of Parks and Forestry; Raymond Teichman, Franklin D. Roosevelt Library; Addison B. Thompson, Tuckahoe Plantation; Anne Thompson, Milton Historical Society (Massachusetts); Lynn Todd-Crawford, Jimmy Carter Library; Edward Twine, James Buchannan Hotel; Vermont Travel Division; Virginia Department of Transportation; Virginia Plantation Country; Alycia J. Vivona, Franklin D. Roosevelt Library; Nancy Vodry, Richland County Historic Preservation Commission (South Carolina); Jana M. Wallace, Public Museum of Grand Rapids (Michigan); Faye A. Watters, Harrisonburg-Rockingham Historical Society (Virginia); Richard Werstler, McKinley Museum of History, Science and Industry; Westchester County Office of Cultural Affairs & Tourism (New York); Westmoreland County Council for Travel and Tourism (Virginia); George M. White, Architect of the Capitol; Reverend J. Douglas Wigner, Jr., St. Peter's Parish Church (Virginia); Lawrence E. Wikander, Forbes Library (Massachusetts); Constance E. Williams, Civil War Library and Museum; Steven M. Wilson, Abraham Lincoln Museum; Winchester-Frederick County Historical Society; Allen Yale, Vermont Division for Historic Preservation; Nancy L. Zerbe, Office of New Jersey Heritage; Benedict K. Zobrist, Harry S. Truman Library.

Leo E. Leavers of Buffalo, New York, and Clearwater, Florida, Founder and Chairman, Preserve our Presidential Sites, Inc., and lecturer on the Presidents, kindly supplied photographs of all Presidential burial sites.

A special note of thanks, appreciation, and admiration to the National Park Service, United States Department of the Interior. For more than seventy-five years, the National Park Service has performed outstanding service to the country by its administration of our nation's national parks, monuments, memorials, historic sites, and other areas entrusted to its care. The Presidential-related sites it administers are among the most significant and most professionally operated in the country. The local superintendents in charge of each site and their rangers are extremely knowledgeable. Our sincere thanks for their friendly attitude and valuable help.

Special recognition is also appropriate for the Presidential Libraries of the National Archives. Franklin D. Roosevelt devised the concept of the Presidential library and it has been followed by all succeeding Presidents and by his predecessor, Herbert Hoover. Two special libraries, unaffiliated with the National Archives, hold the records of Presidents Rutherford B. Hayes and Richard M. Nixon.

An outstanding feature of all these libraries is their professional museum exhibits usually devoted to the lives and careers of their namesakes. Priceless gifts from foreign governments, memorabilia, old photographs, rare historical documents, with other unique material on display offer a special treat for visitors. For writers, historians and other researchers, Presidential libraries are an invaluable source of information and professional librarians to help locate needed documents or audiovisual material. Their help is gratefully acknowledged.

A final word of loving appreciation to our very own First Ladies, Gladys Kruh and Mauzy Stafford, whose encouragement and forbearance with the manuscript, which often took precedence over many social activities, will be impossible to repay.

George Washington, 1st President, 1789-1797

Memorial House. Washington Birthplace National Monument

George Washington's Grist Mill

Aerial View of Mount Vernon with the Potomac River and Maryland shore in the background

George Washington Masonic National Memorial

Washington's Headquarters Museum

Washington Monument

Washington's Tomb

George Washington
First President
1789 - 1797

Sometime around 1656, a ship, crusing up the Potomac river, ran aground in what we today call Virginia. By the time it had been repaired, ship's mate John Washington had decided he liked the area (and one particular woman) so much that he would settle and marry there. By the time his great-grandson George was born on February 22, 1732, the Washington family had amassed thousands of acres of rich farmland in the region.

George received a basic education, but due to his father's death when the boy was 11, was unable to attend college. His skills in mathematics proved useful, however, helping him earn money as an assistant to some local surveyors. At the age of fourteen, restless and seeking adventure, George was dissuaded from joining the Royal Navy, and was instead given the opportunity to join an expedition to survey the land owned by Lord Fairfax in 1748. The following year he helped lay out the new town of Alexandria, Virginia.

As a surveyor, Washington had intimate knowledge of the land in and around Virginia. He used this knowledge to his advantage, and much of his earnings went towards the purchase of land he found favorable.

At 21, George Washington inherited some family property known as Ferry Farm, which he ran successfully for many years. He worked hard, but is also known to have enjoyed the life of a country gentleman in Virginia, becoming an expert horseman, dancer, and a writer of love poems.

But the urge for adventure had not left him, and so in February of 1753 George Washington applied for and received a commission in the militia. It was while in that service that Washington is said to have first become aware of the British attitude towards the American colonists, as he and his American counterparts were being paid less than the British regulars. At one point he even threatened to resign over the disparity.

Washington's actions during the French and Indian War (1754 - 1761) were exemplary, and his rank rise from major to colonel. Although his first military engagement ended in the surrender of Fort Necessity, his bravery in the face of overwhelming odds was widely praised. He later took the job as aide to General Edward Braddock without pay because he saw it as an excellent opportunity to learn military tactics from an expert. Although ill, Washington rode with Braddock at the British defeat

at Fort Duquesne. Washington had gained some notoriety for his actions there, despite the fact that this and a later attack were both failures. In 1758 he left the army and returned to Mount Vernon.

On January 6, 1759, George Washington married a widow named Martha Dandrige Custis. Soon after their wedding they moved to Williamsburg, where George was to serve in the Virginia House of Burgesses, a post to which he was elected while still on the frontier. He was returned for fifteen years to that legislative body, where he learned about representative government while becoming acquainted with many of Revolution's future leaders, among them Thomas Jefferson and Patrick Henry.

When the British governor of Virginia disbanded the legislature for its protest over the Townshend Acts, Washington and others met to discuss a plan to boycott British goods. Washington was elected to attend both the First (1774) and Second (1775) Continental Congresses in Philadelphia. At the Second Congress, which was held following the Battles of Lexington and Concord, Washington advocated military action, and his popularity among the delegates led to his appointment as commander in chief of the army. "I do not think myself equal to the command," he said, and though he accepted the post, refused the monthly stipend offered him.

Washington's actions during the next eight years would serve to increase his stature among the colonists. Often outnumbered and lacking supplies, he commanded an army made up of soldiers of the Continental Army and state militia men, many of whom simply walked away as soon as their enlistments were up. But using his experience with the British Army on the frontier, Washington formulated a battle plan which at times called for outright retreat (as with Philadelphia in 1777) or outright daring (his Christmas 1776 attack on the Hessians at Trenton).

In 1781, with the assistance of the French navy, British troops under Lord Cornwallis were forced into surrender. Two years later the Treaty of Paris was signed, giving the Americans their freedom from the British crown. Washington returned home to Mount Vernon, where he happily returned to the life of a planter, canal promoter, conservationist, and family man.

When it became clear in 1786 that the Articles of Confederation were not up to the task of holding the new country together, a Constitutional Convention was held in Philadelphia, and Washington was elected to head the Virginia delegation. That summer, although he took little part in the debates, Washington helped keep the convention from falling apart over a number of issues. When the members of the first Electoral College met at the beginning of 1789 to choose a President, Washington was the unanimous choice as the country's first chief executive. On April 30, 1789, he was inaugurated in New York City.

His first major bill was handed to him, on all days, July 4, 1789. It called for the setting of import taxes to run the government.

"I walk on untrodden ground," Washington said of his new office. Nothing could be truer, for everything he did was precedent. For instance, the first cabinet was not run as it is today. It was not even called a cabinet until 1793, when the first regular meetings were held. Washington allowed Jefferson (his Secretary of State), Hamilton (Treasury), Knox (War), and Randolph (Attorney General) to act independently, even using their own influences on Congress to get things done.

Under Washington the huge debt the country had incurred was assumed by the national government, which slowly began paying it off. His signing of the charter for the First Bank of the United States was controversial, because many considered its powers to be beyond those mentioned in the Constitution. Washington's first use ever of the power of the veto came in 1792, when the House of Representatives, after the first census had shown a marked increase in the country's population, tried to increase the number of members in the lower chamber. They failed to override the President's veto and eventually settled on a smaller number which was accepted.

Though he desired retirement, Washington was convinced that the country needed him to continue as president for another term. Once again he was elected without a dissenting vote. But the next four years would prove to be difficult for him.

He was faced first with the specter of a European war which involved several countries allied against France. Although America had signed an alliance with the French king in 1778, revolutionaries had taken the country over since then. Realizing the jeopardy a young America would face if it got involved in the war, he signed the Neutrality Proclamation in 1793, which among other things forbade any U.S. ship from carrying war supplies to a belligerent.

The first test of the power of the federal government came in 1794 when a band of farmers in western Pennsylvania refused to pay taxes on the manufacture of whiskey. When they attacked federal officials, Washington ordered 15,000 troops to the region to crush the revolt. The Whiskey Rebellion, as it became known, was the first real test of the power of the national government.

Relations with Great Britain strained during Washington's second term, as its war with France prompted the naval power to take action against American ships it feared were carrying supplies to their enemy. American seamen were also being taken off American ships and impressed into British service. Meanwhile, in the western territories of the United States, the British maintained control of several frontier forts they were supposed to have given up under the Treaty of 1783.

To solve these disputes Washington sent the Chief Justice of the Supreme Court, John Jay, to Britain negotiate a settlement. Unfortunately, the treaty that Jay sent back created more problems than it settled. Instead of addressing the issues of impressment and free trade, it called for trade between the two countries and the removal of British troops from the frontier. The country was divided over the treaty. Federalists like Alexander Hamilton supported the treaty because it opened trade with England. Republican-Democrats like Thomas Jefferson opposed it because it would harm the French.

Though it was unpopular to do so (Hamilton was stoned by an angry mob in New York City over his support) Washington realized that conflict with Great Britain could only harm the young country. He suffered strong criticism in the first few months following his signing of the treaty eventually the country came to realize it was a wise thing to do.

Washington's popularity returned, helped by his negotiation of a treaty with Spain which opened the Mississippi River to trade and the signing of a peace treaty with several Native American tribes. He also reached an agreement with the pirates of the Barbary States for the release of prisoners and for the payment of a tribute which would allow for the continued passage of American ships.

Washington decided not to seek a third term and he retired to Mount Vernon, eager to resume the life of a country gentleman. He supported, but did not campaign for John Adams, his Vice-President, who ran and barely defeated Thomas Jefferson for the presidency in 1796.

George Washington was called to service once more by his country in 1798, when during a period of tense relations with France, President Adams asked him to plan and lead an army. After a short time in Philadelphia, Washington was able to return home to Mount Vernon again, where he lived until December 14, 1799. That night he died at the age of 67 from an infection of the throat.

Historical Landmarks

Birthplace of George Washington
Pope's Creek, now Wakefield, Virginia

About 1726, Augustine Washington, George's father, completed a house on land he had purchased along Pope's Creek, 1 mile southeast of his old Bridges Creek home. Three years later his wife, Jane Butler, died, leaving him with four children: Lawrence, Butler, Augustine, Jr., and Jane. On March 6, 1730, Augustine married again; his bride was Mary Ball. Their first child, George, was born at the Pope's Creek home on February 22, 1732.

George Washington spent the first three years of his life at Pope's Creek. In 1735, Augustine moved his family to the Hunting Creek plantation now known as Mount Vernon. Four years later the family moved to the "Strother estate" (Ferry Farm) on the Rappahannock River opposite Fredericksburg. Augustine died there in 1743 and his body was brought back to Bridges Creek to be buried besides his ancestors.

Upon the death of his father, the birthplace of George Washington (known as "Wakefield" in its last years) was passed on to Augustine, Jr. Subsequently his son, William Augustine Washington, inherited the farm and was living in the birthplace house when it accidentally burned down around December 25, 1779. It was never rebuilt. In 1931, as a memorial to George Washington, a reconstruction of the house was built near the site of the original house. Because reliable information about the appearance of the birthplace home was lacking, the memorial house is only a general representation of a Virginia plantation residence of the 18th century. It is a 1 1/2-story Georgian design brick mansion with furnishings from the first half of the 18th century.

About a mile northwest of the memorial mansion, on the banks of Bridges Creek, are the family burial plot and the site of the home that John Washington, American progenitor of the family and George Washington's great-grandfather, purchased in 1664. The burial plot includes the graves of George Washington's father, grandfather, great-grandfather, and half-brother, Augustine, Jr.

Visitor's Information

The George Washington Birthplace National Monument, the site's official name, is administered by the National Park Service which operates it as a colonial farm, recreating the sights, sounds, and smells of 18th century plantation life. A Visitor Center features exhibits and a film, "A Childhood Place" about life at the Pope's Creek plantation.

Open daily 9:00 a.m.-5:00 p.m., closed January 1 and December 25.
Admission: $1.00 for adults 17-61. Telephone: (804) 224-1732.

The Birthplace Monument is on the Potomac River, 38 miles east of Fredericksburg. Virginia and can be reached via State Routes 3 and 204.

George Washington's Home, Mount Vernon
Mount Vernon, Virginia

Washington was 16 when he came to live permanently at Mount Vernon, the 1 1/2-story house built in 1743 by his half-brother, Lawrence. The house sat on the foundations of an earlier house erected by his father which was destroyed by fire. Two years after Lawrence's death George leased the 2,600 acre property from Lawrence's widow, who had a lifetime right to it, and upon her death in 1761 George inherited it.

In 1757-58, in preparation for his marriage the following year to Martha Curtis, George thoroughly rebuilt the 1 1/2-story Georgian structure, which then contained four rooms bisected by a central hall on each floor. He enlarged the residence to 2 1/2-stories and remodeled it to a more impressive Palladian form. For the next 15 years after his marriage in 1759, Washington lived as a prosperous planter and made few changes to his home.

He decided to enlarge the house in 1773, but soon left for Philadelphia to serve in the Continental Congress. While he was away during the War for Independence, a distant relative, Lund Washington, carried out his plans. Lund enlarged the modest main house from five to nine bays; constructed the piazza; added the detached, flanking wings, which connected to the central mansion by means of curving light arcades; built outbuildings; landscaped the grounds; and extended the gardens. After George returned to Mount

Vernon he finished the remodeling and placed the large octagonal cupola on the center of the roof. At its peak, during Washington's lifetime, the plantation contained more than 8,000 acres, and was partitioned into five farms with almost 250 people on the estate.

In the 50 years after the deaths of George and Martha, the estate became run down, land was sold and the property dwindled to 200 acres. In 1858, the Mount Vernon Ladies' Association was formed to acquire and restore the property. This has been accomplished in magnificent fashion, including the addition of 300 acres. Washington's elegant mansion has been meticulously restored to its appearance in the last year of his life, from the actual paint colors on the walls to the actual arrangement of the furnishings, many of which are original. The exhibition area contains more than 30 acres of beautiful gardens and wooded grounds. Near the mansion are the outbuildings where much of the day-by-day domestic activity on the plantation took place; bread was baked, wool and flax fibers were woven into cloth, laundry was washed and ironed, paints were mixed, and meats were cured. The estate also includes a museum where a large number of personal possessions of the Washingtons are on display.

Visitor's Information

Open daily 9:00 a.m.-5:00 p.m., March-October; 9:00 a.m.-4:00 p.m., rest of year.

Admission: Adults $6.00; over 61 with proof of age $5.50; ages 6-11, $3.00. Telephone: (703) 780-2000.

Mount Vernon is at the southern end of the George Washington Memorial Parkway, overlooking the Potomac River, 8 miles south of Alexandria, and 16 miles from downtown Washington, D.C.

George Washington's Office Museum
Corner of Braddock and Cork Streets
Winchester, Virginia

This is a small log building that served as Washington's military office from September 1755 to December 1756 when he was a commissioned officer in the Virginia militia and built Fort Loudoun. In 1748, Washington came to Winchester to work for Thomas Lord Fairfax as a surveyor and spent the next four years surveying and exploring the region. The Office Museum contains artifacts from the colonial period including rare surveying instruments and a scale model of Fort Loudoun.

Visitor's Information

Open daily, 9:00 a.m.-5:00 p.m., April-October. Telephone: (703) 662-4412.

Admission: Adults $2.00, ages 6-12, $1.00.

Directions: On I-81 take Exit 80, then right onto Pleasant Valley Road, continue to Cork Street, make left and continue to Braddock Street where museum is located.

George Washington's Grist Mill Historical State Park
5514 Mount Vernon Memorial Highway
Alexandria, Virginia

In colonial times, owners of large plantations often built merchant mills to augment the farm's income. George Washington selected a spot on Dogue Creek for just this purpose and outfitted it with the best machinery available. Though it proved to be somewhat less than profitable, Washington's mill did produce meal and flour of excellent quality, much of it which was shipped direct to the West Indies.

Washington operated the mill during most of his adult life, including the eight years as the First President of the United States. In 1799, he rented it to a nephew, Lawrence Lewis. Later that year Washington died, leaving the mill to Lewis in his will. Lewis died in 1839, and his son sold the mill to a group of Quakers in 1846. By this time the mill needed repairs which would cost $2,000 and the Quakers decided it was not worth it. In 1850 the walls fell and in later years the stones were used for other buildings.

The present mill is a reconstruction of the mill Washington built. It was a stone building of 3 1/2-stories with a wheel on the inside and an arch over the tailrace. Interest in its reconstruction was developed during plans for the Washington Bicentennial Birthday Celebration in 1932.

Visitor's Information

The restored mill is on the original foundation. Replicas of machinery are displayed and a slide show gives the history of the mill.

Open daily, 9:00 a.m. to 5:00 p.m., from Memorial Day to Labor Day.
Telephone: (703) 339-3383

Admission: Adults (13 and up) $2.00
　　　　　　 Children (6-12) $1.00

The Park is 16 miles south of Alexandria via the George Washington Memorial Parkway to Mount Vernon, then 3 miles west on SR 235.

Mary Washington House
1200 Charles Street
Fredericksburg, Virginia

George Washington purchased this house for his mother, Mary Ball Washington, on September 18, 1772. As he stated in a letter, "Before I left Virginia (to make her comfortable and free from care), I did at her request but at my own expense purchase a commodious house and garden lotts (of her own choosing) in Fredericksburg that she might be near my sister Lewis, her only daughter." Mrs. Washington was 64 years old and spent her last 17 years in this home. It was here that the President came to receive his mother's blessing before his inauguration in 1789.

In the garden, the same sundial still marks the passing time, as when Mrs. Washington passed the hours among her beloved plants. The large boxwoods she planted line a brick walkway that separates a well-tended vegetable garden from the picturesque English-style flower garden.

George Washington

Visitor's Information

Tours are provided by costumed guides and last about 30 minutes.

Open daily, 9:00 a.m.-5:00 p.m., March through November; rest of year, 8:00 a.m.-4:00 p.m. Closed January 1, Thanksgiving, December 24-25 and 31.

Admission: $3.00 adults, $.75 students, children under 6 free.

The house is in downtown Fredericksburg at Charles and Lewis Streets, a few blocks north of SR 3.

Washington's Headquarters Museum
Virginia Road
North White Plains, New York

When downtown White Plains was overrun by the British, General George Washington used Elijah Miller's 1738 colonial style farmhouse as his headquarters. It was here that he planned the strategy that successfully concluded the battle.

The house has been restored and furnished.

Visitor's Information

Open Wednesday-Sunday, 10:00 a.m. to 4:00 p.m. Telephone: (914) 949-1236.

Admission: Free.

The Museum can be reached via the Bronx River Parkway; Exit 26 (Virginia Road) and go east for 1/4 mile.

George Washington

Brandywine Battlefield Park
U.S. 1
Chadds Ford, Pennsylvania

On the eve of the Battle of Brandywine, Washington established his headquarters in the farmhouse of Benjamin Ring, a Quaker farmer and miller. The house stood within easy access of Chadds Ford where the British were expected to cross the river. Washington held a council of war with his generals in the Ring house on September 9th, 1777 to plan his strategy. The battle took place September 11.

Although Washington was defeated at Brandywine, the courage of the Americans helped to convince France to form an alliance with the rebels; a union which turned the tide in favor of the Americans.

Visitor's Information

A permanent interpretive exhibit and an audio-visual presentation tell the story of the Battle of Brandywine. Changing exhibits cover other topics of interest pertaining to the American Revolution. The Benjamin Ring house, which was damaged by fire in the early 1930's, has been reconstructed and furnished so visitors see it much as it was on that late summer day in 1777.

Visitor Center: Tuesday-Saturday, 9:00 a.m. to 5:00 p.m.; Sunday, Noon to 5:00 p.m.

Historic Houses (including Ring house): Tuesday-Saturday, 9:00 a.m.-4:00 p.m.; Sunday, Noon to 4:00 p.m.

Brandywine Battlefield Park Grounds: Tuesday-Saturday, 9:00 a.m.-8:00 p.m.; Sunday, Noon to 8:00 p.m.; Memorial Day to Labor Day; rest of year, 9:00 a.m. to 5:00 p.m.

All facilities closed January 1, Martin Luther King, Jr.'s Birthday, Presidents Day, Easter, Columbus Day, Thanksgiving, December 25.

Admission to battlefield and historic buildings $1.00; senior citizens $.75; ages 6-17, $.50. Telephone: (215) 459-3342.

George Washington

Valley Forge National Historical Park
Route 23
Valley Forge, Pennsylvania

On December 19, 1777, when Washington's army struggled into camp at Valley Forge, tired, cold, and ill-equipped, it was lacking in much of the training essential for consistent success on the battlefield. No battles were fought here, no bayonet charges or artillery bombardments took place but during the winter of 1777-78 thousands of American soldiers died during the severe winter weather. But on June 19, 1778, after a 6-month encampment, this same army emerged to pursue and successfully engage the British army at the Battle of Monmouth in New Jersey.

The Park, which is administered by the National Park Service, contains extensive remains and reconstructions of major forts, and lines of earthworks, Washington's Headquarters, quarters of other officers, reconstructed huts, memorials, monuments, and markers.

Visitor's Information

About 90 percent of the 1758 Isaac Potts stone farmhouse, used by Washington as his headquarters, is completely original with period furnishings and an iron candlestand owned by Washington. The Visitor Center has an audio-visual program and exhibits to tell the story of the winter encampment of 1777-78.

Visitor Center and Washington's Headquarters open daily, 8:30 a.m. to 5:00 p.m.; park open during daylight hours. Closed December 25. Telephone: (215) 783-7700.

Admission: Washington's Headquarters, $1.00 adults, ages 12-61. Visitor Center and Park free.

Valley Forge National Historical Park is about 20 miles west of Philadelphia. Entrances from major highways are marked. From Pennsylvania Turnpike, take Exit 24 (Valley Forge); stay in right lane for toll booth and take the next right onto North Gulf Road which goes to the Visitor Center at intersection of Valley Forge Road and Route 23.

George Washington

Museum of the Valley Forge Historical Society
Route 23 (in Valley Forge National Historical Park)
Valley Forge, Pennsylvania

The Society's collection of George and Martha Washington's memorabilia is large and interesting. It ranges from the General's "Marquee" (sleeping and office tent) to locks of his hair in pins and rings. There are important collections of paintings, maps, engravings and documents including letters from Washington and period items relating to Lafayette, James Monroe, Lord Cornwallis and others.

Visitor's Information

Open Monday-Saturday, 9:30-4:30 p.m.; Sunday, 1:00 p.m.-4:30 p.m. Closed January 1, Easter, Thanksgiving, December 25.

Admission: Adults $1.50; senior citizens, $1.00; children, $.50. Telephone: (215) 783-0535.

The Museum is located on private property within the Park next to the Washington Memorial Chapel on Route 23. Follow directions above to Park's Visitor Center and continue on Route 23 to Museum.

Wallace House
38 Washington Place
Somerville, New Jersey

Washington and his wife, Martha, occupied the two-story, eight-room, Georgian style Wallace House from December 1778 to June 1779. There he planned the Sullivan expedition that destroyed New York Iroquois settlements in 1779.

Visitor's Information

The house contains period furnishings, Revolutionary War relics and Washington's metal campaign chest.

George Washington

Open: Wednesday-Friday 9:00 a.m.-Noon, 1:00 p.m.-6:00 p.m.; Saturday 10:00 a.m.-Noon, 1:00 p.m.-6:00 p.m.; Sunday 1:00 p.m.-6:00 p.m. Telephone: (908) 725-1015.

Admission: Free.

The house is located 1/2 mile from the Somerville Circle off Middaugh Street.

Morristown National Historical Park
230 Morris Street
Morristown, New Jersey

George Washington arrived in Morristown in a severe hail and snow storm on December 1, 1779. It was the worst winter of the century with twenty-eight blizzards which made the previous year's encampment at Valley Forge seem like a picnic. Washington made his headquarters at the house of Jacob Ford's widow and Morristown's finest house became a center of the American Revolution. The large Georgian mansion was built by Colonel Jacob Ford, Jr. between 1772 and 1774. About 80 percent of the furnishings are original to the house and short explanations on doorways describe the use of each room.

Adjacent to the house is a historical museum and library with perhaps the best collection of Washington's personal items in the country. The museum displays material relating to the 1779-80 encampment, valuable historical objects, documents, and a collection of military weapons. The library contains about 40,000 manuscripts and more than 20,000 printed works dealing with the colonial and Revolutionary eras.

Visitor's Information

Washington's Headquarters and adjacent museum are open daily 9:00 a.m. to 5:00 p.m. Closed January 1, Thanksgiving, and December 25. Telephone: (201) 539-2085.

Admission: $1.00 adults, ages 17-61.

Best approach to Washington's Headquarters is via I-287. Southbound, use Exit 32; northbound use Exit 32A and follow directional signs. Morristown is also reached by US 202 or by NJ 24.

George Washington

Dey Mansion
199 Totowa Road
Wayne, New Jersey

When the Continental Army was encamped throughout the Preakness Valley, Colonel Theunis Dey, a friend of General Washington, offered him use of the eastern half of his home for his headquarters. The Dey mansion is a Georgian manor built by Theunis's father in the 1740's. Washington used the mansion in July and again in October and November 1780. While there Washington was told by American spies that the British planned to kidnap him. Colonel John Simcoe and his raiders were dispatched on that mission by the British but they were routed by American forces at Totowa Bridge.

Visitor's Information

The house is one of a very small number of pre-Revolutionary houses built by the Dutch. The combination of materials, huge oak timbers pegged with wooden pins, brownstone, and brick, shows the Dutch influence. The house and detached kitchen display 18th century antiques and artifacts and is furnished as it would have been when Washington made it his headquarters.

Open: Wednesday-Friday, 1:00 p.m.-4:30 p.m.
  Saturday and Sunday, 10:00 a.m.-noon, 1:00 p.m.-4:30 p.m. Closed major holidays. Telephone: (201) 696-1776.

Admission: $1.00.

Directions: Route 80 or Route 46 to the Union Boulevard/Totowa exit. North on Union Boulevard. Left onto French Hill Road. Take second left onto Totowa Road.

On the Garden State Parkway use Exit 159/Route 80 West and follow Route 80 directions above.

George Washington

Washington's Headquarters State Historic Site
84 Liberty Street
Newburgh, New York

On April 1, 1782, Washington established his military headquarters in a rented fieldstone farmhouse at Newburgh, sixty miles north of Manhattan and a dozen miles north of West Point. The house, owned by Jonathan Hasbrouck, who began to build it in 1750, adding more rooms over the next 20 years, served as the center of the Continental troops' final winter encampment at New Windsor (1782-83). Washington lived here for 17 months, longer than he spent at any other headquarters. It was here that he rejected the proposal that he become king, he also quelled an incipient mutiny called the Newburgh Conspiracy, and he created the Order of the Purple Heart.

The house is original except for the kitchen and dining room floors and is furnished to reflect the time when the Washingtons lived here. It was open to the public on July 4, 1850, representing the first public historic site in the nation. Adjacent to the house a museum was opened in 1910 to display a growing collection of artifacts. Exhibits on two floors illustrate American Revolutionary and Hudson River themes.

Visitor's Information

Open April through December, Wednesday-Saturday, 10:00 a.m.-5:00 p.m.; Sunday, 1:00 p.m.-5:00 p.m.; rest of year, Saturday 10:00 a.m.-5:00 p.m.; Sunday 1:00 p.m.-5:00 p.m. Telephone: (914) 562-1195.

Admission: Free.

Directions: From New York State Thruway Exit 17 or I-84 Exit 10 to Route 17K to downtown Newburgh; follow signs.

Rockingham State Historic Site
Route 518
Rocky Hill, New Jersey

When the war ended in 1783, Rockingham, also known as the Berrien Mansion, a twenty-room mansion with some rooms dating from 1710, became Washington's residence for three months just before he retired to Mount Vernon. Congress was convening at Nassau Hall, Princeton University, awaiting the signing of the peace treaty with England. Washington was invited to attend the sessions and Congress rented Rockingham for his use during this period.

Washington entertained extensively with guests including Hamilton, Jefferson, Madison, and Paine among other notables. To plan, prepare and serve the many banquets he hosted, he obtained a cook from the noted Fraunces Tavern in New York City. It was also here that Washington wrote his "Farewell Address to the Armies."

Visitor's Information

The mansion has been moved six-tenths of a mile from its original site to protect it from quarry blasting, and restored with authentic furnishings of the period.

Open Wednesday-Friday, 9:00 a.m.-noon, 1:00 p.m.-5:00 p.m.;   Saturday, 10:00 a.m.-noon, 1:00 p.m.-5:00 p.m.;
  Sunday, 1:00 p.m.-5:00 p.m.
Closed January 1, Thanksgiving, and December 25. Telephone: (609) 921-8835.

Admission: Free.

Rockingham is located east of Rocky Hill on County Highway 518 just west of the State Highway 27 junction.

George Washington

Federal Hall National Memorial
26 Wall Street
New York City, New York

The site of the first United States Capitol where Washington, standing on a half-enclosed, open-air balcony on the second floor, took the oath of office on April 30, 1789 and became the first President of the United States, and where Congress met from April 1789 to August 1790.

The original building was demolished in 1812 and replaced in 1842 by the present structure, an outstanding example of Greek Revival architecture, that served as the New York Custom House until 1862 when it became the U.S. Sub-Treasury building. Later it housed the Federal Reserve Bank of New York before the idea of preserving the structure as a memorial to the founding of our federal from of government was conceived. A larger than life-size statue of Washington by John Quincy Adams Ward was placed on the steps of the memorial in 1883 to celebrate the 100th anniversary of the last British solders leaving New York City and Washington's troops entering.

Visitor's Information

Exhibits include Washington's inaugural bible and the suit he wore when he took the oath of office, and an orientation film, "Journey to Federal Hall," a history of Federal Hall through the eyes of Washington. The Inaugural Stand on display in the rotunda was built for President George Bush's use when he participated in the bicentennial celebration of Washington being sworn in as the nation's first President. The Inaugural Stand incorporates a piece of the railing from the balcony where Washington took the oath of office. Another display illustrates the history of the Memorial.

Open daily 9:00 a.m.-5:00 p.m.; closed federal holidays except Washington's Birthday and July 4. Telephone: (212) 264-8711.

Admission: Free.

The Memorial, operated by the National Park Service, is located at the corner of Wall and Nassau Streets, 1 block east of Broadway, in lower Manhattan. Public transportation is recommended and the site is easily reached by bus or subway.

Deshler-Morris House
5442 Germantown Avenue
Philadelphia, Pennsylvania

Late in the summer of 1793 a yellow fever epidemic struck Philadelphia, the U.S. Capitol at that time. President Washington, watching the progress of events from Mount Vernon, decided to return in late October, if not with safety to the city, then to Germantown. He asked the Attorney General to rent him a house there and selected one owned by Colonel Isaac Franks because it was "more commodious for myself and the entertainment of company."
Washington stayed there for about two weeks and held several cabinet meetings in the house. The following summer, Washington found that his schedule would not permit him to go to Mount Vernon for more than a few days. Therefore, to avoid the Philadelphia heat he returned to the house in Germantown with his wife and children, this time for more than seven weeks.

The house had been built by David Deshler in 1772 and the name Morris comes from the family that owned it for over 114 years before bequeathing it to the United States in 1948. The house is part of Independence National Historical Park administered by the National Park Service and is furnished in the period.

Visitor's Information

Open April 1-December 15, 1:00 p.m.-4:00 p.m., Tuesday-Sunday; closed legal holidays. Telephone: (215) 596-1748.

Admission: Adults $1.00, students $.50.

From the Pennsylvania Turnpike the easiest route is to exit at Interchange 25 (Norristown) at Germantown Pike which becomes Germantown Avenue going south.

George Washington

Gadsby's Tavern Museum
132 Royal Street
Alexandria, Virginia

The older portion of this building, known for years as City Tavern, was built about 1752 and used intermittently by Washington as military headquarters during the French and Indian War. A taller brick addition was built onto the two-story tavern in the last decade of the 18th century. The buildings are named for Englishman John Gadsby who operated them from 1796 to 1808. Mr. Gadsby's establishment was a center of political, business and social life in early Alexandria. The annual Birthday Ball in celebration of George Washington's birthday was held here during Washington's lifetime and is reenacted each year. The Washingtons twice attended the annual Birthday Ball held in his honor.

Washington reviewed the Alexandria militia from the tavern steps in November 1799, one of his last public appearances.

Visitor's Information

Guided tours available of rooms in both buildings which have been restored to their 18th century appearance. Archaeological excavation, paint analysis and research of surviving documents have provided an accurate picture of the furnishing and use of the buildings in the period 1770-1810.

Open Tuesday-Saturday, 10:00 a.m.-5:00 p.m.; Sunday, 1:00 p.m.-5:00 p.m. Last tour each day at 4:15 p.m.; closed holidays. Telephone: (703) 838-4242.

Admission: Adults $2.00, ages 6-17, $1.00.

Located at Royal and Cameron Streets, in downtown Alexandria, near City Hall.

The George Washington Masonic National Memorial
Shooter's Hill, west end of King Street
Alexandria, Virginia

George Washington was the first Worshipful Master of Alexandria Lodge No. 22 under its 1788 charter. He retained that office until December 1789. The 333-foot-high memorial is based on the design of the ancient lighthouse at Alexandria, Egypt. The memorial contains a 17-foot bronze statue of Washington as Worshipful Master and Washington memorabilia including a chair from his library at Mount Vernon, his bedchamber clock stopped by the doctor at the moment of Washington's death, the silver trowel used at the laying of the cornerstone of the Capitol, the Washington family bible and many paintings, documents and other artifacts.

Visitor's Information

Open daily, 9:00 a.m.-5:00 p.m. Closed January 1, Thanksgiving, December 25. Scheduled Tower Tours, 9:15 a.m. until 3:45 p.m.
Telephone: (703) 683-2007.

Admission: Free.

From U.S. 1, west on King Street to Shooter's Hill.

1815 Masonic Lodge
Princess Anne & Hanover Streets
Fredericksburg, Virginia

Washington was initiated as a Mason on this site in 1752. Portions of the lodge where his initiation took place are incorporated in this later structure. A George Washington Masonic Museum on the second floor of the lodge features a Gilbert Stuart portrait of Washington and the Bible he used to take his Masonic oath.

Visitors Information

Open Monday-Saturday, 9:00 a.m.-4:00 p.m.; Sunday, 1:00 p.m.-4:00 p.m. Closed January 1, December 25.

Admission: adults, $2.00; ages 6-12, $.50.

The 1815 Masonic Lodge Museum is in downtown Fredericksburg on Princess Anne Street which is U.S. Bus. Route 1 and 17.

Anderson House Museum
2118 Massachusetts Ave. NW
Washington, District of Columbia

Headquarters, museum and library of The Society of the Cincinnati whose members are direct male descendants of the officers who served in the Continental Army or Navy during the American Revolutionary War. Its first president from 1783 until his death in 1799, was George Washington.

Anderson House, one of the best remaining examples of great Washington residences of a bygone era, was completed in 1905 by the Honorable Larz Anderson, a career diplomat and member of the Society. On his death in 1937 his wife gave the house to the Society for use as its headquarters. The Museum of the American Revolution containing portraits, weapons and other relics commemorates the Continental Army and its commander, George Washington. A fascinating collection of military miniatures is on display, and a comprehensive library on the American Revolution is open to the public.

Visitor's Information

Museum open Tuesday-Saturday, 1:00 p.m.-4:00 p.m.
Harold Leonard Stuart Memorial Library open weekdays, 10:00 a.m.-4:00 p.m., appointments advisable. Telephone: (202) 785-2040.
Closed on national holidays.

George Washington

Admission: Free.

Located in downtown Washington, the building is 1 1/2-blocks west of the Dupont Circle Metro (subway) stop.

Washington Monument
National Mall between 15th and 17th Streets
Washington, District of Columbia

The construction of a monument to honor George Washington was first considered by the Continental Congress in 1783. But it was not until July 4, 1848, that the cornerstone was laid with elaborate Masonic ceremonies. Work progressed favorably until 1854 when the building of the monument became involved in a political quarrel. Then the Civil War intervened and it was not until 1880 that work resumed on the shaft. The new Maryland marble used at that point came from the same vein as the original stone but from a different stratum which explains the "ring" noticeable on the shaft. The monument was dedicated on February 21, 1885 and opened to the public on October 9, 1888. It is operated by the National Park Service.

Visitor's Information

The top of the 555 feet, 5 1/8 inch high monument may be reached by elevator or by an iron stairway consisting of 50 landings and 897 steps. Inserted into the interior walls are 188 carved stones presented by individuals, societies, cities, states, and nations of the world.

Open daily, 8:00 a.m.-midnight, April 1-Labor Day; 9:00 a.m.-5:00 p.m., rest of year. Closed December 25. Telephone: (202) 485-9880.

Admission: Free.

The Monument is located on the National Mall between 15th and 17th Streets and Independence and Constitution Avenues. From Virginia follow Route 50 east or I-395 north to Washington.

George Washington

Burial Site
Mount Vernon
Mount Vernon, Virginia

In the early morning, December 14, 1799, George Washington awoke with a sore throat and he had difficulty speaking. He did not allow Martha to call a doctor until dawn. The diagnosis was "inflammatory quinsy" and following the practice of the day, the doctor bled him. Present day doctors believe he had a streptococcal infection of the throat. Other doctors arrived in the afternoon and also bled him. About 10 p.m. on December 14, Washington whispered, I am just going. Have me decently buried, and do not let my body be out in the vault in less than two days after I am dead. Do you understand me?" His secretary answered, "Yes sir." Washington said, "Tis well." He felt for his own pulse. Then he died.

On December 18, Washington was given a military funeral and his body was laid to rest in the family tomb at Mount Vernon. The tomb is planned according to directions left in his will which includes position, dimensions, and the material, brick. On a stone tablet above the vault's iron gates is the inscription: "Within this enclosure rest the remains of General George Washington."

Visitor's Information

See Mount Vernon information above for details.

John Adams, 2nd President, 1797-1801

Birthplace of John Adams

First Parish Unitarian Church, burial site of Presidents John Adams and his son, John Quincy Adams, and their wives

Adams Mansion or the "old House," Adams National Historic Site

John Adams

Second President
1797-1801
Federalist

It has been written that no man enjoyed his time as President less than John Adams. Following in George Washington's footsteps was difficult enough, but Adams' administration was beset by political maneuvering, the first rumblings of sectionalism, and an undeclared war with France.

John Adams was born on October 30, 1735 to Deacon John Adams, a farmer, and his wife Susanna Boylston in what was then called Braintree, Massachusetts. Farming the hard, stony soil of what would soon be called Quincy did not appeal to young John, and so he chose a career in the law, becoming the second Adams to attend Harvard (class of 1755), passing the bar in 1758. He married the daughter of a Congregational minister from Weymouth, Massachusetts named Abigail Smith on October 25, 1764.

Although a member of the Sons of Liberty and a fervent defender of colonial rights to representation, he successfully defended the British officer in charge of the Boston Massacre. He was chosen as a delegate to the first Continental Congress which was held in Philadelphia in 1775. There he proposed Washington for the position of Commander-in-Chief. He later sat on the committee which drafted the Declaration of Independence, and was one of the signers of that document. With Benjamin Franklin and John Jay he negotiated the treaty of peace with Great Britain in 1783, and two years later became the first independent American to serve as Minister to England, 1785 to 1788.

Returning to New York, he served for two terms as George Washington's Vice-President (1788 - 1796) earning the distinction of being the first person to hold that office. When Washington announced he would step down from the presidency in 1796, America's first real campaign for the office began between Adams and Jefferson. There was no political love lost between the two men, since the former was a Federalist, (meaning he believed in a strong central government and a loose interpretation of the Constitution), and the latter was a Republican (who counted himself among men who feared an American monarchy and chose to interpret the Constitution strictly).

America's first presidential campaign ended on the floor of Congress, where electors, who were themselves chosen by state legislators, cast their votes for President and Vice-President. An attempt by the Republicans (in concert with some Federalists who disliked

Adams) to place Adams second on the ticket backfired, resulting in the election of John Adams as President and Thomas Jefferson as Vice-President.

During Washington's administration relations with France had been deteriorating. The French believed (correctly) that America favored England and they began attacking American shipping during the end of Washington's administration. One of Adams' first acts as president was to send three diplomats to France to try and settle the dispute. An attempt by French agents (publicly identified by Adams by the letters X, Y, and Z), to extort money from the U.S. for cooperation in the dispute inflamed the Americans, and preparations for war were begun.

A cabinet level Department of the Navy was formed, American ships were authorized to attack French ships, trade with that country was suspended, and Washington came out of retirement to command the army once again. For two years this country was essentially at war with France. But Adams, seeing signs of conciliation and believing that foreign entanglements would be detrimental to the young country, sought for and achieved a treaty with France in 1800. It was a brave stand to take, for most of the country was in favor of war.

Fueled by anti-French sentiment, the Sedition Act was signed by Adams in 1798, further spelling doom for him and his party. By making it illegal to write or speak anything that was "false, scandalous, and malicious" against the government, Adams was unfairly charged with trying to eradicate the right to free speech. Most of these acts were never enforced, although they left the country suspicious of the Federalists in general and of Adams in particular.

One of John Adams' last official acts turned out to be one of his most lasting, the appointment to Supreme Court of John Marshall of Virginia, a staunch Federalist who served thirty-four years as the Chief Justice.

Near the end of his term, Adams became the first president to serve in the nation's new (and still incomplete) new capital city, when the 150 employees of the federal government moved from Philadelphia to Washington, D.C. Adams was also the first president to live in the White House.

Adams lost the 1800 election to Thomas Jefferson, and so became the first incumbent president to suffer that political fate. On inauguration day Adams, anxious to depart the city where he had endured a most unhappy term of office, left Washington, D.C. before Jefferson had even taken the oath.

Adams returned to Quincy where he lived to see what no president had seen before or since, a son in the White House. His feud with Thomas Jefferson had previously ended, and the two men enjoyed a wonderful correspondence up to the end of their lives. On July 4, 1826, fifty years to the day after he signed the Declaration of Independence, John

Adams died. His last words are said to have been "Thomas Jefferson lives." What the ninety year-old Adams did not know was that his former comrade-in-arms and political nemesis had died earlier that same day in Monticello, Virginia.

Historical Landmarks

Birthplace of John Adams
133 Franklin Street
Quincy, Massachusetts

John Adams was born October 19, 1735, in the original homestead of the Adams family. Built about 1681, it was purchased by John Adams' father, "Deacon" John Adams, in 1720 and remained in the possession of the family until it was given to the city in 1940. Although not architecturally impressive, it is historically notable as the place where Adams grew to manhood. It is also, along with the adjacent birthplace of the 6th president of the United States (his son, John Quincy Adams), the earliest presidential birthplace to have survived.

The original house, a typical New England saltbox structure of frame construction with a massive central chimney, was probably built about 1681. It consisted of two lower and two upper rooms. Extensive alterations were made over the years and the rear lean-to, built sometime in the 18th century, added two downstairs rooms and two small upper ones, separated by a large attic.

Adams lived in his birthplace house until he was married in 1784, when he moved to 141 Franklin Street, a residence that he had inherited from his father in 1761. The reason for the move was to better accommodate his library and to set up a law office. In 1767, his son, John Quincy, was born in the house. In his law office, Adams drafted the Massachusetts Constitution of 1780, which served as a model for the constitutions of other states and the United States.

John Adams

In 1788, when John Adams returned home from Europe, the family settled in a house he had purchased the previous year.

Visitor's Information

The Adams National Historic Site is administered by the National Park Service and consists of the birthplaces of John Adams, John Quincy Adams, and the Adams Mansion (Peacefield).

Open daily, 9:00 a.m.-5:00 p.m., April 19-November 10. Telephone: (617) 773-1177.

Admission: adults, $2.00 for all three houses; under 17, free.

The birthplace is 9 miles south of Boston. Take Exit 8 (Furnace Brook Parkway interchange) of Southeast Expressway (Route 3) to Adams Street East to Hancock Street through Quincy Center to School Street. Turn right onto School Street, then left on Franklin Street.

Peacefield-Adams Mansion
135 Adams Street
Quincy, Massachusetts

The Adams Mansion was named Piecefield by John Adams but it was known to some as the Vassall-Adams house and later, to the Adams family, as the "Old House."

The oldest part of the house was built in 1730-31 as a country villa by Leonard Vassall, a sugar-planter from Jamaica, and was the front western section of the present house. It was a 2 1/2-story frame structure of Georgian design with clapboarded walls and gambrel roof. The first floor contained two rooms separated by a central stair hall; the second floor, two bedrooms and center hall; and the dormered attic, three smaller rooms. The kitchen and servants' quarters were detached.

When Adams took possession he apparently attached the 2 1/2-story kitchen and servants' quarters to the rear, or northwest corner of the main structure. In 1800, near the end of his presidency, he doubled the size of the house by adding a large, 2 1/2-story, L-shaped wing of frame at the eastern end. It was constructed in the same Georgian style as the original residence. On the first floor it had a second entry hall and staircase and the "Long Room" to the east of the hall. Adams' large study-library was on the second floor.

Other additions were made in the 19th century. In 1836, John Quincy Adams built the passage along the back, or north, side of the structure connecting the two rear service ells. In 1869, Charles Francis Adams. son of John Quincy, added 30 feet to the kitchen ell for additional servants' quarters; the following year, a detached stone library overlooking the garden; and in 1873, the stone stable. Brooks, one of Charles Francis Adams' four sons, constructed the present entrance gates in 1906.

After the end of his presidency in 1801, John Adams lived in the house until his death in 1826. Succeeding generations resided in the house until Brooks' death in 1927. As a result, the "Old House: was the home to the second U.S. President, John Adams, and the sixth U.S. President, John Quincy Adams, our Civil War Minister to England, Charles Francis Adams, and two literary historians, Henry and Brooke Adams, a truly distinguished family.

Visitor's Information

In 1946, the Adams Memorial Society donated the property to the Federal Government and it became the Adams National Historic Site, administered by the National Park Service.

Peacefield was home to the Adams family for 140 years over four generations, and it remains just as it was when they lived here, with the furnishings, family memorabilia and the home itself reflecting all four generations.

Subsequently, the birthplaces of John Adams and John Quincy Adams became part of the National Historic Site.

See above for admission details.

John Adams

The Adams Mansion is about 8 miles south of Boston. Take Route 93 south (Southeast Expressway) to Exit 8 (Furnace Brook Parkway). Once on Furnace Brook Parkway, at third set of traffic lights turn right onto Adams Street and proceed for 1 mile to site at corner of Adams Street and Newport Avenue. To reach it via Rapid Transit, take the Red Line from Boston to Quincy Center.

Burial Site
United First Parish Church
1306 Hancock Street
Quincy, Massachusetts

John Adams died at age ninety at the family home on July 4, 1826, the fiftieth anniversary of the day on which he had voted for the Declaration of Independence.

The tombs of Adams and his wife, Abigail, are in the crypt of the United First Parish Church (Unitarian) in Quincy, a handsome Greek Revival style building erected in 1828 and designated a National Historic Landmark for its architecture. It is the only edifice in the country that is the burial place of two presidents of the United States and their wives; John Quincy Adams and his wife, Louisa Catherine are also entombed there.

Visitor's Information

Open Monday through Saturday, 10:00 a.m.-4:00 p.m., Memorial Day-Labor Day; rest of the year by appointment only. Closed January 1, Thanksgiving Day, December 25 and during special church functions. Telephone: (617) 773-1290.

The Church is at 1306 Hancock Street in downtown Quincy.

Thomas Jefferson, 3rd President, 1801-1809

Tuckahoe Plantation

Monticello

Jefferson's Poplar Forest

Tomb of Thomas Jefferson

Cherry Blossoms and the Thomas Jefferson Memorial

Thomas Jefferson

Third President
1801-1809
Republican

Thomas Jefferson was quite possibly our most diverse President. An accomplished architect, violinist, inventor, scientist, farmer, and politician, his intellectual prowess led John Kennedy to call a group of Nobel Prize winners meeting at the White House "the most distinguished gathering of talent ever assembled in the Executive Mansion except for when Thomas Jefferson dined there alone."

Thomas Jefferson was born on April 13, 1743 in Shadwell, Virginia to a Virginia planter and his wife. After graduating from William and Mary College in 1762, he studied law. An accomplished musician, he played violin duets with his friend, Patrick Henry. He moved to Monticello, a home of his design, in 1770.

On January 1, 1772, Monticello gained a nickname: Honeymoon cottage, when he married widower Martha Skelton. Although she and Jefferson had six children, her health was not good, and she died in 1782 at the age of 33. Jefferson never remarried, and during his administration it was his daughter Martha and Dolly Madison, the wife of his Secretary of State, who carried out the duties of a first lady.

Jefferson was active in the struggle for Independence, beginning with his membership on the Virginia "Committee of Correspondence," along with Patrick Henry and Richard Lee. Along with Washington and Adams, he was a delegate to the Second Continental Congress. In 1776 he performed what he considered to be his greatest act of public service (including the presidency), the writing of the Declaration of Independence. Jefferson was also the author of the statute of Virginia for religious freedom. He was a member of the Virginia House of Burgess, a member of Congress twice, and the Governor of Virginia from 1779 to 1781. At the close of the Revolutionary War, Thomas Jefferson was sent as American Minister to the Court of France. Under Washington he became America's first Secretary of State, and then under Adams its second Vice-President.

He ran for the presidency against Adams in 1796 and lost, trying again in 1800. When the electoral votes had been counted, however, the system had once again proved to have a glaring weakness...Republican Thomas Jefferson and his running mate, Aaron

Burr of New York, had received the same number of votes, seventy-three. According to the Constitution, the House of Representatives would have to chose between the two candidates. It took thirty six votes, but Jefferson was finally elected. Because of this election the twelfth amendment, which called for separate ballots for both President and Vice President, was adopted.

Thomas Jefferson, the first chief executive to be inaugurated at the Capital, brought a great change to the presidency. Unlike the formal and erudite Federalists, Jefferson was a man of the people who eschewed the imperial formalities of office. His appearance was so casual (rather than don the powdered white wigs that Washington and Adams wore, he preferred to display his own locks which he cut himself) that a Senator once mistook him for a servant. His Republican philosophy ran counter to the previous administration, favoring States rights and showing sympathy towards the French Revolution.

Under Jefferson the national debt was reduced and all federal bonds were paid off. Shifting the tax burden to the rich, he repealed all excise taxes, (including the infamous Whiskey Tax), while increasing tariffs, land sales, and postal services fees.

Jefferson, while desiring balance in the country's budget, jumped at the chance to purchase the Louisiana Territory from France for $15 million. He had two outstanding reasons for doing so. With one purchase he eliminated the French threat in North America and doubled the land area of the country. In 1804 he sent an army expedition led by Meriwether Lewis and William Clark to explore the new territory.

Jefferson's economizing reduced the size of the United States Navy, which left him unable to eliminate the continuing threat by the Barbary Pirates of Algiers, Tunis, Morocco, and Tripoli, who demanded that merchant ships make a yearly payment of a "tribute." After a daring raid into the Tripoli harbor by Stephen Decatur in 1804 (in which he destroyed the frigate Philadelphia which had been seized by the pirates) and a naval blockade in 1805, the Americans reached a new agreement with the pirates.

Jefferson easily won a second term in 1804. His first Vice-President, Aaron Burr, had been replaced by George Clinton of New York. After Burr lost an election for the governorship of New York, he became involved in a bizarre scheme to form a new country out of the American west. When Jefferson was subpoenaed to be a witness at the trial, he refused, becoming the first president to exercise executive privilege. This, however, was not Jefferson's first tangling with the judiciary. Early in his first administration, in an attempt to remove the "midnight justices" appointed by Adams in the last months of his presidency, Jefferson abolished Adam's appointments. One of those Adams appointees, William Marbury, went all the way to the Supreme Court for his job. The principle of judicial review, while abhorrent to Jefferson (he wrote often of his fears of the judiciary's power), was to become a fundamental part of our national process.

During Jefferson's second term there were conflicts with the British and French over American trade with the other. This included attacks on American merchant vessels and blockades. Though many Americans called for war, Jefferson (whose scaled down navy was in no position to force any issue) opted to forbid all American ships from international trade with the passage of the Embargo Act of 1807. It was a failure, and three days before he left office in March of 1809, Congress revoked the Embargo Act.

Washington's refusal to run for a third term was a precedent that an office-weary Thomas Jefferson was glad to follow. But he did remain the leader of the Republican Party after leaving office, the only president to do so.

Jefferson spent his remaining years at Monticello, not only establishing the University of Virginia in Charlottesville, but designing much of the campus himself. His finances in later life were in poor shape, and after a friend defaulted on a loan he was forced to sell his magnificent library to the government. It became the nucleus of the Library of Congress.

In the early morning hours of July 4, 1826, Thomas Jefferson died at his home in Monticello, Virginia, on the fiftieth anniversary of the signing of his most cherished public act, the Declaration of Independence.

Historical Landmarks

Birthplace of Thomas Jefferson
Shadwell
Charlottesville, Virginia

Jefferson was born April 13, 1743 at his father's plantation house, Shadwell, in Albemarle County, on U.S. 250, about two miles southeast of Charlottesville, Virginia. Jefferson's father, Peter, had built it about 1737 on land he had purchased a year or so earlier from William Randolph.

Jefferson lived at Shadwell for the first two years of his life, and again during the years 1752-1770 on an intermittent basis. Fire destroyed the home in 1770 and afterwards the site was lost. In 1955, however, archaeologists, after a 14-year search, located it. The style of the original house is unknown but architects, under the auspices of the Jefferson

Birthplace Memorial Park Commission, designed and built a 1 1/2-story clapboard home faithful to the era and mode of life of Jefferson's parents. Subsequently, it was removed because it lacked authenticity.

An historic marker containing some of the above details designates the site.

Tuckahoe Plantation, Jefferson's Boyhood Home
12601 River Road
Richmond, Virginia

After two years at Shadwell, Jefferson spent the next seven years of his boyhood, from 1745 to 1752, living with his parents at Tuckahoe, home of his cousins, the Randolphs. The home was constructed between 1712 and 1730, with its present H-plan achieved through the construction of a T-shaped addition onto the earlier central-hall house. There are elaborately carved interior woodwork of pine and black walnut, a delicate stairway and small formal entrance porches on the land and river facades.

Tuckahoe is considered by architectural historians to be the finest existing early 18th century plantation in America and it still stands in its virtually undisturbed setting on a bluff overlooking the James River valley. In his forward to the book, *Tuckahoe Plantation*, University of Virginia Professor of Architecture Frederick Nichols, wrote, "Not only is the house priceless because of its completeness, but it contains some of the most important architectural ideas of the early Georgian Period. Probably unique in American architecture are the rare outbuildings, including paired structures which were the office and schoolhouse where Thomas Jefferson went to class."

Visitor's Information

The plantation is privately owned but open by appointment.
Admission $5.00 per person to tour the house and grounds; $1.00 per person for grounds only. Telephone: (804) 784-5736.

Tuckahoe is 7 miles west of Richmond city limits. From Interstate 64, just west of Richmond, take Parham South exit. Continue until Parham ends at River Road. Turn west, right, on River Road, go just over 4 miles, turn left into first lane past Route 649.

Thomas Jefferson

Monticello, Home of Thomas Jefferson
Charlottesville, Virginia

"Monticello," Italian for "Little Mountain," is an enduring tribute to the genius and versatility of Thomas Jefferson, who personally designed and supervised erection of this splendid mansion.

Jefferson inherited the 1,053-acre Shadwell Plantation when his father died in 1757 and after clearing and leveling a nearby hilltop, he began construction of Monticello in 1769. He moved into it upon Shadwell's destruction the following year. Architecture was one of Jefferson's chief delights and the house was built and subsequently remodeled over a period of 40 years, reflecting the pleasure he found in "putting up and pulling down."

Often described as one of America's foremost architectural masterpieces, Monticello remains today as a testimony to its creator's ingenuity and breadth of interests. Visitors are surprised to find that the entrance hall functioned as a museum containing fossil bones, a buffalo head, elk antlers, and a seven-day clock which indicated the day in addition to the hour.

The mansion consists of 2 1/2-stories over a basement and contains 35 rooms. The drawing room contains one of the first parquet floors in the United States and the house also has a dumbwaiter. It is largely furnished with Jefferson belongings.

Jefferson's attention to garden design paralleled his interest in architecture. Both ornamental and vegetable gardens, as well as two orchids, a vineyard, and an eighteen-acre "grove" or ornamental forest, were included in his plans. Few early American gardens are as well documented as those at Monticello and Jefferson's detailed records, along with recent archaeological discoveries, have made possible an accurate recreation of his gardening scheme.

Visitor's Information

Monticello is owned and operated by the Thomas Jefferson Memorial Foundation, Inc., a private, nonprofit organization formed in 1923 to purchase, preserve and maintain Monticello as a national monument to Thomas Jefferson.

Guided tours are offered daily except December 25 from 8:00 a.m. to 5:00 p.m. Winter hours are 9:00 a.m. to 4:30 p.m. from November 1 through February 28. Adult admission $7.00 per person; senior citizens (age 60 and over) $6.00 per person; children, ages 6-11 $3.00 per child. Telephone: (804) 295-8181.

Monticello is located on State Route 53, three miles southeast of Charlottesville. Exit 24A on I-64, then 1/2 mile south on State Route 20 and 1 1/2 miles east on State Route 53.

The Thomas Jefferson Visitors Center, located on State Route 20 just south of exit 24 off I-64, about two miles west of Monticello, features an exhibition called Thomas Jefferson at Monticello that focuses on Jefferson's domestic life at Monticello. It features an assortment of personal and family memorabilia and includes nearly 400 objects and artifacts, many of which were uncovered during archaeological excavations at Monticello, plus architectural models and drawings, and two audiovisual presentations. The exhibit complements the guided tour of the house and grounds. Daily 9:00 a.m. to 5:30 p.m. Winter hours are 9:00 a.m. to 5:00 p.m. from November 1 through February 28. Closed January 1, Thanksgiving and December 25. Admission free. Telephone: (804) 977-1783.

Poplar Forest
Forest, Bedford County, Virginia

Jefferson had inherited the land in Bedford County from his father-in-law, John Wayles. He first visited the property in 1773 and although Jefferson owned several plantations in Albermarle and Bedford counties, he built an elaborate house for his personal use at only two of them, Monticello and Poplar Forest. It was during his second term as president, in 1806, that Jefferson himself assisted his masons in laying the foundation for Poplar Forest, the dwelling that today is considered one of Jefferson's most creative and original architectural designs.

For his house at Poplar Forest Jefferson created an octagonal building based upon his own interpretation of the French Palladian style of architecture. Writing in 1812, Jefferson revealed his pleasure in the quality of the design, especially as a design for a purely private house: "When finished, it will be the best dwelling house in the state, except that of Monticello; perhaps preferable to that, as more proportioned to the faculties of a private citizen."

Poplar Forest became Jefferson's personal retreat. Overwhelmed by an almost perpetual round of visitors at Monticello, he escaped several times a year to find at Poplar Forest what he called the "solitude of a hermit." At his retreat he indulged in his favorite pursuits: reading, studying, and thinking. In addition, Jefferson oversaw the operation of his plantation, the embellishment of the house, the planting of the vegetable garden, and the adornment of the grounds with a variety or ornamental plants and trees.

Visitor's Information

Poplar Forest remained private property until 1984 but when the home became endangered, a nonprofit organization was formed to rescue this landmark for the public.

Tours are conducted Wednesday through Sunday and major holidays, from 10:00 a.m. to 4:00 p.m. (last tour begins at 3:45), April through October. Admission fees range from $1.00 for youth to $5.00 for adults. Telephone: (804) 525-1806.

Poplar Forest is just southwest of Lynchburg on Rt. 661, 1 mile from Rt. 221. To reach the entrance, take either Rt. 221 to Rt. 661, or take Rt. 460 and follow Routes 622 (Waterlick Road) and 811.

Thomas Jefferson Memorial
Washington, D.C.

In preparation of the plan for the memorial, the architects were clearly influenced by Jefferson's own taste as expressed in his writings and demonstrated by his designs of the rotunda at the University of Virginia and his famous home, Monticello. Thus the circular colonnaded structure is an adaptation of the classic style which Jefferson himself is credited with having introduced into this country.

The central memorial room contains a heroic bronze statue of Jefferson by sculptor Rudulph Evans, surrounded by panels inscribed with Jefferson's most significant writings.

The height of the statue is 19 feet and it stands in the center of the room on a pedestal of black Minnesota granite reaching 6 feet above the floor. The domed ceiling of Indiana limestone reaches approximately 67 feet above the head of the statue. The memorial was dedicated on April 13, 1943, the 200th anniversary of Jefferson's birth, and is administered by the National Park Service.

Visitor's Information

Open daily 8:00 a.m. to midnight; closed December 25. Free admission. Telephone: (202) 619-7222.

The Memorial is on the south bank of the Tidal Basin, 900 Ohio Drive SW, near downtown Washington. From Virginia, take the George Washington Parkway to Memorial Bridge, cross the bridge and follow Ohio Drive to the Memorial.

Jefferson National Expansion Memorial
St. Louis, Missouri

The vision of President Thomas Jefferson, the great architect of westward expansion, led to the purchase of the vast French empire of Louisiana from Napoleon in 1803. This brilliant act doubled the land area of the infant republic and assured the United States of a major role in the settlement of the North American continent.

With the Louisiana Purchase, St. Louis, which was founded in 1764 by French fur traders from New Orleans, became part of the United States. For many decades thereafter, the city was a key one on the western United States frontier. Its strategic location convenient to the Ohio, Missouri, and other river approaches made St. Louis the hub of mid-continental commerce, transportation, and culture, and a gateway to the wilderness beyond.

To dramatize the westward expansion and rich cultural, political and economic benefits that accrued to the Nation from the Louisiana Purchase, a memorial was established on the site of the original St. Louis settlement. In 1947, a national competition to select a suitable design for the memorial was won by the late Eero Saarinen's Gateway Arch. This colossal 630-foot high stainless steel arch, 75 feet higher than the Washington Monument, symbolizes the historic position of St. Louis as the gateway to the West. A special passenger tram within the Arch carries visitors in a four-minute ride to an observation deck at the top of the Arch. In the underground visitor center at the base of the arch is the Museum of Western Expansion. It uses exhibits, films and artifacts to depict the Nation's epic march to the West and is organized by themes that fan out chronologically from a central bronze statue of Thomas Jefferson. There is also a film on the construction of the arch.

Visitor's Information

The Memorial is administered by the National Park Service.

The visitor center which houses the Museum of Westward Expansion is open daily 8:00 a.m. to 10:00 p.m., Memorial Day-Labor Day; and 9:00 a.m. to 6:00 p.m. rest of the year. Closed January 1, Thanksgiving and December 25. Admission: Ages 17-61, $1.00; maximum $3.00 per family.

The tram to the observation deck at the top of the Arch is open daily 8:30 a.m. to 9:30 p.m., Memorial Day-Labor Day; and 9:30 a.m. to 5:30 p.m. rest of the year. Closed January 1, Thanksgiving and December 25. Fare for tram $2.50; ages 3-12, 50 cents.

The Memorial is located on the waterfront at Market Street within easy walking distance of downtown St. Louis. Telephone:
(314) 425-4465.

Burial Site
Monticello
Charlottesville, Virginia

On July 4, 1826, the fiftieth anniversary of the Declaration of Independence, its author, the third president of the United States died in his home at Monticello. The graveyard on the estate, where he is buried, was laid out by Jefferson in 1773, and it continues to be reserved as the family burial ground for his descendants. Over Jefferson's grave ia an obelisk inscribed as he had instructed:

Thomas Jefferson

Here was buried Thomas Jefferson
Author of the Declaration of American Independence
Of the Statute of Virginia for Religious Freedom
And Father of the University of Virginia

Visitor's Information

See information above for Monticello.

James Madison, 4th President, 1809-1817

Montpelier

Madison's Tomb

The Octagon Museum

James Madison

Fourth President
1809-1817
Republican

James Madison was born on March 16, 1751 at the home of his maternal grandmother in Port Conway, Virginia. (Among his ancestors was great-grandfather James Taylor, whose great-grandson Zachary would also become president.) After graduating from the predecessor to Princeton University in New Jersey in 1772, he studied the law and was soon engaged in politics, speaking out against the Stamp Act.

In 1794 he married a young widow, Dolley Payne Todd, who was 17 years his junior when they were introduced by Aaron Burr.

At the age of 25, he was a member of the Virginia Assembly serving at the same time as Thomas Jefferson. He was a participant in the Constitutional Convention in 1787, where he drafted the original articles and the first ten amendments, and became known as the "father of the Constitution." Madison's other contribution to the story of the Constitution was the painstaking record he made of the proceedings, which amazingly were kept secret until his death.

Aside from his work in securing ratification in his own state of Virginia, Madison, along with Alexander Hamilton and John Jay, successfully argued for the ratification of the Constitution in a series of articles printed in New York newspapers. These were later released together in a volume called *The Federalist*. Madison also served the as a member of the Continental Congress ,and during Washington's administration was elected from Virginia to the House of Representatives.

After serving for eight years as Thomas Jefferson's Secretary of State (during which time he negotiated the Louisiana Purchase), James Madison was elected president of the United States in 1808, beating Charles Pinckney of South Carolina by a decisive margin. His Vice-President was George Clinton, who had also served under Jefferson in his last term. (This makes Clinton the first of two Vice-Presidents to serve under two different presidents.)

Despite being a self-proclaimed student of political philosophy, Madison was not an adept politician. He encountered difficulty with Congress almost from the very beginning of his administration, and found himself forced to accept a Cabinet not of his choosing.

But it was events taking place beyond American shores which directed Madison's actions as president.

He was beset by problems stemming from the war between Britain and France. American ships, goods, and men were still being seized by the belligerents, and pressure for war came from many parts of the country. The northwestern states and territories saw war as a way to annex Canada, thus gaining fertile farmland and remove the threat many felt from British fur traders whom they believed were arming Indians against the Americans. Southerners saw it as an excuse to annex Florida, which was owned by British ally Spain. An agricultural depression, getting worse since it began in 1808, had caused the price of southern and western goods to plummet. These parts of the country were anxious for the chance to export their goods again.

On June 18, 1812, Congress declared war on Britain, not knowing that two days earlier the British Parliament suspended the offending Orders of Council, which had upheld Britain's right to search American ships that were suspected of trading with France. But the vote had been taken, and "Mr. Madison's War," as some Federalists called the War of 1812, had begun.

The war itself was a near disaster for the country. Madison's re-election in 1812 revealed a country deeply divided over the war, as he carried only one New England state (Vermont) and one Middle Atlantic state (Pennsylvania), while carrying all the southern and western states. The navy was small, and the entire war effort underfinanced. Not only were attempts at Canadian conquest foiled, but it was only through the gallantry and heroism of men such as Oliver Perry, who secured Lake Eire, that the British were prevented from possibly occupying America permanently.

With the abdication of Napoleon in 1814, Britain was free to send her troops across the Atlantic to fight the Americans. In August of 1814 they sacked Washington, and for the first (and only) time forced the president to flee the capital. It was Madison's wife Dolley who saved many of Madison's papers as well several paintings, among them the portrait of George Washington that hung in the White House.

The most decisive American victory of the War of 1812 took place weeks after the Treaty of Ghent was signed on Christmas Eve in 1814, when Andrew Jackson routed the British forces at New Orleans in January of 1815. The peace treaty, while solving none of the major points which led to the war, was submitted to the Senate by Madison and quickly ratified in early 1815.

During Madison's administration the Indian Confederacy under Chief Tecumseh had been crushed, and that, combined with the removal of the British from the west after the War of 1812, opened up the American frontier to farmers and settlers. The National Road, which went from Cumberland, Maryland to Ohio, was begun in 1811, although

Madison vetoed a bill appropriating money for improvements to the road in 1817. Despite his Republican heritage, Madison saw to the establishment of a national bank in 1816 which gave Americans a sound currency. The War of 1812 also caused a great revival of patriotism in America, as the nation become more prosperous and self-sufficient.

After almost forty-five years of uninterrupted public service, James Madison returned with Dolley to Montpelier, where they entertained guests such as Lafayette and Daniel Webster. Madison served as rector of the University of Virginia, and at the age of seventy-eight took part in Virginia's Constitutional Convention. Madison died on June 28, 1836 at the age of 85, his last message to the nation a stern warning about America's own "Pandora's box," slavery.

Dolley returned to Washington where she remained a social fixture, assisting other First Ladies in their duties. History also records that Dolley was present when Samuel B. Morse demonstrated the electric telegraph, and was the first woman to send a message through that device.

Historical Landmarks

Birthplace of James Madison
Belle Grove
Port Conway, Virginia

James Madison, the fourth president of the United States was born March 16, 1751 at Port Conway, King George County, Virginia. An historic marker at the site notes that Madison's mother "was staying at her paternal home, Belle Grove," when the future President was born.

Visitor's Information

The birthplace of James Madison is no longer standing. An historic marker on U.S. 301, 4 miles north of Port Royal, Virginia, identifies and gives information on the site.

Montpelier, Madison's Home
Route 20
Orange County, Virginia

Montpelier was Madison's residence for nearly all his life. Soon after his birth at his grandparent's home in King George County, he traveled with his mother to his father's farm in Orange County which had been in the family since 1732. There he first lived in a modest wooden house constructed by his grandfather, Ambrose Madison, about 20 years earlier. The early, or central, portion of the present Georgian mansion was built by his father, also named James, about 1760, probably a half mile north of his first home. When his father died in 1801, he bequeathed the house and part of the estate to his oldest son, James.

Madison's frequent absences were mainly for education or public service but on completion of his second term as president, he and his wife, Dolley, retired to Montpelier. They held court for a succession of distinguished visitors including the Marquis de Lafayette, James Monroe, Thomas Jefferson, and Daniel Webster.

The mansion was originally a brick rectangular structure, two stories in height over an elevated basement. It had two large rooms and a central hall on each floor. Madison had the home remodeled during his first term as president, in 1807-1811. The main building was enlarged and step-down one story wings were added. The huge Doric portico was added at a later date. In 1907, the wings were enlarged to 2 1/2-stories. Madison, who was interested in horticulture and agriculture, planned the gardens and landscaping of the estate.

After Madison died there in 1836, at age 85, Dolley Madison returned to Washington. She sold Montpelier in 1844. Title to the estate changed hands six times between 1844 and 1901, when it was purchased by William du Pont, Sr. In 1984, following the death of du Pont's daughter who had inherited the property, the National Trust for Historic Preservation acquired Montpelier.

The mansion and the beautifully landscaped grounds have been carefully maintained. Three-bay wings flank the seven-bay central section of the hip-roofed mansion. Four huge Doric columns support the two-story portico, which has a triangular pediment containing a semicircular window. The double-door front entrance is framed by sidelights and a fanlight. A pair of chimneys stand at either end of the main building, and a chimney at the end of each wing. A dentiled cornice adorns the roofline and the pediment.

Visitor's Information

In 1987, after decades as a private hunt country residence, the 2,700-acre estate, with its breathtaking views of the nearby Blue Ridge Mountains, was open to the public. Visitors may take guided tours of the estate which include a shuttle bus drive through part of the 2,700 acres, the 55-room mansion, more than 100 other structures and features, the Madison graves, and an audiovisual presentation on Madison and his importance to our nation.

Tours are conducted daily, 10:00 a.m. to 4:00 p.m.; closed Thanksgiving, December 25, January 1, mansion closed Montpelier race day.
Admission: adults, $5.00; over age 60, $4.00; ages 6-11, $1.00. Telephone: (703) 672-2728.

Montpelier is four miles southwest of Orange, VA, on Route 20. From Washington, D.C.: west on U.S. 66 to U.S. 29 to Culpeper, VA, then south on U.S. 15 to Route 20, Orange, VA. From Charlottesville, VA: northeast on Route 20 to Montpelier Station four miles before Orange.

James Madison Museum
129 Caroline Street
Orange, Virginia

Four permanent exhibits deal with the life and times of Madison and detail his important contributions to the American political system. Madison artifacts highlight the museum's main exhibit and include furnishings from Montpelier, presidential correspondence, fashions associated with his wife, Dolley, books from Madison's library, and other select pieces of Madisonia. There ia also an audiovisual presentation on Madison's Montpelier, his home for almost 85 years.

James Madison

In addition to the permanent Madison exhibits, special exhibits are presented on a regular basis.

Visitor's Information

The museum, operated by the James Madison Memorial Foundation, is open March-November: Weekdays 10:00 a.m. to 5:00 p.m., weekends 1:00 p.m. to 4:00 p.m. December-February: Weekdays 10:00 a.m. to 4:00 p.m., weekends closed.

Closed: January 1, Memorial Day, July 4, Labor Day, Thanksgiving, December 25.

Admission: Adults, $2.00; over 60, $1.75; ages 6-16, $.50.
Telephone: (703) 672-1776.

The museum is about 5 miles from Montpelier, in Orange at 129 Caroline Street, which runs off Main Street. It is diagonally across from the President Madison Inn.

The Octagon,
Temporary White House during Madison's Presidency
1799 New York Avenue NW
Washington, DC

When the British burned the White House during the War of 1812, President Madison and his wife accepted the invitation of Colonel John Tayloe, a wealthy Virginia planter, to live in his 18th century Georgian townhouse. They lived there in 1814-1815.

The house was considered one of the finest in the nation and presidential life quickly resumed a normal pace, though wartime anxieties cast a pall over social gatherings. The Madison's living quarters were on the second floor, in the southeast suite, which consisted of a small vestibule, a large bedroom with a fireplace, and a smaller dressing room. The president used the adjoining circular tower room as a study and, at times, as a meeting place for his cabinet. There, on February 17, 1815, he signed the Treaty of Ghent which ended the War of 1812.

James Madison

In 1815, the Madisons moved to "Seven Buildings" on Pennsylvania Avenue (no longer in existence) where they lived for the rest of the President's term of office.

Visitor's Information

Despite its name, Octagon House is actually an irregular hexagon broken by a dominant semicircular bay projecting from the front, or southeast face. There are eight sides only if the front bay is counted as three.

The house, now a museum, is owned by the American Architectural Foundation, open to the public with guided tours provided. In President Madison's study, the first rotunda on the second floor, is the pivoted circular table on which he signed the treaty of Ghent. Displayed on it is the small leather bound trunk in which the document was brought back from Europe. Other second floor rooms, including the area used by the Madisons for living quarters, are now exhibit galleries with changing exhibitions related to architecture, decorative arts and Washington history.

Open weekdays except Mondays, 10:00 a.m. to 4:00 p.m.; weekends, 12:00 p.m. to 4:00 p.m. Closed on major holidays. Suggested donation $2.00. Telephone: (202) 638-3105.

The house, on New York Avenue and 18th Street, is easily reached by public transportation.

Burial Site
Montpelier
Route 20
Orange County, Virginia

Madison died quietly in bed at Montpelier, June 28, 1836. His wife, Dolley, died in Washington, July 12, 1749. They are both buried in the Madison family cemetery on the Montpelier estate.

James Madison

The Madison monument is a tall shapely stone with the following simple inscription on its face:

Madison
Born, March 16, 1751
Died, June 28, 1836

Neither his first name nor any reference to his having served as the fourth president of the United States for two terms is noted.

Visitor's Information

See Montpelier above for details.

James Monroe, 5th President, 1817-1825

Oak Hill

Tomb of James Monroe

James Monroe Museum and Memorial Library

James Monroe

Fifth President
1817 - 1825
Democrat-Republican

James Monroe was born to Spence Monroe (a carpenter and farmer) and Elizabeth Jones in Port Conway, Virginia on April 28, 1758. As a boy he used to walk to school with his friend, future Supreme Court Chief Justice John Marshall. While at William and Mary he listened to speeches by fellow classmate Patrick Henry. In 1775, at only seventeen years of age and apparently filled with the fervor of Independence, he joined Benjamin Harrison, Jr, (the father of future president William Henry Harrison), and others in seizing ammunition being stored at the royal governor's palace in Richmond, Virginia. The following year he joined the Third Virginia Regiment, in whose company he was wounded. At the age of nineteen he was at Valley Forge with Washington, and soon held the rank of major. Monroe would be the last man to be elected president who had fought in the Revolutionary War.

After American Independence he studied law, and in 1786, the same year that he was admitted to the bar, he married Elizabeth Kortright, the daughter of a New York City merchant. He later served in the Continental Congress, the Virginia Constitutional Convention, and the United States Senate. He was Washington's envoy to France, but was recalled for failing to hide his French leanings at a time when neutrality was the order of the day. Later, he served as Jefferson's minister to England.

James Monroe was the third Virginian in a row to be elected to the presidency when he beat New Yorker Rufus King in 1816, and was the last of the so-called "Virginia Dynasty." So strong were the feelings of nationalism following the War of 1812 that he was overwhelmingly re-elected in 1820 with only one electoral vote cast against him. Having served as Madison's Secretary of State, (before becoming Secretary of War in 1814) he became the second man in a row to ascend to the presidency from that position. (John Quincy Adams, who served as his Secretary of State, would be the third when he became president after Monroe.)

Monroe, a Republican, was fortunate to preside over a country still feeling euphoric over the outcome of the War of 1812. He began his first term with a tour of New

England, a region once known as a strong Federalist stronghold. There he was greeted with such enthusiasm by crowds wherever he went that the Federalist newspaper the *Columbian Sentinel* described his election as the beginning of an "Era of Good Feelings."

But the "Era of Good Feelings" quickly eroded. In 1819 America experienced its first economic depression. The South and North began squabbling over the implementation of a protective tariff, which was later passed (in a mild form) by Congress in 1824. The issue of slavery in the new states began to create hard feelings among Americans. The argument continued until 1820 when Maine, which had just separated itself from Massachusetts, was admitted as a free state and Missouri as slave. More importantly, it limited slavery in the Louisiana Purchase to below the 36 degree 30 minute line, effectively eliminating it in the western part of the country. Known as the Missouri Compromise, it preserved the delicate balance of slave and free states for a while longer.

The Western Hemisphere at the time of Monroe's inauguration was part independent country, part colony, and part territory claimed by one or more powers. After Napoleon's France conquered Spain in 1808, many Latin American countries revolted, seeking independence. Monroe wanted to recognize these new countries, but feared reprisal from European powers bent on retaining their colonies.

To meet the threats from European powers, most notably Russia, Prussia, Austria and Britain, (who had organized themselves into the Quadruple Alliance), Monroe, in a December 2, 1823 message to Congress, enunciated the Monroe Doctrine. It asserted that 1) the Western Hemisphere was closed to colonization, 2) any attempt at colonization would be considered an unfriendly act toward the United States, 3) the United States would not interfere in European Affairs or any established colony in the Western Hemisphere, and 4) no European country must involve itself politically in any free country here, either.

Though much of what the Monroe Doctrine sought to achieve was, through independent avenues, becoming part of the international status quo, it was nevertheless an important stand for the still young nation to take, and remains the most important contribution made by the Monroe presidency.

Monroe lived for six years after his retirement from the presidency on his estate in Oak Hill, Virginia. He became a regent of the University of Virginia, served as co-chairman of the State constitutional convention of 1829-30, and acted as a local magistrate. His wife Elizabeth passed away in 1830, and a year later, facing bankruptcy, he moved to the home of his daughter and son-in-law in New York City. He died there on July 4, 1831 at the age of 73, the third president to die on Independence Day.

Historical Landmarks

Birthplace of James Monroe
Monrovia
Colonial Beach, Virginia

James Monroe was born April 28, 1758, on his parent's small plantation, "Monrovia," near Colonial Beach, Westmoreland County, Virginia. The area has been called the "Athens of America" because it has been the birthplace of so many distinguished Americans including Washington, Jefferson and Madison.

The house in which Monroe was born and lived in until 1769 has entirely disappeared. An historic marker on State Highway V.A. 205 between Oak Grove and Colonial Beach, Virginia, states, "In this vicinity stood the Monroe home where James Monroe, the fifth president of the United States, was born."

James Monroe Museum and Memorial Library
908 Charles Street
Fredericksburg, VA

After the Revolutionary War, Monroe returned to Virginia to read law under the guidance of Governor Thomas Jefferson. In February, 1786, he married Elizabeth Kortright of New York and established a law practice in Fredericksburg, Virginia, where he was a Town Councilman and a representative to the Continental Congress.

The restored early ninteenth century brick building on property Monroe owned is now a museum and library owned by the Commonwealth of Virginia, and administered by Mary Washington College. The museum contains more Monroe-related items than any other institution in the nation including a Louis XVI desk, with its secret compartments. On this desk, in 1823, President Monroe signed his annual message to Congress, a section of which became known as the Monroe Doctrine. Other exhibits include Louis XVI furniture he purchased in France and used in the White House, costumes and gems owned by Mrs. Monroe and an variety of other possessions that belonged to the Monroes. The old-fashioned walled garden contains a bronze bust of James Monroe.

The library contains thousands of books and historical manuscripts with the emphasis of the collection on the life and times of James Monroe.

Visitor's Information

Open daily, 9:00 a.m. to 5:00 p.m. except Thanksgiving, December 24, 25, 31 and January 1.

Admission: adults, $3.00, ages 7-16, $1.00. Telephone: (703) 899-4559.

Fredericksburg is located on I-95 just 50 miles south of Washington and 55 miles north of Richmond. The Route 3 exit from I-95 leads to the downtown historic area and the Law Office-Museum is near its intersection with Charles Street.

Ash Lawn-Highland
Charlottesville, Virginia

In 1796, Thomas Jefferson designed the rambling, hilltop Highland for his friend and neighbor on 800 acres that Monroe has purchased within sight of Jefferson's Monticello in 1789.

Monroe's move to the two-story, L-shaped house that he called Highland, perhaps because of his Scottish ancestry or possibly because it was his "upper" plantation (he owned other tracts of land in the county) resulted from his friendship with Jefferson who wished to create "a society to our taste" near Monticello. Jefferson personally selected the site for the house and sent his gardeners to start orchards. On November 23, 1799, James Monroe and his wife, Elizabeth, moved to their new home where frequent guests included James Madison and his wife, Dolley.

For 25 years Monroe's residence was his beloved "cabin-castle" but by 1825 his debts forced him to sell the farm to which he had hoped to retire. After changing hands several times, Jay Winston Johns, a Pittsburgh industrialist, bought Ash Lawn in 1929 (it had been renamed in 1838). He recognized the historic importance of the home, opened it to the public in 1931, and spent the rest of his life collecting Monroe furnishings and appropriate period pieces for display. He died in 1974 and bequeathed Ash Lawn-Highland, its furnishings, and 535 acres to James Monroe's alma mater, the College of William and Mary. The College initiated an ongoing restoration and today visitors can find the atmosphere of an early 19th-century working plantation.

Visitor's Information

Guided tours of the main house are available and periodic cooking and spinning demonstrations and other activities are offered. Telephone: (804) 293-9539.

Open: Daily 9:00 a.m. to 6:00 p.m., March-October; 10:00 a.m.-5:00 p.m., rest of year. Closed: January 1, Thanksgiving, December 25.

Admission: Adults, $6.00, Senior Citizens, $5.50, Children (6-11), $2.00.

Ash Lawn-Highland is 2 1/2 miles past Monticello off State Route 53 on County Road 795.

Oak Hill
Aldie, Loudoun County, Virginia

James Monroe built this palatial mansion at the height of his career, during his first term as president (1817-1821), drafted the Monroe Doctrine in it, and retired there at the end of his public career in 1825. In 1808 Monroe had inherited the property on which the mansion stands from an uncle, but lack of funds prevented him from beginning construction of a home for at least a decade. Thomas Jefferson designed the mansion, and James Hoban, architect of the White House and Capitol, provided architectural assistance. Constructed of brick kilned nearby, the structure was completed in 1823. Monroe furnished it with pieces from his Highland estate which he later sold. On the grounds, among the numerous locust and polar trees, he planted an oak for each state in the Union and thereby gave the estate its name.

The mansion originally consisted of a two-story central portion with small, one-room wings. In 1923, the owner enlarged the wings to two full stories. The south portico, two stories high and supported by seven doric pillars, is the most striking feature of the residence. On the first floor are an entrance hall, two drawing rooms, dining room, sitting room, library, master's room, guest room, and pantry. Bedrooms, servant's quarters, and four sun decks occupy the second floor. A number of outbuildings remain, including a smokehouse, springhouse, law office, and "Monroe's Cottage," which is a small frame structure that served as his residence before he built the present mansion.

Visitor's Information

Oak Hill is a working farm and private residence. It is open for groups of 20 or more on a pre-arranged basis through the Loudoun Visitor's Center, 108 South Street SE, Leesburg, Virginia.
Admission: $5.00 per person. Telephone: (703) 777-0519.

Burial Site
Hollywood Cemetery
Cherry and Albermarle Streets
Richmond, Virginia

Long years of public service had left Monroe in poor financial straits and shortly after his wife died at Oak Hill, September 23, 1830, he went to live with his daughter and son-in-law in New York City. It was in their home that he died on July 4, 1831.

The funeral was held at St Paul's Chapel on Broadway and his body was interred in Marble Cemetery, Second Street, in New York City. In 1858, the 100th anniversary of his birth, Virginia officials decided that the remains should be returned to his home state for reburial. On July 5 the body accompanied by the 7th Regiment of the New York National Guard, arrived in Richmond and an impressive ceremony was held on that day at the grave site, on a high bluff overlooking the James River, in Richmond's Hollywood Cemetery. The tomb is an ornate Gothic Revival structure in the form of a rectangular "cage" surrounding Monroe's simple granite sarcophagus. It sits on a solid but elaborately decorated base and a low stone wall encircles the tomb.

Visitor's Information

Hollywood Cemetery is the burial place for many of Virginia's greatest men, including President John Tyler, Jefferson Davis, General J.E.B. Stuart, and many others. A granite pyramid honors 18,000 Confederate soldiers buried there.

Open daily 8:00 a.m. to 6:00 p.m., mid-May to mid-October; rest of the year, 8:00 a.m. to 5:00 p.m. Telephone: (804) 648-8501.

The cemetery is located at Cherry and Albermarle Streets, Richmond. Take U.S. 1 (Chamberlayne/Belvidere Streets) south to Cumberland, turn right and proceed to Laurel, turn left for two blocks and turn right onto Albermarle.

John Quincy Adams, 6th President, 1825-1829

Birthplace of John Quincy Adams

Tombs of John Quincy Adams and his wife

John Quincy Adams

Sixth President
1825 - 1829
Democrat-Republican

There is, in America, no royalty. That is, in part, what the revolution was about, letting the people govern themselves. Yet there is no doubt that some families, through their consistency of service, seem to be almost fixtures in the national political scene. The Adams family is one such example, having given us two presidents, an ambassador, congressmen and notable historians.

The oldest of John Adams' children, John Quincy Adams was born at the Adams homestead in Braintree (now Quincy) on July 11, 1767. Perhaps no child had public service instilled in him as did John Quincy Adams. By the time he was twelve he had, with his father, run the British blockade four times on his way to Paris. At fourteen he was given the job of secretary to the Ambassador to Russia. He studied in Europe before returning to pursue law at Harvard, which he graduated from in 1787. He was admitted to the bar in 1790, but was soon asked by George Washington to be the Minister to the Hague. Later, he became Minister to Prussia before returning to Massachusetts and running for (and winning) the office of Senator in 1802.

While in London as American Consul in 1795 he met a twenty year old English born woman named Louisa Catherine Johnson, whose father was an American businessman and whose mother was British. They were married two years later, and when Adams became president she became our only First Lady born in another country.

John Quincy Adams returned to the diplomatic corps as Minister to Russia from 1809 to 1814, and was then appointed to the commission which negotiated the Treaty of Ghent which ended the War of 1812. John Quincy Adams was a skilled negotiator, and as Monroe's Secretary of State, he helped draft the Monroe Doctrine and worked out the joint occupancy of Oregon with the British. One of his greatest moments came after General Andrew Jackson, who had been authorized to eradicate marauding Indians, crossed over the Florida border and quickly seized most of the Spanish outposts in their territory. Adams managed to turn this into America's advantage, successfully negotiating the Adams-Onis Treaty, in which Spain gave in to the American demands for all territory east of the Mississippi and relinquished any of her claims to Oregon.

John Quincy Adams

The election of 1824 was a study in sectionalism, as each of the three sections of the country was represented by a candidate. War hero Andrew Jackson represented the western states, Georgian William Crawford, who had served as Monroe's Secretary of Treasury, represented the Southern states, and Secretary of State John Quincy Adams of Massachusetts represented the north. Also running was Henry Clay, who represented Kentucky in the Senate but viewed himself as a national candidate.

When none of the four candidates culled the necessary votes for a majority, (Jackson had 99, Adams 84, Crawford 41, and Clay 37), the Twelfth Amendment went into effect, sending the top three vote getters to the House of Representatives. With Clay's support (though he was no great fan of Adams, he did not think Jackson qualified), John Quincy Adams became president. South Carolinian John C. Calhoun became Vice-President. When Adams appointed Clay as his Secretary of State, Jackson was enraged, and charged (quite incorrectly) that there was a "corrupt bargain."

Adams advocated a number of nationally sponsored improvements. He succeeded in establishing a uniform standard of weights and measures and appropriating several million investing dollars for improvements to the National Road and investing in several private canal companies. But his quest for a National University and an astronomical observatory failed, as did his attempts to create a Cabinet level Department of Interior.

The tariff question continued to create sectional friction. Trying to please everybody while helping to forge an independent American economy, Adams got a tariff passed in 1828. But it was so badly pieced together from regional requirements that it only served to create even more dissent, especially in the South, where Adams' enemies labeled it the "Tariff of Abominations."

As adept as Adams was as a negotiator before becoming president (witness the Adams-Onis Treaty), once in office he failed to display the same brilliance. When the British opened a small part of the lucrative West Indies to American ships, Adams demanded better terms. The British simply rescinded their offer and closed the ports to Americans once again.

Adams gained a great many enemies during his administration and was defeated at a try for a second term by Andrew Jackson in 1828. He became the first and only president to serve in the House of Representatives after leaving our nation's highest office. He served there for sixteen years, gaining the nickname "Old Man Eloquent." In the House he became a champion of the anti-slavery movement, opposed the Mexican War, and sponsored the establishment of the Smithsonian Institution. It was on the floor of the House of Representatives that he was fatally stricken with paralysis, and died on February 23, 1848.

Historical Landmarks

Birthplace of John Quincy Adams
141 Franklin Street
Ouincy, Massachusetts

John Quincy Adams was born July 11, 1767 in his parent's home. His grandfather, "Deacon" John Adams had acquired the residence in 1744 and the oldest part may date to 1663. The house is well preserved. Like John Adams' birthplace, it is of typical New England saltbox design, originally comprised of two upper and two lower rooms arranged around a huge central chimney but it has been extensively altered.

Visitor's Information

The birthplace is part of the Adams National Historic Site administered by the National Park Service.

See John Adams section for details.

Peacefield-Adams Mansion
Adams Street and Newport Avenue
Quincy, Massachusetts

Like his father before him, the Adams Mansion became home to John Quincy Adams. He celebrated his 50th wedding anniversary at Peacefield as did his father and his son. The house abounds with priceless heirlooms and furnishings from the four generations of Adams family members who lived there. (See section on John Adams for further information on Peacefield.)

Visitor's Information

See John Adams section for details.

John Quincy Adams

Burial Site
United First Parish Church (Unitarian)
1306 Hancock Street
Quincy, Massachusetts

Adams, elected to Congress after his presidency, suffered a stroke at his desk in the House of Representatives on February 21, 1848. He was carried into the Speaker's room because he was too ill to be taken from the building. He died there two days later.

John Quincy Adams and his wife are interred in the same crypt as his father and mother in the United First Parish Church (Unitarian).

Visitor's Information

See John Adams section for details.

Andrew Jackson, 7th President, 1829-1837

Springfield Plantation

The Hermitage

Jackson's Burial Site

Andrew Jackson

Seventh President
1829- 1837
Democrat

Andrew Jackson was born on March 15, 1767 in the Waxhaws region along the North and South Carolina border, just two days after his father, a poor farmer, died. The Revolution cost the lives of his two brothers and mother, who died while tending to wounded soldiers. Captured, he was scarred for life by the sword of a British officer whose boots he refused to brush.

Jackson had attended a country school, and began studying the law when he was in his teens. He was admitted to the bar when he was twenty. In 1791 he married the daughter of a member of the Virginia House of Burgess, Rachel Donelson.

When Tennessee became a state in 1796, Jackson was elected its first Congressman, a position he later resigned to accept a judgeship in that state's Supreme Court. He became a general in the Tennessee militia and a major general in the regular army. In March of 1814, during the War of 1812 he beat the Creek Indians at the Battle of Horseshoe Bend, captured Pensecola, Florida (to prevent the British from using it as a base), and engaged the British at New Orleans, winning a decisive victory. Unfortunately, due to slow communication, the Battle of New Orleans was actually fought *after* the Treaty of Ghent was signed. But to the American public Andrew Jackson became, next to George Washington, its greatest hero.

He continued to serve in the army and in 1818 he invaded Spanish Florida in pursuit of marauding Seminole Indians. By the time his attack was over, he had captured all but one Spanish fort and hung two British soldiers he accused of providing arms to the Indians. After negotiations with Spain turned Florida over to the United States, he was appointed the territory's military governor. In 1822 he went to Washington as a Senator from Tennessee, and two years later lost his first bid for the presidency when he won a plurality but failed to received a majority of electoral votes. Charging Adams with a "corrupt bargain," Jackson quit the Senate to devote himself full time to a run for the White House.

Andrew Jackson's election to the presidency in 1828 represented the beginning of a new era in American politics, for by this time most states had opted for direct election of presidential electors by the people, rather than by state legislators. Jackson was also the first of the "log cabin" presidents, and by making the trek from poor farmer all the way to the White House, he seemed to epitomize all that was possible in the country. He became the nation's first president not born in either Virginia or Massachusetts and its first non-aristocrat. His Vice President was John C. Calhoun, who had already served four years under John Quincy Adams, making Calhoun the second Vice President to serve under two different presidents.

Jackson's inauguration day left many wondering if the people's candidate was not the predecessor to mob rule, for after his inauguration speech the gates of the White House were flung open so that the people could join in the celebration. A melee ensued, resulting in White House property being damaged and the President forced to flee the mansion for fear of being injured.

Part of Jackson's philosophy about government was that officeholders should be "rotated" out to prevent indifference and improve performance. He also saw it as a chance to give ordinary people the chance to participate in their government. He was also honest in his other reason for removing many officeholders- they had supported his opponents. This program became known by its critics as the "Spoils System," and it resulted in political patronage, the professional politician, and the political "boss."

One of Jackson's innovations was the "Kitchen Cabinet," a group of advisors who served in an unofficial capacity. Among these men were some newspaper editors, whom Jackson used to mold public opinion for his policies.

Jackson, whose abilities to lead were questioned by some who had supported John Quincy Adams, managed to succeed in one area of foreign affairs where Adams had failed when he negotiated trade rights in the West Indies with the British. He also forced the French to deliver payments owed for damages incurred during the Napoleonic Wars.

As a warrior, Jackson had led troops against many Native American tribes. As president, he saw to a massive, often brutal removal of Native Americans from their homelands. In an act disregarding two Supreme Court rulings which declared their treaty rights had been violated, thousands of Native Americans were forcibly moved to land west of the Mississippi.

Despite the National Bank of the United States' accomplishments, Jackson, like many of his fellow Westerners and Southerners, distrusted it and resented its strict lending policies. And scornful of a Supreme Court decision to the contrary (McCulloch vs.

Maryland, 1819) he also professed his belief that the bank was unconstitutional. Henry Clay, seeking an issue to use against Jackson in the 1832 election, got the bank president to apply for a renewal of his charter. It passed both houses of Congress, and went on to the president, who vociferously vetoed it. It became the major campaign issue of 1832, with Clay in support of the bank and Jackson against. But Andrew Jackson had read public sentiment correctly, and he easily won re-election over Clay and America's first third-party candidate, William Wirt, a Baltimore lawyer who ran as the standard bearer of the Anti-Mason (and anti-Jackson) party.

A hint of the great conflict between the North and the South came in 1836 when South Carolina threatened to secede from the United States because of the high tariffs. Jackson mobilized federal troops to enforce the tax, and when South Carolina failed to gain the support of any other Southern states, its leaders accepted a compromise tariff drafted by Henry Clay.

Andrew Jackson was devoted to the country and committed to the Union. The delicate balance between the free and slave states is what kept Jackson, and several presidents who followed, from taking action on the request by the newly formed Republic of Texas for admission to the Union. He waited until the last day of his administration, March 3, 1837, to formally recognize the new Republic.

One of the tributes to the impact of Andrew Jackson's presidency comes from the fact that historians chose his name as a description for his eight years in office- the Jacksonian Era. His attacks on the National Bank, his defense of the Union in the nullification crisis, his support of the nominating convention (which forever ended the practice of secret Congressional nominating caucuses), and his frequent use of the veto gave the average American a sense that the government was truly in the hands of the people.

Following tradition, Andrew Jackson chose not to run for a third term. He was the first president to actively campaign for his successor, helping Martin Van Buren win the White House in 1836. Jackson retired to his plantation, The Hermitage, near Nashville, Tennessee. He died there on June 8, 1845.

Historical Landmarks

Birthplace of Andrew Jackson

Andrew Jackson was born on March 15, 1767, in either North Carolina or South Carolina, no one really knows for sure. Jackson believed that he was born on the farm of his uncle, James Crawford, near Waxhaw settlement, South Carolina. The Crawford's log cabin home stood on the west side of the road that formed the boundary between the two states at that time.

The debate on the matter of where Jackson was born began about 1815 when he emerged as the "Hero of New Orleans" after defeating the British army. At various times four states and Ireland have claimed his birth.

An historical marker in Andrew Jackson State Park says he was born "near this site on South Carolina soil ... at the plantation whereon James Crawford lived and where Jackson himself said he was born."

North Carolina claims his birth took place in the log cabin of another uncle, George McCamie, in Union County (formerly Mecklenburg).

Springfield Plantation
Miss. Route 553
Fayette, Mississippi

While living in the Nashville boarding house of the widow Donelson, Jackson became attracted to her daughter, Mrs. Rachel Donelson Robards, who was separated from her husband. Later to escape her family situation she went to visit the Greens, old family friends who owned Springfield Plantation near Natchez. And, when she and Jackson heard that her husband had obtained a divorce they were married at Springfield in August, 1791. In December, 1793, however, they learned that the divorce had only been granted in September 1793, and they were remarried in Nashville. This marriage issue was raised in the presidential election of 1828 where Jackson was called a "paramour husband" and Rachel accused of being a "convicted adulteress." This unintentional illegal marriage was the source of some gossip and the spark for Jackson's participation in more than a few duels.

The combination of this historic event and the major architectural significance of this house makes the Springfield Plantation, with its 1,000 acres, one of the country's most notable landmarks. Springfield was one of the first houses in America to have a full colonnade across the entire facade and is the first such mansion to be built in the Mississippi Valley. Still a working plantation after more than two centuries, Springfield remains almost entirely original, including magnificent Georgian-Adams-Federal woodwork and mantles hand carved in Virginia in the 18th century.

Visitor's Information

Guided tours daily 10:00 a.m. to 6:00 p.m., May-September; 10:00 a.m. to 5:30 p.m., March-April and October 1-November 15; call for hours, rest of year. Closed December 25. Overnight guests accepted by reservation. Telephone: (601) 786-3802.

Admission: adults $5.00; senior citizens $4.50; ages 5-11, $2.50.

Directions from the north: U.S. Highway 61 south or Natchez Trace to Miss. Route 553, at Fayette Junction; right on Route 553 , 9 miles. One mile past the Natchez Trace.

Directions from the south: U.S. Highway 61 north to Natchez Trace. Left onto Trace for 2 miles to junction with Miss. Route 553; left onto 553 for 12 miles.

Andrew Jackson State Park
U.S. 521
Lancaster, South Carolina

Allegedly built on Andrew Jackson's birthplace, the park contains a museum with his letters, last will and testament, and many antiques and artifacts from his era. The park reflects the period from 1750 to 1850 which includes the time when Jackson spent his early years in this rugged pioneer area which once belonged to the Waxhaw Indians. The museum also houses a collection of Indian arrowheads and artifacts, an antique spinning wheel and weaving loom, along with a period bedroom and kitchen furnishings from the Jackson era. Besides the five museum rooms filled with furnishings and memorabilia from the period of Jackson's youth, there is a frontier schoolhouse, a meeting house and an equestrian statue of the "Boy of the Waxhaws." This is a larger than life-size statue of Andrew Jackson as a youth astride his horse, a gift from famed sculptress Anna Hyatt Huntington on the 200th anniversary of Jackson's birth.

The park also contains a marker noting what may be the birthplace of Andrew Jackson. Visitor's Information

Park open daily during daylight hours.
Museum open Saturday-Sunday, 1:00 p.m.-5:00 p.m., other days by appointment. Telephone: (803) 285-3344.

Admission: Free.

From Charlotte, North Carolina: Take I-77 south to U.S. 21/S.C. 5 south (Exit 77) and follow signs to Andrew Jackson State Park on U.S. 521, 8 miles north of Lancaster.

The Hermitage
4580 Rachel's Lane
Hermitage, Tennessee

For more than 40 years, during which Andrew Jackson rose from a frontier military commander to the Presidency, he made this estate his home.

In 1804, Jackson purchased 1,200 acres of land in central Tennessee and planted groves of peach and apple trees. He and his wife, Rachel, moved into a two-story cabin already on the property, which he called The Hermitage. Jackson added a lean-to back of the cabin and to the rear erected a group of log structures, including slave cabins, storerooms, and a smokehouse. Soon afterwards he settled down to the life of a plantation farmer. The War of 1812 intervened and he became a national hero. He returned to The Hermitage whenever he could and in 1818-19 Jackson had erected a brick house to replace the log structure he had lived in for 15 years. The new residence was a square building two stories high. On each floor were four rooms, each with fireplace, divided into pairs by large central halls.

During his first term as president he enlarged his home and added wings on both sides. In 1834 fire destroyed much of the interior of the home but Jackson rebuilt and refurnished it, and it was ready for occupancy in May 1835. At the end of his second term, in 1837, Jackson retired to The Hermitage, where he lived out his days as an elder statesman. His beloved wife, Rachel, had died on December 28, 1828, a few weeks before his inauguration as president.

Except for the tree-lined, guitar-shaped driveway, which dates from 1837, The Hermitage appears today as it did after the 1835 reconstruction. From the broad front portico with flagstone floor, double doors lead to the central hall, which is dominated by a circular staircase. The walls of the hall are covered with scenic French wallpaper. To the left of the hall are double parlors connected by folding doors. Each of these chambers has a marble mantlepiece. The grounds include an early 19th century garden designed for Jackson's wife, Rachel, with landscaping and plantings representative of the era.

Visitor's Information

The mansion is furnished with many of the original furniture and fixtures; nearly all of President and Mrs. Jackson's personal effects are here. A short distance from the house are two of the log houses where the family lived from 1804 when Jackson purchased the property, until 1821 when the family moved into the main house.

Tours include the mansion and grounds, log houses, dependencies and slave quarters, a visitor's center and museum which displays personal artifacts belonging to the Jackson family and a biographical film of the seventh president.

Included in the tour is Tulip Grove, residence of Andrew Jackson Donelson, the president's nephew and confidante who was Jackson's secretary and whose wife, Emily, became hostess for the widowed Jackson during the White House years.

Open 9:00 a.m. to 5:00 p.m. every day of the year except Thanksgiving and December 25. Telephone: (615) 889-2941.
Admission: Adults $7.00; over 65, $6.50; ages 6-18, $3.50.

The Hermitage is about twelve miles east of Nashville. Take I-40 to Old Hickory Boulevard exit and proceed to Rachel's Lane.

Burial Site
The Hermitage
4580 Rachel's Lane
Nashville, Tennessee

While at The Hermitage, on June 8, 1845, Jackson fell unconscious. Upon awakening he saw his weeping slaves crowded around him. He looked at them and said, "Oh, do not cry, be good children, and we will all meet in heaven." Jackson died that evening and he was buried beside his wife in a corner of the Hermitage garden. The tomb was built by Jackson long before his death and was erected over his wife, with a crypt left for himself. A lengthy inscription on the tomb of his wife who had died 17 years earlier bears evidence of his devotion. His own simple inscription reads:

General
Andrew Jackson
Born on the 15th of March, 1767
Died on the 8th of June, 1845.

Visitor's Information

See The Hermitage above for details.

Martin Van Buren, 8th President, 1837-1841

Lindenwald, Home of Martin van Buren

Burial Site of Martin Van Buren

Martin Van Buren

Eighth President

1837 - 1841
Democratic

Born December 5, 1782, Martin Van Buren was the first president born after the Declaration of Independence and the first under the U.S. flag. He was also the first born in New York, in a town called Kinderhook. Martin studied hard to achieve his goal of becoming a lawyer, and began the study of law at the age of fourteen. At seventeen he left for New York City, took a job as a law clerk, and was admitted to the bar four years later.

In 1807 he married Hannah Hoes, a girl with whom he had grown up in Kinderhook. They soon moved to Hudson, New York, where Martin began practicing law. Hannah died after delivering Van Buren's fourth son in 1819, and he never remarried.

He loved politics, and was a delegate to a political convention at the age of twenty-one. He became a State Senator, New York Attorney General, and in 1820 a United States Senator. After his re-election to the Senate in 1826, he resigned to become Governor of New York. After only two months in office he resigned that job to become Andrew Jackson's Secretary of State. His political acumen gained him several appellations, among them "The Flying Dutchman," "The Little Magician," and the "Red Fox of Kinderhook."

Martin Van Buren faced an unusual challenge in the Presidential election of 1836. Anointed by Andrew Jackson as his successor (whom he served as Secretary of State during the first term and Vice-President in the second), Van Buren was opposed by three men all running under the banner of the Whig party. The Whig Party was a coalition of former Republicans, Jackson foes, as well as commercial and other special interests. Their own lack of unity forced the party's leaders to adopt the "favorite son" tactic, whereby each ran sectional candidates who, it was hoped, would draw enough votes from Van Buren to throw the election to the House of Representatives.

The plan failed, and Van Buren was elected by a comfortable margin. But much like another future president, Van Buren would be forced to spend much of his time dealing with a serious depression that hit the country soon after he took office. The 1837 depression was, much like the one over which Herbert Hoover presided, brought on by speculators, in this case men who invested heavily using borrowed money from Jackson's pet banks. This money, it turned out, had little real value. Van Buren, who believed in the Jacksonian theory of less government, did not intercede to ease the depression. "The less government interferes with private business the better the general prosperity," he once said. Recognizing the need for reform, however, he proposed an independent treasury system, whereby the country's banking business would be carried out by private banks regulated by the states. The measure, after much debate, was finally passed just as Van Buren's only term in the White House ended.

Martin Van Buren succeeded twice in averting war with England during his term, once over the aid the United States provided to a failed Canadian insurrection by Americans, and again when a disputed timber-rich area known as the Aroostook River valley was claimed by both Maine and the British. This was later resolved with the Webster-Ashburton Treaty.

One of Van Buren's other accomplishments was significant for the Labor movement in this country. In 1840 he established a 10 hour working day for all federal employees.

Martin Van Buren was renominated by the Democrats in 1840, but the effects of the depression (he was labeled Martin Van "Ruin" by the Whigs) and opposition from war hero William Henry Harrison led to defeat by a large margin. Van Buren sought the presidency again, but was first turned away by the Democrats, who failed to nominate him in 1844, and then by the general electorate, when he lost in 1848 running as a third party candidate under the Free Soil banner.

Martin Van Buren retired to his home at Lindenwald, where he lived with his son and daughter-in-law (the daughter of writer Washington Irving) and their children. He spent some time in Europe studying and writing before returning to his home in 1855. A supporter of Lincoln's efforts at limiting slavery and preserving the Union, he passed away on July 24, 1862.

Historical Landmarks

Birthplace of Martin Van Buren
46 Hudson Street
Kinderhook, New York

On December 5, 1782, Martin Van Buren was born in his father's tavern, 46 Hudson Street, in the Dutch community of Kinderhook, New York. His father, Abraham Van

Buren, who had fought in the War for Independence, was a farmer and tavern owner. The tavern was popular in those days as a gathering place for local residents and as a hostel for stage coach travellers between New York and Albany. As a child, Martin enjoyed listening to the tavern patrons arguing politics in the Dutch language. The tavern was torn down in 1926 and an historical marker has been placed on the site.

Lindenwald
Route 9H
Kinderhook, New York

This large, two-story red brick house had been built by wealthy judge Peter Van Ness following a simple square plan, which emphasized a Palladian window illuminating the second story hallway. The Georgian style carried over to the inside as well; pilasters and entablatures framed six-panel molded doors, and finely carved cornices edged the ceilings. Adorning the entrance was a silver plated door-knocker inscribed with "1797," the year the house was completed.

William Van Ness, Van Buren's lifelong friend and mentor, inherited the house from his father but lost it to creditors in 1824. Fifteen years later, in 1839, during his presidency, Van Buren decided he eventually wanted to retire in Kinderhook and bought the house, which had been neglected, and about 130 acres of land for $14,000. After his defeat for a second term in 1841, he retired to the home which he named Lindenwald after the linden groves on the property.

In 1845, Van Buren acquired 90 more acres and in 1849, because his son, Smith, agreed to move in and help manage the estate, he agreed to alterations to accommodate his growing family. Architect Richard Upjohn was hired to renovate the exterior and create a "Venetian villa" appearance in addition to providing more room. Dormers were installed to provide an additional half-story for servants' quarters; a four-room library wing, two kitchens and a four-story Italianesque tower added at the rear of the house overlooking the Hudson River; the eaves laced with Victorian trim; and a Victorian porch attached to the front. Finally, the red brick was plastered over and Lindenwald was painted yellow. Of the changes, Van Buren said, "the idea of seeing in life, the changes which my heir would be sure to make after I am gone, amuses me."

Martin Van Buren

Van Buren lived happily at his estate until his death in 1862.

Visitor's Information

The Martin Van Buren National Historic Site, administered by the National Park Service, features 22 acres of land from Van Buren's original holdings, as well as the mansion.

Open daily, 9:00 a.m.-5:00 p.m., May-October; Wednesday-Sunday, 9:00 a.m.-5:00 p.m., April and November; closed Thanksgiving. Telephone: (518) 758-9689.

Admission: Adults, ages 17-61, $1.00.

Lindenwald is located in Columbia County, just southeast of Kinderhook, and 25 miles south of Albany, on Route 9H.

Burial Site
Kinderhook Cemetery
Albany Avenue
Kinderhook, New York

Van Buren suffered from bronchial asthma and finally succumbed to the disease at Lindenwald on July 24, 1862, at age 79. He was buried in Kinderhook cemetery along with his wife Hannah, his parents, and his son, Martin, Jr.

Visitor's Information

Open daily during daylight hours.

The cemetery dates from 1817 and occupies a triangle of land on Albany Avenue (Route 21) in Kinderhook.

William Henry Harrison, 9th President, 1841-1841

Berkeley Plantation

Grouseland built 1803-04 by William Henry Harrison, first Governor of Indiana Territory

William H. Harrison's Tomb

William Henry Harrison

Ninth President
1841
Whig

The son of a signer of the Declaration of Independence (Benjamin Harrison V) and the grandfather of a president (Benjamin Harrison), William Henry Harrison was born on February 9, 1773 in Berkeley, Virginia. He studied for a time to be a doctor, but his father's death left the family poor, so he accepted a commission in the nation's new army.

Along with Meriwether Lewis and William Clark, William Henry Harrison served under General "Mad Anthony" Wayne during the period of bloody fighting with Native Americans in the Northwest Territory. Harrison was instrumental in getting Indiana Territory to split off from the Northwest Territory, and at the age of twenty six was elected a territorial delegate to Congress, where he saw to the passage of a land act which allowed more people to purchase property in the territory. A year later, at the age of 27, he was appointed the Territorial Governor of Indiana.

While serving under Wayne, Harrison met and married Anna Symmes, the daughter of Cincinnati Supreme Court Judge John Symmes, who, it has been noted, did not think much of the young soldier's ability to support a family. While Governor of the Indiana Territory William and Anna lived in the frontier settlement, Vincennes.

Harrison's military career was filled with battles against Native Americans, notably with Chief Tecumseh of the Shawnee tribe. A great battle with Tecumseh at Tippecanoe in 1811 made Harrison a national hero. During the War or 1812 he was promoted to major general and led his forces to victory over the British in Canada at the Battle of the Thames.

After the war he resigned from the army and moved to North Bend, Ohio, and was elected to the House of Representatives, and then to the Senate. He was unsuccessful in his first attempt at the presidency in 1836, since Jackson's popularity made the election of his chosen successor, Martin Van Buren, virtually assured. Harrison returned to Ohio to take a position as clerk of the Hamilton County Court. His continuing popularity as a war hero made him the perfect candidate for the Whigs to run again against Van Buren in 1840.

Even though he now owned a prosperous farm, Harrison was extolled as a poor man of the people as well as a war hero. His running mate was John Tyler of Virginia, and the Whigs ran one of the most boisterous campaigns in history, shouting "Tippecanoe and

Tyler too!" Coonskin hats, miniature log cabins, and plenty of hard cider could be found at a Harrison-Tyler rally. Their victory was decisive.

It was an extremely cold rainy day when Harrison was inaugurated and he refused to wear a hat or coat while giving the longest inaugural address on record: one hour and forty minutes. As a result, the 68-year-old Indian fighter, exhausted from his arduous presidential campaign, caught a cold, and some weeks later, when he went walking in slush on another raw day, developed pneumonia. After only 30 days in office, he died on April 4, 1841, the shortest presidential tenure in history. Ralph Waldo Emerson wrote, "He died of the presidency in one month." He was the first president to die within the White House and the first to lie in state in the East Room.

Historical Landmarks

Birthplace of William Henry Harrison
Berkeley Plantation
Charles City, Virginia

William Henry Harrison was born on February 9, 1773, at "Berkeley," his father's plantation where he spent part of his boyhood.

The land on which it stands was part of a grant made in 1619 by King James I to the Berkeley Company and was designated "Berkeley Hundred." On December 4, 1619, the settlers stepped ashore there and in accordance with the proprietors' instructions that "the day of our ships' arrival ... shall be yearly and perpetually kept as a day of Thanksgiving" celebrated the first Thanksgiving Day more than a year before the Pilgrims arrived in New England.

The early Georgian mansion, which occupies a beautifully landscaped hilltop site overlooking the historic James River, was built in 1726 by Benjamin Harrison. His son, Colonel Benjamin Harrison, inherited it. He was a member of the Continental Congress, Signer of the Declaration of Independence, three-time governor of Virginia and father of William Henry Harrison, the ninth President of the United States and great grandfather of our twenty-third President, Benjamin Harrison.

When he was elected as the ninth President of the United States, William Henry Harrison returned to write his inaugural address at Berkeley in the room in which he was born.

Visitor's Information

One of America's most historic homes, this James River plantation is a beautiful restored example of the mansions that graced Virginia's "Golden Age." The rooms are furnished with a magnificent collection of eighteenth century antiques and Berkeley's ten acres of formal terraced boxwood gardens and lawn extend a full quarter-mile from the front door to the James River.

This home had been sacked by a British force led by Benedict Arnold in 1781. Later, during the Civil War, General George McClellan used Berkeley as his headquarters, and while quartered here with McClellan in 1862, General Daniel Butterfield composed the famous bugle call, "Taps."

Open daily 8:00 a.m.-5:00 p.m.; closed December 25.   Telephone: (804) 829-6018.

Admission: Adults $8.00; children $3.00.

Berkeley is located on Virginia State Route 5 between Richmond and Williamsburg, Virginia, 8 miles west of Charles City. From Richmond follow Main Street east to Route 5; from Williamsburg take Route 31 to Route 5.

Grouseland
3 West Scott Street
Vincennes, Indiana

When Harrison was appointed Governor of Indiana Territory he went to the small Territorial capital of Vincennes in January 1801 and purchased a 300-acre tract just northeast of town. Here he built his spacious home, 1803-04, in a grove of walnut trees, near the Wabash River. Tradition holds that Harrison's home was the first brick building in Vincennes. While he lived there it was called the "White House of the West."

Grouseland is a 2 1/2-story, brick Georgian house containing 26 rooms and 13 fireplaces. It resembles Berkeley, Harrison's birthplace and boyhood home in Virginia and may have been designed by him. Concern that Vincennes was still under threat of Indian attack and combined with the fact that he had five children in the house, there were many features built for protection. The outer walls, eighteen inches thick, were slit for portholes, and the attic had windows designed for sharpshooters; the roof originally had a lookout post. There were two false windows in the front of the house, heavily barred basement windows, a powder magazine in the cellar, and a basement well. For emergency escapes, there was a trapdoor on the second floor leading to a hidden closet on the ground floor, as well as an underground passage leading to one of the buildings at the rear.

It was at Grouseland in 1810 that Harrison met with the Shawnee Indian Chief Tecumseh. The following year they met in battle at Tippecanoe where Harrison emerged victorious. Harrison and his family remained at Grouseland until 1812.

Visitor's Information

The house was rescued from demolition by the local chapter of the Daughters of the American Revolution 1909. It has been a memorial and museum since 1911 and is furnished with Harrison possessions and pieces of the period.

Open daily 9:00 a.m.-5:00 p.m., March through December; 11:00 a.m.-4:00 p.m., January-February. Closed January 1, Thanksgiving, and December 25. Telephone: (812) 882-2096.

Admission: Adults $2.00; ages 12-18, $1.00; ages 6-11, $.50.

Grouseland is located at the intersection of Scott and Park Streets

Burial Site
Harrison Tomb State Memorial
Loop Avenue, North Bend, Ohio

Harrison had indicated that he wanted to be buried on Mt. Nebo in North Bend, Ohio, on the Harrison Plantation where he had retired to in 1829 and had lived until he entered the White House in 1841. He was buried in a plain tomb without a monument or any inscription. In 1871, when the Harrison estate had passed out of the hands of the Harrison family, with the exception of the three acres containing the tomb of the president, (the house had burned down in 1858) his only surviving son, John Scott Harrison, father of President Benjamin Harrison, offered the property to the State of Ohio on condition that it be preserved as a memorial to William Henry Harrison. The offer was accepted and a gubernatorial appointed Harrison Memorial Commission was responsible for the Harrison Tomb State Memorial. The Memorial, about three hundred yards from the Ohio River, overlooks three states, Ohio, Kentucky and Indiana, and contains the bodies of President Harrison, his wife Anna, their son, John Scott Harrison, and other family members.

Visitor's Information

Open daily, sunrise to sunset.

The Harrison Tomb State Memorial is located on Loop Avenue south of Harrison Avenue, North Bend, Ohio. It is 17 miles southwest of Cincinnati, Ohio on U.S. Highway 50.

John Tyler, 10th President, 1841-1845

Sherwood Forest Plantation

Tomb of John Tyler

John Tyler

Tenth President
1841-1845
Whig

John Tyler was born on March 29, 1790 in Greenway, Virginia. He had a great interest in poetry and music and was an accomplished violinist. His father was a judge, and the law was in his blood, and after graduating from William and Mary in 1806, he studied under his father and was admitted to the Virginia bar in 1809 while still a teenager.

When his father was Governor of Virginia, John was elected to the Virginia legislature. At the age of twenty-three he was finally permitted by his fiancee's parents to marry, taking Letitia Christian as his wife in 1813. She bore him eight children before suffering a stroke in 1838. She passed away in 1842.

Meanwhile, Tyler's political career progressed. Elected as a Congressman from Virginia, he then held the office of governor of the Commonwealth for one term. He was then elected to the United States Senate, and was in the midst of his second term when he resigned over a dispute with the Virginia Legislature, which had instructed him to rescind his censure vote of Andrew Jackson over the President's actions regarding the National Bank. Tyler, although a Democrat during Jackson's administration, found other issues over which he disagreed with the president. Tyler was pro-slavery and an advocate of States rights, leading him to disagree with Jackson over his handling of the state's rights issue brought on by the nullification controversy. Yet despite these fundamental disagreements, he supported Jackson in the 1832 election, seeing him as the lesser of two evils.

By 1836 his rift with the Democrats caused Tyler to switch parties and run for the vice-presidency on the Whig ticket. After his ticket lost, he returned to Williamsburg, Virginia, where he served again in the House of Delegates. In 1840 he was again chosen by Clay and the Whigs to run as vice-president to balance out the ticket with William Henry Harrison, (who, although born in Virginia, lived in Ohio) and to attract votes from the slave-holding South.

After his election, Tyler expected, quite correctly, that he would play a minor role in the Harrison administration. But when Harrison died after only a month in office, Tyler became the first vice-president to ascend to the presidency. There was much talk of whether or not he should be addressed as "Acting President." Tyler dismissed such talk, moving swiftly and deliberately to take the office as if he was elected to it, establishing a tradition of succession that was to be followed many times to come.

Tyler followed the Whig line when he repealed the independent Treasury started by Van Buren. The navy was reorganized under Tyler, and the forerunners of the Naval Observatory and Weather Bureau were established. The United States negotiated its first trade agreement with China and the Webster-Ashburton Treaty which settled territorial disputes between the United States and Canada, was signed.

John Tyler, who had displayed pro-South sentiment in the Senate, shocked the South when he signed a revision of the tariff which raised the rates, rather than lowering them, as had been promised in the compromise of 1833. The Whigs were no less shocked when Tyler, in attempt to gain control of the party, vetoed the charter to a new National Bank. Tyler's cabinet, loyal Whigs all, were furious. When he vetoed the bill a second time they all resigned, except for Daniel Webster. Henry Clay then held a Whig caucus in which Tyler was read out of the party. Tyler continued to exercise his veto powers throughout the remainder of his term, and on the final day of his administration became the first president to have a veto overridden by Congress.

On February 28, 1844, the President was traveling on the warship USS Princeton, which possessed a new gun, dubbed the Peacemaker, which as the most powerful of its day. During a second firing of the gun (the first had gone off without a hitch), the gun exploded, killing the ship's captain, two members of the cabinet, and David Gardiner of New York. Gardiner's daughter, Julia, whom Tyler had been courting at the time, was uninjured, as was Tyler himself. Tyler's actions that day supposedly solidified young Julia's feelings for the President, and in June they were married, the first wedding of a sitting President. At the time, Tyler was fifty-four and Julia twenty-four, and their age difference caused quite a stir in Washington. Julia would bear him seven children, and combined with the eight his first wife Letitia bore, makes Tyler our most prolific president.

Tyler, aware that the Whigs feared the annexation of Texas would strengthen slavery, completed negotiations for the Republic to join the Union in February of 1844. Northern and Western states, smelling a plot by the South to promulgate slavery, vetoed annexation. By this time the election of 1844 had resulted in the election of a pro-annexation candidate, James Polk, and Tyler, determined to complete the annexation himself, asked for a joint resolution of Congress (which required a simple majority) instead of approval of a treaty (which requires a two-thirds majority for passage). The resolution passed both houses of Congress by small margins and Tyler signed it a few weeks before he left office in 1845.

Left without a party, John Tyler was unable to run for re-election in 1844, and he retired from politics. He and Julia moved to a home he was building not far from his birthplace in Greenway, Virginia, which he called Sherwood Forest.

After retiring to Sherwood Forest, Tyler lived quietly until just before the Civil War. When the first southern states seceded from the Union in 1861, Tyler led a compromise mission to Washington which failed. At the Virginia secession convention Tyler voted in favor of Virginia leaving the Union and he won election to the Confederate House of Representatives in November 1861. Before taking his seat, however, in January 1862, while waiting the convening of that body in Richmond, Virginia, Tyler was suddenly stricken ill and died there a few days later on January 18, 1862.

Historical Landmarks

Birthplace of John Tyler
Greenway
Charles City, Virginia

John Tyler, a lifelong Virginia resident, and the first vice president to succeed to the presidency through death, was born on March 29, 1790, at Greenway, a 1 1/2-story frame house on the family's 1200-acre estate in Charles City, Virginia. It was built ca. 1776 for Tyler's father, Judge John Tyler, governor of Virginia 1808-11. The future president lived there until his marriage to Letitia Christian in 1813. He returned in 1821 and made Greenway his home while he was governor 1825-27. Tyler sold Greenway in 1829. The house has survived without significant alteration and the interior preserves its original woodwork, including paneled chimneypieces in the principal rooms.

Visitor's Information

Greenway is located west of Charles City, Virginia, on State Route 5. The house is privately owned and visiting is not permitted.

John Tyler

Sherwood Forest Plantation
State Route 5
Charles City, Virginia

The estate, originally called Creek Plantation, was purchased by Tyler while he was president. He named it Sherwood Forest as he likened himself to Robin Hood, a political outlaw. The original house, which was built in 1780, was renovated by President Tyler in 1844. He connected the old kitchen and laundry to the house on the east end by a covered colonnade and added a corresponding west wing for his office and a ballroom. The dwelling is 300 feet long and one room deep with the central portion of three stories. It is considered the longest frame house in America.

The house looks much as it did when Tyler left the White House in 1845 and brought his second wife (his first wife had died in 1842), Julia Gardiner, of Gardiner's Island, New York, who he had married in 1844, to Sherwood Forest. Since that time, the plantation has been continuously occupied by members of the Tyler family and has been a working planation for over 250 years. All of the original 1,600 acres are still in the Tyler name.

The house contains a private ballroom 68 feet in length, and is superbly furnished with family heirlooms of the 18th and 19th century. President Tyler's porcelain, china, silver, mirrors, girondoles, tables, chairs, and other furnishings are still in use at Sherwood Forest. In the library are the books of Governor Tyler (President Tyler's father), President Tyler, and President Tyler's son, Dr. Lyon Gardiner Tyler, President of the College of William and Mary. Opposite one end of the house is the 18th century wine house and opposite the other end is the old dairy. The buildings are in a twelve-acre yard with an exceptional number of century old trees.

Visitor's Information

The grounds are open daily 9:00 a.m.-5:00 p.m. Admission: $2.00 per person.

Mansion available by appointment: $30.00 minimum includes 4 people, $6.50 each additional person. Telephone: (804) 829-5377.

Sherwood Forest in on State Route 5, 35 miles east of Richmond, 18 miles west of Williamsburg.

John Tyler

Burial Site
Hollywood Cemetery
Cherry and Albermarle Streets
Richmond, Virginia

John Tyler was buried in the Hollywood Cemetery in Richmond where a great public funeral witnessed the interment. In 1911, Congress approved the erection of a monument over the grave of the former president which was unveiled October 12, 1915.

Visitor's Information

Hollywood Cemetery is the burial place for many of Virginia's greatest men, including President James Monroe, Jefferson Davis, General J.E.B. Stuart, and many others. A granite pyramid honors 18,000 Confederate soldiers buried there.

Open daily 8:00 a.m. to 6:0 p.m., mid-May to mid-October; rest of the year, 8:00 a.m. to 5:00 p.m. Telephone: (804) 648-8501.

The cemetery is located at Cherry and Albermarle Streets, Richmond. Take U.S. 1 (Chamberlayne/Belvidere Streets) south to Cumberland, turn right and proceed to Laurel, turn left for two blocks and turn right onto Albermarle.

James Knox Polk, 11th President, 1845-1849

Polk's Birthplace (replica)

Polk's Home

James K. Polk's Burial Site

James Knox Polk

Eleventh President
1845 - 1849
Democrat

The oldest of ten children, James Knox Polk was born on November 2, 1795 in Mecklenberg County, North Carolina. Polk attended the Mufreesboro Academy and was salutatorian of the 1818 graduating class of the University of North Carolina, delivering his speech in Latin. He studied law and was admitted to the bar in 1820. The same year he was elected to the Tennessee Legislature he married Sarah Childress, a woman of intellect who became Polk's confidential secretary and part-time speech writer.

A year later Polk was elected to the United States Congress from Tennessee. He served for fourteen years with such hard work and tenacity that he became known as "Polk the Plodder," and was ultimately elected Speaker of the House in 1835. This makes him the only House Speaker to reach the Presidency. He returned to Tennessee where he was elected Governor in 1836. After losing two attempts at re-election, he seemed relegated to political obscurity.

But in 1844 James Polk was chosen by Democratic Party leaders to run against Martin Van Buren for the Democratic nomination. Van Buren had opposed the annexation of Texas and the party, sensing public support for it, turned to the expansionist Polk, who sought not only Texas, but the Oregon territory as well. "Fifty-four forty or fight," his western supporters shouted, referring to the border line they desired for Oregon. Polk won the Democratic nomination, becoming America's first "Dark Horse" candidate. His lack of recognition around the country prompted Whig candidate Henry Clay to ask "Who is James K. Polk?". When the votes were counted, the answer was President, and Polk, at the age of forty-nine, became the youngest man to be elected to the nation's highest office up to that time.

Polk was a Southerner and slaveowner, but while he did not advocate or encourage the expansion of slavery, he did insist on its right to exist. With the Walker Tariff in 1846 he succeeded in getting a reduction in the tariffs which helped to expand the Southern economy. Though he vetoed internal improvement bills, he did reinstate the national Treasury and saw the establishment of the U.S. Naval Academy. But Polk's most important achievement as president, the achievement which many historians believe place him among one of our greatest presidents, was his policy towards territorial expansion.

If anyone doubted that Polk was an unabashed expansionist, he made his feelings quite clear as soon as he stepped up to the podium to deliver his inauguration address, when he spoke of the "right of our territory which lies beyond the Rocky Mountains." He was referring to two potential political powderkegs; Oregon, which the British claimed, and California and the Southwest, which was claimed by Mexico.

While taking the hard line for the fifty-fourth parallel for Oregon in public, he was more than willing to compromise using the forty-ninth parallel, and made such an offer to the British envoy soon after taking office. When the offer was turned down in April of 1846, Polk had Congress give a one-year notice to Britain that America would terminate the joint occupation of Oregon which had been in effect since 1818. Britain turned around and proposed Polk's own original offer of the forty-ninth parallel. Polk turned the issue over to Congress, which accepted the compromise, and the Oregon Territory now belonged to America.

The questions surrounding the Southwest and California were not solved as peacefully. It was obvious to the Mexican government that America had its eyes fixed firmly on California. When Texas was admitted to the Union, Mexico broke off diplomatic relations in a dispute over which river, the Nueces (preferred by Mexico) or the Rio Grande (150 miles to the south and the preference of the Americans) would be the border between Texas and Mexico. When Mexico sent troops into the area, Polk countered with a force led by General Zachary Taylor. Still desiring a peaceful settlement, he sent John Slidell of Louisiana with an offer of thirty million dollars for California and the Southwest. The Mexican government refused to see Slidell.

By March of 1846 General Taylor was, under orders from Polk, preparing to attack when one of his mounted patrols was ambushed while still on the north side of the Rio Grande. With this incident inflaming the country, Polk asked for and received a declaration of war on May 13, 1846. It was to be the first war in which the Commander-in-Chief actually directed the military action. After a number of American victories, a peace treaty was signed just before Polk left office in 1848, giving America everything it had sought in the Slidell negotiations.

Polk only served one term, but it was a remarkable one by anyone's account. The United States now extended from coast to coast and could claim over half a million more square miles of territory, including California, the Southwest, and a Texas border which extended to the Rio Grande. He had even tried, in the last full year of office, to buy Cuba from Spain for $100 million. The Spanish foreign minister replied that he would rather see Cuba sunk than sold.

James Polk, had promised he would serve only one term as President. Exhausted and weak from his four years in office, he retired to his home in Nashville, Tennessee, where he died only three months later, on June 15, 1849 at the age of 53.

Historical Landmarks

Birthplace of James Knox Polk
U.S. 521
Pineville, North Carolina

James K. Polk was born one-half mile from Pineville, North Carolina, November 2, 1795, in an unpretentious farmhouse, on his parents' 250-acre farm. He spent most of his childhood among the gently rolling hills of Mecklenburg County. When he was eleven, the family sold the homestead and moved west to join James' grandfather in Tennessee.

The farmhouse is no longer standing but there is a stone pyramid with an inscribed tablet marking the site, which was erected in 1904 by Mecklenburg Chapter, Daughters of the American Revolution. Also on the site is the James K. Polk Memorial developed by the State's Division of Archives and History. The Memorial includes a reconstruction of his birthplace and subsidiary buildings, authentically furnished to the period when the Polks lived there. A Visitor Center contains exhibits and shows a film on Polk's life and career.

Visitor's Information

Open: April 1 through October 31: Monday-Saturday, 9:00 a.m. to 5:00 p.m.; Sunday, 1:00 p.m. to 5:00 p.m.; November 1 through March 31: Tuesday-Saturday, 10:00 a.m. to 4:00 p.m.; Sunday, 1:00 p.m. to 4:00 p.m. Closed Monday. Telephone: (704) 889-7145.

Admission: Free.

The James K. Polk Memorial is located a half mile south of Pineville, North Carolina, on U.S. Route 521.

Polk Home
301 West 7th Street
Columbia, Tennessee

Although James K. Polk lived in this house for only a few years during his early manhood, it is the only extant structure closely associated with him. Now preserved as a memorial, it contains many items and furnishings commemorating him and his career. Constructed by Polk's father in 1816, it is a two-story brick structure typical of the Federal style. The residence features a gable roof and a handsome doorway with fan shaped transom. The bricks, woodwork, window frames, and sashes are all handmade.

The furnishings include an outstanding collection of historical portraits, prints, lithographs, engravings, and photographs; items originally used in the house; furnishings used by President and Mrs Polk in the White House including the inaugural bible, pieces of china service used for state dinners, Mrs. Polk's ball gown, designed and made in Paris, and the fan which the president had made for Mrs. Polk to carry to the inaugural ball. On the front of the fan are pictures of the first eleven presidents and on the reverse side is a print of the signing of the Declaration of Independence.

Adjacent to the Polk Home is the Sisters' House, where two of the President's sisters lived at different times. It is now a museum which depicts Polk's career chronologically with exhibits and a film on his life and accomplishments. Many artifacts are also displayed.

Visitor's Information

Open: April through October: Monday through Saturday, 9:00 a.m.-5:00 p.m.; Sunday, 1:00 p.m.-5:00 p.m.; November through March: Monday through Saturday, 9:00 a.m.-4:00 p.m.; Sundays, 1:00 p.m.-5:00 p.m.
Closed January 1, Thanksgiving, December 24, 25. Telephone: (615) 388-2354.

Admission: (includes the Sisters' House) Adults $2.50; over 60, $2.00; ages 6-18, $1.00.

Telephone: (615) 388-2354.

James Knox Polk

Burial Site
State Capitol Grounds
Sixth and Charlotte Avenues
Nashville, Tennessee

In 1847, for his retirement, Polk had purchased the colonnaded mansion of his old law mentor, Judge Felix Grundy, U.S. Attorney in the Van Buren administration. The mansion's extensive formal gardens occupied an entire city block in Nashville, Tennessee. After his successor, Zachary Taylor, was inaugurated, Polk, prematurely white-haired and aged before his time, returned to Grundy Place, now known as Polk Place. He soon took ill with cholera and died June 5, 1849, only three months after his retirement. He was buried in the city cemetery and later in the garden tomb east of his estate. His wife died at Polk Place 42 years later, August 14, 1891, and was buried beside him. Unfortunately, despite Polk's specific instructions to give the estate to the state of Tennessee, it was sold to another family and demolished in 1893. Because the President's final resting place seemed inappropriate on someone else's property, the tombs of President Polk and his wife were moved to the grounds of the Tennessee capitol in Nashville.

Open: Monday-Saturday, 9:00 a.m.-4:00 p.m.; Sunday, 1:00 p.m.-3:00 p.m.; closed January 1, Easter, Thanksgiving, December 25. Telephone: (615) 741-2692.

Admission: Free.

The tomb is located at Sixth and Charlotte Avenues on the State Capitol grounds in Nashville.

Zachary Taylor, 12th President, 1849-1850

Zachary Taylor's Boyhood Home

Zachary Taylor's Burial Site

Zachary Taylor

Twelfth President
1849 -1850
Whig

A second cousin to James Madison, America's fourth president, Zachary Taylor was born on November 24, 1784 in Orange County, Virginia. His father, an officer in the Continental Army, soon moved the family to the Kentucky frontier. But Zachary did not want to be a farmer, he had always dreamed of life in the military, and when he was twenty three he joined the regular army.

By the end of the War of 1812 he was a major. Taylor then went on to distinguish himself in campaigns against Native Americans in the Old Northwest during the Blackhawk War and Florida in the Seminole War. In 1846, when he was a major general, President Polk sent him to Texas to defend its border, and he was in command during the opening engagement of the war with Mexico at Palo Alto. In 1846, he fought the Battle of Resaca de la Palmo, and captured Monterrey. Taylor became a national hero, when his forces, outnumbered by Santa Anna, were victorious at the Battle of Buena Vista.

After the war, "Old Rough and Ready," (as he was known to his troops), retired from the military to the plantation he had bought in 1842, with his wife, the former Margaret Smith. They had met in Kentucky after Taylor had joined the army, and were married in 1810. Margaret spent most of the rest of her life as a soldier's wife, following him from post to post across America.

The Whigs, desperate to retake the White House in 1848, nominated Zachary Taylor, although he possessed only some of the party's views on the issues of the day. The "Hero of Buena Vista" beat two men, Democrat Lewis Cass and Martin Van Buren, who ran under the banner of the Free Soilers, an anti-slavery party. Taylor became the first professional soldier to occupy the White House and the first without any elective experience. His lack of experience in the electoral process was glaring; he once admitted to never having voted in a presidential election.

The slavery issue dominated Taylor's administration, and although he was a slave holder, all of his actions were of a man committed to the preservation of the Union. Secession, he said, was treason, and he threatened to lead an army against any rebellion.

His desire to admit California to the Union horrified Southerners who sought to preserve the 15 slave state/15 free state balance which existed in the Senate. Taylor also advocated that the citizens of a new territory be allowed to decide for themselves whether or not it would be free or slave. This added to southern frustration, and led to a bitter fight in the Senate over the slavery question.

Early in 1850 Taylor negotiated the Clayton-Bulwar Treaty with Britain. The treaty helped to resolve American and British disagreements in Central America.

Zachary Taylor never saw the questions surrounding slavery settled. On July 4, 1850, he attended the ceremony laying the cornerstone of the Washington Monument. Under a broiling sun, he listened to hours of oratory and consumed large quantities of iced drinks, cold cherries and pickled cucumbers. He died five days later, only sixteen months after taking office, possibly of gastroenteritis. Some medical experts suspect that he died of typhus or cholera. His last words were "I expect the summons soon. I have endeavored to discharge all my official duties faithfully. I regret nothing, but am sorry that I am about to leave my friends."

Historical Landmarks

Birthplace of Zachary Taylor
Montebello
Gordonsville, Virginia

Zachary Taylor was born on November 24, 1784, in an 18th century frame house "Montebello" near Gordonsville, Virginia. His birth occurred when his family was migrating to Kentucky and illness necessitated a stopover with a cousin. The house is no longer standing but a roadside marker erected by the state says: "Here was born Zachary Taylor, 12th President of the United States, November 24, 1784. Taylor, commanding an American Army won the notable Battle of Buena Vista in Mexico, 1847."

Visitor's Information

The site is on Highway 33, about three miles west of Gordonsville.

Springfield
5608 Apache Road
Louisville, Kentucky

In 1785, when Zachary Taylor was less than 1 year old, his father, Richard Taylor, moved from Orange County, Virginia to a 400-acre farm outside the village of Louisville. The family first lived in a small log structure but within a few years construction of Springfield began. It was a 2 1/2-story brick house with a basement which provided quarters for servants. A large central hall divided the first floor into twin parlors on the east, and dining room and kitchen to the west. Four bedrooms were on the second floor and quarters for coachmen comprised the top floor, an unfinished attic. It was more substantial than most homes on the frontier, even including handsome carved walnut paneling.

Zachary Taylor lived at Springfield, his boyhood home, until the beginning of his military career in 1808. He was married there two years later, and probably returned periodically until the death of his father in 1829. For nearly all of the thirty-nine years from 1808 to 1847 that Taylor was in the U.S. Army, he and his wife, Margaret Mackall Smith, moved constantly from one frontier army post to another.

After his father's death, the house passed to Zachary's oldest brother, Hancock Taylor, and left the Taylor family in 1867. It now occupies a small plot with a nearby housing development.

Visitor's Information

Springfield is at 5608 Apache Road, seven miles east of Louisville on US 42.

The house is privately owned and visiting is not permitted.

Zachary Taylor

Burial Site
Zachary Taylor National Cemetery
4701 Brownsboro Road
Louisville, Kentucky

Following Taylor's death, his body was brought back to Springfield and interred in the family burial ground which later became the nucleus of Zachary Taylor National Cemetery. In 1925, Congress authorized the building of a mausoleum of classic Roman design. In 1926 the remains of President Taylor and his wife were transferred from the original family vault to the new mausoleum. The inscription over the entrance simply says, "1784 Zachary Taylor 1850."

Visitor's Information

Open 24 hours; office hours daily 8:00 a.m.-4:30 p.m.; 8:00 a.m.-7:00 p.m. on Memorial Day. Telephone: (502) 893-3852.

Zachary Taylor National Cemetery is located at 4701 Brownsboro Road, seven and one-half miles east of Louisville on US 42.

Millard Fillmore, 13th President, 1850-1853

Millard Fillmore Cabin (Replica of Birthplace)

Millard Fillmore's House

Burial Site of Millard Fillmore

Millard P. Fillmore

Thirteenth President
1850-1853
Whig

Millard Fillmore was born to a poor farmer and his wife in Summer Hill, New York on January 7, 1800. He began working as an apprentice to a woolcarder, but at the age of seventeen he fell in love with his eighteen year old school teacher, Abigail Powers. She was apparently a great inspiration to the young Fillmore, and in 1819 bought his freedom from the woolcarder for thirty dollars. Encouraged by Abigail, he studied law, and he passed the bar in 1823. They were married in 1826.

He served in the state legislature, and was elected (and re-elected four more times) as a United States Congressman, eventually winning the Chairmanship of the powerful Ways and Means Committee. In 1843 he returned to Buffalo to practice law, and a year later was defeated in an attempt to win the governorship of New York. However, three years later he did become Comptroller. In 1848 he was placed on the ballot with Zachary Taylor as a "ticket-balancer" to help the Whigs secure the White House.

When President Zachary Taylor died July 9, 1850, Vice-President Millard P. Fillmore became the second President to ascend to the Presidency in such a manner. He also became the first President born in the nineteenth century.

The issues surrounding slavery and the expansion of the American frontier took up much of Fillmore's Presidency. He disliked slavery and wanted to see the Union strengthened. One of his first acts was to support Henry Clay's Compromise of 1850, which settled, for a few years anyway, the questions surrounding slavery and its extension into the territories. Among its points were that California was to be admitted as a free state, that all other territories would have their own say in whether they would allow slavery, and that the Fugitive Slave Law would be strengthened, forcing the return of runaway slaves. This last provision would have a great impact on events leading up to the Civil War as the Underground Railroad came into being.

In the foreign arena Fillmore restored diplomatic peace with Mexico, began negotiations for a canal through Nicaragua, and in one of his most lasting acts, sent Commodore Matthew Perry to Japan to open up trade.

Fillmore was unable to gain his party's nomination for the presidency in 1852, nor could he win four years later when, in 1856, he was nominated by both the Whig Party and the American (Know-Nothing) Party. In 1858 Fillmore re-married, (his first wife Abigail had died after catching a cold during Franklin Pierce's inauguration), taking Caroline McIntosh as his wife in 1858. She joined him in retirement at his home in Buffalo. Millard Fillmore died on March 8, 1874, at the age of 74.

Historical Landmarks

Birthplace of Millard Fillmore
Fillmore Road
Summer Hill, New York

In 1795, Nathaniel Fillmore, Father of Millard Fillmore, left Bennington, Vermont, where he was born, to move with his wife, Phoebe Millard Fillmore, to what was then known as the "Far West." In reality it was Summer Hill, Cayuga County, New York, where his farm was located in a dense forest. He built a log cabin and five years later, on January 7, 1800, Millard Fillmore was born. At the time of his birth, the cabin home was shared with Nathaniel's brother, Calvin, and his wife. Their nearest neighbor lived four miles away, and the nearest doctor was seven miles away.

About two years later, the elder Fillmore lost his farm because of a faulty title and the family moved to another part of Cayuga County; New Hope, where he rented a better piece of land which was closer to neighbors.

Visitor's Information

The log cabin in Summer Hill, in which Fillmore was born, was torn down in 1852. The site on Fillmore Road, a very rural section, consists of a mowed picnic area with a wooden fence typical of his era and an historical marker.

To reach the site, take Interstate 81 to Homer, New York. Go north on 281 to Route 41, turn left and continue to Route 41A, turn left and proceed to the third left, Eaton Road, which becomes Fillmore Road and the site is on the right.

The log cabin has been recreated at Fillmore Glen State Park. It is a 21 x 16 foot replica containing period furnishings from 1800-1830 which can be only viewed from the outside.

The park is open from 8:00 a.m.-10:00 p.m. without charge, except on weekends, from mid-May to mid-October, when the entrance fee is $3.00 per vehicle. Telephone: (315) 497-0130.

Fillmore Glen State Park, five miles west of his birthplace, is located one mile south of Moravia on State Highway 38.

Fillmore's boyhood home (1802-1819) on Carver Road in New Hope was demolished in 1937. On the site are trees, a picnic table and an historical marker

To reach the site, follow above instructions to Summer Hill but on Route 41A continue until you reach the village of New Hope. Turn right onto Glen Haven Road, then take the first left onto Carver Road and the site is immediately on the right.

The Millard Fillmore House
24 Shearer Avenue
East Aurora, New York

This one and one-half story clapboard dwelling was built by Fillmore with the help of neighbors, in 1826, for his bride, Abigail Powers Fillmore. He and his wife lived there until 1830. The house was originally at 681 Main Street and was later moved to the rear of that lot. It stood in disrepair for many years until artist Margaret Price (Mrs. Irving Price of Fisher-Price Toys) became enchanted with the house and its history. She purchased it in 1930, had it moved to the present site and remodeled for her studio. After she died, the Aurora Historical Society acquired it in 1975 and began restoring it.

The house now typifies a small frame dwelling of the Federal period with much of Millard Fillmore's hand labor in it. The rooms are furnished with authentic Fillmore or period pieces. Front windows are twelve over eight, original panes. The living room walls are stenciled with original designs traced from Aurora homes of the same period. A carriage barn was erected next to the house to hold Millard Fillmore's sleigh as well as a period tool collection.

Millard P. Fillmore

Visitor's Information

The house is owned, maintained and staffed by volunteers from the Aurora Historical Society.

Open: Wednesday, Saturday and Sunday; 2:00 p.m.-4:00 p.m., June 1-October 15.
Telephone: (716) 652-8875 or (716) 652-3280.
Admissions: Adults, $1.00

East Aurora is twenty miles from Buffalo, New York, and Route 400 goes to the center of the village.

Burial Site
Forest Lawn Cemetery
1411 Delaware Avenue
Buffalo, New York

Before leaving for Washington, Fillmore had lived in Buffalo and he returned there after leaving the White House. He purchased a large home on Buffalo's Niagara Square, then the city's most exclusive residential quarter. (The house was torn down in 1929 to make way for the Hotel Statler.) His wife died in Washington, less than a month after he left office. He remarried in 1858, to a widow, Mrs. Caroline Carmichael McIntosh. Fillmore died in Buffalo on March 8, 1874, at age 74, and was buried in his family plot in Forest Lawn Cemetery. As a memorial to him and his family, there is an obelisk of pink granite inscribed with the birth and date of death of Millard Fillmore, his wife Abigail, his wife Caroline, who died seven years after her husband, and his two children, Millard and Abigail. At his own grave there stands a simple granite memorial marker with only two letters, "M F."

Visitor's Information

Forest Lawn Cemetery is open every day from 8:30 a.m.-4:30 p.m.
Telephone: (716) 885-1600.

The Cemetery is located at: 1411 Delaware Avenue at Delavan Avenue in Buffalo, New York.

Franklin Pierce, 14th President, 1853-1857

Homestead of Franklin Pierce, Fourteenth President of the
United States, Hillsboro, N. H.

Homestead of Franklin Pierce

Pierce Manse

Franklin Pierce's Burial Site

Franklin Pierce

Fourteenth President
1853-1857
Democrat

Franklin Pierce was born in Hillsboro, New Hampshire on November 23, 1804. Although his father was a military man, Franklin was enrolled in Bowdoin where he studied with fellow class of 1824 members, Nathaniel Hawthorne and Henry Wadsworth Longfellow. He then studied law at Northampton in Amherst, Massachusetts, and was admitted to the bar in New Hampshire in 1827.

The following year he got involved in politics, not for himself, but to help get his father elected governor. In 1829 Franklin not only helped his father get re-elected but successfully campaigned for his own seat in the State Legislature. He was soon the Speaker, and in 1834, as a supporter of Andrew Jackson, was elected to the United States Congress. After two terms in the House, he won a seat in the United States Senate.

In 1836, Pierce married Jane Appleton whom he had been courting for six years. Jane was a frail, shy woman who disliked Washington, D.C. After Franklin's one term as Senator came to a close in 1842, they returned to a home they had bought in Concord, New Hampshire. For the next ten years Pierce turned down more offices than he had ever held, refusing a seat in Polk's cabinet, a nomination as an interim Senator, and the governorship of New Hampshire. He did, however, accept the position of Federal District Attorney for New Hampshire in 1845. Franklin Pierce enlisted in the army to fight in the Mexican War. Rising from private to brigadier general in only a year, he commanded troops in the battles of Contreras and Churubusco, serving with distinction with Winfield Scott, Robert E. Lee, Jefferson Davis, and Ulysses S. Grant.

After returning to Concord, Pierce resumed his law practice. But in 1852 a deadlocked Democratic convention, desperate for a candidate offensive to the fewest number of voters, sought and found, after forty nine ballots, somebody to run against the Whig's General Winfield Scott. America's second "dark horse" candidate, Franklin Pierce, ran with his party's promise to support the Compromise of 1850 and to oppose further debate on the slavery question. The American voting public responded in support of these policies and Pierce overwhelmed Scott in the electoral college.

Franklin Pierce

The truth is that Pierce never expected to win and that his family was opposed to the run. In his inauguration address Pierce made these feelings known to the world by saying "I have been borne to a position so suitable to others rather than desirable to myself."

Pierce, like fellow Democrat Polk, advocated continued American expansionism and the acquisition of Cuba became one of the primary objectives of his administration. A recommendation that the United States should take Cuba by force if Spain did not accept an offer of $120 million, known as the "Ostend Manifesto", created such an outcry that Pierce was forced to repudiate it and drop his quest for the island.

The signing of the Clayton-Bulwer Treaty with Great Britain declared that any trans-ocean canal built by either country would be open to all ships of all nations, and would remain unfortified, even during war. This basic agreement would remain the model for agreements surrounding the Panama Canal.

In 1853, at the suggestion of Pierce's Secretary of War, future Confederate leader Jefferson Davis, James Gadsden was sent to negotiate a treaty with Mexico for land south of the Gila river. Forty thousand square miles of territory were purchased for ten million dollars, the only expansion of United States territory during Pierce's administration.

Pierce also reorganized the consular and diplomatic service, signed a treaty with Japan (the first ever with that nation), and had a railroad route to the Pacific surveyed.

During Pierce's term a bill submitted to the Senate by Stephen Douglas proposed that land within the Louisiana Purchase be taken from the Indians and split into two new territories, Kansas and Nebraska. This reopened the issue of slavery in the West, and when the first territorial election was held in Kansas it was marred by several thousand pro-Slavery Missourians who crossed the border and elected pro-slavery legislators. When the Kansas governor tried to disqualify some of the illegally elected legislators, President Pierce overrode the decision and replaced the governor with a man who led the legislature in passing a series of laws intended to force out the anti-slavery factions. The anti-slavery Kansans retaliated by forming their own government and sending their own territorial delegation to Washington. Pierce's actions led to a small explosion of violence between the Free-Soilers and Slavery advocates in what became known as "Bleeding Kansas."

In his attempts to both expand the Union and maintain the peace, Franklin Pierce angered both Northerners and Southerners alike. He was not renominated by his party in 1856, and retired to his home in Concord. After an extensive tour of Europe he returned to New Hampshire. In 1861 he attempted to arrange a meeting of the five living ex-Presidents to try and find a solution to the secession crisis, but failed.

Pierce died on October 8, 1869, at the age of 64.

Historical Landmarks

Birthplace of Franklin Pierce
Hillsboro, New Hampshire

At the close of the Revolutionary War, Captain Benjamin Pierce, the father of Franklin Pierce and the later two-time governor of New Hampshire, bought a farm in the forests of New Hampshire, in what is now called Hillsboro. In 1786, he built a log cabin, and one year later, 1787, he married Elizabeth Andrews. She lived only a year. In 1788, the Captain married Anne Kendrick, who bore him eight children; the sixth child born on this farm, November 23, 1804, was Franklin Pierce.

Visitor's Information

Little is known about the birthplace of Franklin Pierce and some sources even believe he may have been born in his boyhood home described below. The farm house was destroyed many years ago.

The Pierce Homestead
State Highway 31
Hillsboro, New Hampshire

In 1804, Captain Benjamin Pierce, who was almost impoverished when he first came to Hillsboro, was a prosperous and prominent man in the state. That year he built a two-story frame house with large spacious rooms, hand stenciling on the walls, imported wallpaper, and a ballroom occupying the entire length of the second floor, where Captain Pierce drilled local militia groups. Several weeks after his birth, Franklin Pierce was taken to this mansion where he lived for the first thirty years of his life.

Visitor's Information

The mansion, which was restored in 1965, has furnishings of the period during Pierce's boyhood including the original scenic wallpaper. It reflects the graciousness of affluent living in those times and is administered by the State of New Hampshire's Division of Parks and Recreation in cooperation with the Hillsborough Historical Society.

Open: Memorial Day weekend, June, September-October(Columbus Day), Saturday 10:00 a.m.-4:00 p.m., Sunday 1:00 p.m.-4:00 p.m., closed Monday-Friday; July and August, Friday and Saturday 10 a.m.-4:00 p.m., Sunday 1:00 p.m.-4:00 p.m., closed Monday-Thursday.   Telephone: (603) 464-5858.

Admission: Adults, $2.00; under 18, free.

The Pierce Homestead is on State Highway 31 just north of the junction with State Highway 9.

The Pierce Manse
14 Penacook Street
Concord, New Hampshire

This was the Franklin Pierce family home from 1842 to 1848. When he moved into this house with his wife and two children, Pierce had just resigned his post as U.S. Senator to resume his law practice. He left the house to go off to the Mexican War while his wife and son (another son had died of typhus in the house) went to stay with relatives. They probably did not return to the house after the war because the rooms would have been haunted by the memory of their son's death.

The house was originally at 18 Montgomery Street but when threatened with demolition by an Urban Renewal project in 1966, it was saved by The Pierce Brigade which, in 1971, moved it to its present site in Concord's Historic District. The Brigade still owns the house and maintains it as a memorial to New Hampshire's only president.

Visitor's Information

The house has been restored as it must have been when the Pierces lived here. Many of the furnishings in the house belonged to Pierce or other members of his family; some pieces are known as "White House" pieces.

Open Monday to Friday, mid-June to mid-September, 11:00 a.m.-3:00 p.m. Closed on holidays. Telephone: (603) 224-9620.

Admission: Adults $1.50; children and students, $.50.

The Pierce Manse is at 14 Penacook Street at the very end of North Main Street. Exit 15W off I-93, at light make sharp right onto North Main Street and continue to end (about 1/4 mile).

Pierce House
52 South Main Street
Concord, New Hampshire

While in Washington, Pierce had a spacious mansion built, from 1854 to 1857, in the prevailing French manner, with mansard roof and stucco finish. This was his retirement home from 1857, when he left the White House. His wife, Jane, died there in 1863 and he followed in 1869.

Visitor's Information

The house was privately owned and it was destroyed by fire in 1985. An historic marker is on the site.

Burial Site
Old North Cemetery
North State Street
Concord, New Hampshire

Franklin Pierce died October 8, 1869, in his bedroom and was buried in Concord's Old North Cemetery beside his wife and three children. A marker says, "Franklin Pierce lies buried in nearby Minot enclosure. Native son of New Hampshire, graduate of Bowdoin College, lawyer, effective political leader, Congressman and U.S. Senator, Mexican War

146

veteran, courageous advocate of States' Rights, he was popularly known as "Young Hickory of the Granite Hills."

The "Minot enclosure" refers to the Pierce's close friends, the Minot family, with whom Pierce's wife and child lived with when he left to fight in the Mexican War.

Due to feelings over his ostensibly pro-slavery actions as president, it was not until 1914 that the state erected a monument in memory of its most distinguished citizen, a bronze statue of Pierce on the State House grounds in Concord. And, it was not until 1946 that the state erected a granite memorial at his grave.

Visitor's Information

Open daily from sunrise to sunset.

Old North Cemetery is on North State Street, near the State Capitol, Concord, New Hampshire. Telephone: (603) 225-3911.

James Buchanan, 15th President, 1857-1861

James Buchanan's Log Cabin Birthplace

Wheatland

Burial Site of James Buchanan

James Buchanan

Fifteenth President
1857-1861
Democrat

James Buchanan was born near Mercersburg, Pennsylvania on April 23, 1791 to a prosperous country-store keeper. James was sent to Dickenson College where he graduated only after first being expelled, then reinstated, in 1809. Studying law, he was admitted to the bar in 1812.

His only love, Anne Coleman, died in 1819 before they could be married. Buchanan would be our first bachelor President and the only one to never marry. Harriet Lane, a niece who had been orphaned at an early age, took the place of a wife at social functions and acted as hostess when James Buchanan reached the White House.

Buchanan served in the War of 1812 as a private, and was the only president with military service not to have a commission. At the age of twenty four he was elected to the Pennsylvania legislature and six years later became a member of the United States Congress. His support of Andrew Jackson won him the post of Minister to Russia in 1832.

Returning to the United States two years later, Buchanan was elected to the Senate for the first of three terms. He then became Secretary of State under Polk and Minister to England under Pierce. As Secretary of State he handled the negotiations which ended the Mexican War and settled the Oregon question with Britain in 1846. He was closely associated with the Ostend Manifesto, which garnered support from the South and suspicion from the North.

Buchanan had been seeking the nomination of his party for the presidency since 1836. In 1856, with the country deeply divided over the slavery issue, the Democrats desperately needed a compromise candidate acceptable to the majority of the electorate. Buchanan, having been away in England and therefore avoided involvement in political squabbles surrounding the Kansas-Nebraska Act, finally got his wish for a nomination. He beat Republican James Fremont and former president Millard Fillmore in the general election, running with the declaration that his administration would wipe out any sectional parties and restore the Union as it had been after the Revolution.

But his administration was, simply put, a period of appeasement to the pro-slavery South masked as compromise. By the time his term was over, war between the states was inevitable. His cabinet was filled with men sympathetic to the promulgation of slavery. He urged a Supreme Court Justice to rule as broadly as possible on the Dred Scott decision, which had denied the slave his freedom. The Court also declared that the Missouri Compromise was unconstitutional. This suited Buchanan, who had previously encouraged the Court to take the power to ban slavery away from Congress.

Although the pro-slavery constitution of Kansas was rejected by both the U.S. House and the Kansas legislature Buchanan insisted that it was legitimate. Buchanan had hoped that the admission of Kansas would ease the strain over the slavery issue, but instead it inflamed members of both parties against him.

Buchanan did not seek re-election in 1860, and Republican Abraham Lincoln was the victor over three other candidates. Members of the southern leadership had previously announced that a Republican victory would mean secession of the slave holding states. Among Buchanan's attempts at preventing secession was his support of the Crittenden Compromise, a series of recommendations by a committee headed by Kentucky Senator John Crittenden, which were ultimately rejected by the South. When secession did occur (shortly after Lincoln's election South Carolina left the Union), Buchanan's response was to announce that while no state had the right to secede from the Union, the federal government had no power to hold any state in the Union against its will.

But in his final months in office Buchanan did display a willingness to commit himself to the Union. He replaced most of his cabinet with Union men, and declared in a speech to Congress that "The Union must and shall be preserved." When South Carolina sent representatives to Washington to demand that Buchanan hand over Fort Sumter, located on an island in the Charleston harbor, he refused, instead sending an unarmed ship to try to resupply the garrison holding out there. The ship was fired upon by Southern batteries, and it was forced to return north. Buchanan could have declared war, but decided to leave that momentous decision to his successor.

James Buchanan retired to his home near Lancaster, Pennsylvania, where he lived for seven years until his death at the age of 77, on June 1, 1868.

Historical Landmarks

Birthplace of James Buchanan
Stony Batter
Cove Gap, Pennsylvania

James Buchanan, Sr., had come to Philadelphia from Ireland and subsequently to Stony Batter, an early trading post in Cove Gap, about two and a half miles west of Mercersburg. He worked as a clerk in a store but he soon opened his own business to take advantage of flourishing trade on a principal route between the east and the west. His son, James Buchanan, was born on April 23, 1791, in a log cabin.

The log cabin in which Buchanan was born has been moved several times and presently stands on the campus of the Mercersburg Academy. The original site of the cabin is part of James Buchanan's Birthplace State Historical Park. There is a monument on the site in the form of a large stone pyramid which was erected in 1911, with money left for that specific purpose in the will of Buchanan's niece, Harriet Lane Johnson, who served as hostess in the White House for the bachelor president. The monument's inscription reads, "This monument marks the birthplace of James Buchanan, fifteenth president of the United States, born 23 April 1791, died 1 June 1868."

An historical marker in the park relates the movement of the log cabin. "James Buchanan. President 1857-1861. Was born April 23, 1791, a half-mile from here. The cabin itself was moved to Mercersburg, 1850, and in 1925 to Chambersburg. In 1953, it was removed to The Mercersburg Academy campus where it may be seen"

Visitor's Information

James Buchanan Birthplace State Historical Park is open daily from sunrise to sunset.

Admission: Free.

Mercersburg is situated on Pa. Route 16 (it becomes Main Street in Mercersburg) approximately 10 miles west of Interstate 81, Exits 2 and 3 (Greencastle). The 18-acre

State Historical Park, which has fishing and picnicking, is one mile northwest of Mercersburg off Pa. Route 16.

The interior of the log cabin on the grounds of Mercersburg Academy can be viewed from the outside, May-November, during daylight hours.

Admission: Free.

Mercersburg Academy is one mile east of the town on Pa. Route 16.

James Buchanan Hotel
17 North Main Street
Mercersburg, Pennsylvania

In 1796, the family moved to Mercersburg where the senior Buchanan built a large handsome brick house which also contained a store operated by the Buchanans. Here the future president spent his boyhood until he entered Dickinson College in Carlisle, Pennsylvania, in 1807. The house has changed hands several times with one owner installing tile floors and a third story with a cornice of Italian design and converting it to a hotel. It was called Hotel Mercer and later renamed James Buchanan Hotel.

Visitor's Information

There is no relevant Buchanan material in the structure. An historic marker on the sidewalk in front of the building contains the following inscription.

Buchanan House

Boyhood home of James Buchanan, Lawyer, statesman, diplomat, fifteenth President of the United States. Buchanan family moved from Stony Batter to Mercersburg in 1796. From here, James entered Dickinson College in 1807.

The building is on Pa. Route 16 (Main Street), see directions above.

James Buchanan

Wheatland
1120 Marietta Avenue (Route 23)
Lancaster, Pennsylvania

The house was built in 1828 for William Jenkins, a wealthy lawyer and banker, who named the estate "The Wheatlands" (later shortened to Wheatland) because of its rural location near wheat fields. James Buchanan purchased the 22-acre farm in 1848 while serving as Secretary of State in President James Polk's cabinet. The price was $6,750, plus $75 for the bookcases that still remain in the library almost 150 years later. Buchanan had great affection for Wheatland and praised "the comforts and tranquility of home as contrasted with the troubles, perplexities, and difficulties" of public life.

In the years before the Civil War, Wheatland was one of the most famous country homes in the nation. Statesmen from all parts of the nation came here in the 1850's to meet James Buchanan and his lovely niece, Harriet Lane, who acted as hostess at Wheatland, and later at the White House.

A large brick structure, Wheatland combines Colonial and later architectural features, but possesses a basic Georgian-style symmetry. The 2 1/2-story central section, with a central hall and matching rooms on each side, is flanked by three-story wings. There are 17 rooms. The front of the main section is dominated by a Doric-columned porch. Except for some interior changes by Buchanan such as installation of a furnace and central heating, replacement of the open hearth in the kitchen with a cast-iron stove and addition of conveniences as a tin bathtub, few changes have occurred.

Visitor's Information

The mansion contains much of Buchanan's furniture, china and silver. One of the interesting pieces in the parlor is Harriet Lane's Chickering piano given to her by her uncle in 1852. Buchanan's quiet study with his original furniture is arranged as in his day. Bedrooms and guest rooms look as though they are ready for the President's return from Washington.

Tours begin in the carriage house with a video film and then well informed guides in period costumes personally conduct visitors through the mansion.

Open every day (except Thanksgiving), April 1 through November 30, 10:00 a.m. to 4:15 p.m. Telephone: (717) 392-8721.

Admission: Adults $4.00; senior citizens and students, $3.00; under 12, $1.75.

Wheatland is at 1120 Marietta Avenue which is Pa. Route 23.

Burial Site
Woodward Hill Cemetery
538 East Strawberry Street
Lancaster, Pennsylvania

Buchanan retired to Wheatland after Lincoln's inauguration and followed the events of the Civil War. There he wrote his only book, *Mr. Buchanan's Administration on the Eve of the Rebellion,* in defense of his policies, and he served on the Board of Trustees of Franklin and Marshall College in Lancaster, a position he held until his death on June 1, 1868. He died at Wheatland, in a plainly furnished backroom on the second floor, and was buried in Woodward Hill Cemetery in Lancaster.

Visitor's Information

A simple monument marks Buchanan's gravesite. It notes his date of birth, date of death and a statement that he served as the fifteenth President of the United States.

Open daily sunrise to sunset.

Woodward Hill Cemetery is at 538 East Strawberry Street in Lancaster. From Lancaster, take Route 272 south to stoplight, left on South Queen Street to cemetery.

Abraham Lincoln, 16th President, 1861-1865

Abraham Lincoln's Birthplace Cabin

Abraham Lincoln Birthplace National Historic Site

Lincoln Boyhood National Memorial

Ford's Theatre

House where Lincoln Died (Petersen House)

Lincoln Memorial

Lincoln Memorial Shrine

Lincoln Monument, Laramie, Wyoming

Abraham Lincoln's Tomb

Abraham Lincoln

Sixteenth President
1861-1865
Republican

That so many presidents made their way from poor "log cabin" beginnings to the White House is testimony to the American system, to be sure. That a poor boy with almost no schooling should rise not only to become our nation's leader, but achieve a place among our the greatest leaders is a testimony to the man himself.

Born in Hodgenville, Kentucky on February 12, 1809, Abraham Lincoln was the first President born in a state that was not one of the original thirteen. His family moved to Indiana when he was seven, and there he worked on his father's farm. Though he attended school for only a short period of time, he was a voracious reader. The family moved to Illinois in 1830, where Lincoln worked as a rail-splitter, store keeper, and ran a flatboat while studying law.

While working as a flatboat operator, his observations of ships running aground inspired him to invent a device that would lift ships over dangerous, shallow waters. His patent for that device was the first and only one ever issued to a President.

Abraham Lincoln fought as a captain in the Blackhawk War in 1832, and afterwards returned to New Salem, Illinois where he unsuccessfully ran for the State Legislature. He then operated a store which failed. In 1833 he became New Salem's postmaster. In 1834 at the age of twenty-five he became a member of the Illinois legislature, where he declared himself for woman suffrage and against slavery, although he questioned the constitutionality of the Federal government's abolishment of slavery within a state.

Lincoln moved to Springfield, Illinois, in 1837, and there he met Mary Todd, the woman he would marry five years later. Todd, who had once rebuked an encroaching Stephen Douglas in favor of Lincoln, once joked that her ambition was to marry a man who would be president.

Lincoln was a member of the Whig party when elected to the House of Representatives in 1847 and again in 1854, but he switched to the Republican Party after the repeal of the Missouri Compromise. It was Stephen Douglas, the author of that repeal, whom Lincoln ran against in 1858 for a seat in the U.S. Senate. Douglas was nationally known and a powerful Democratic leader. Lincoln challenged him to a series of seven debates which attracted national attention. Though the debates were supposed to focus on seven different issues, slavery always seemed to end up as the focus. It was in these debates that Lincoln publicly condemned slavery as morally wrong, and forced Douglas to explain his support of "popular sovereignty" and the Dred Scot decision.

Though he lost the election, these debates made Abraham Lincoln nationally known, and so was chosen by the Republican party in 1860 as its standard bearer after only three ballots. His public opposition to slavery caused an anxious South to threaten secession of he was elected. In November of 1860, facing three other sectional candidates, Lincoln won the presidency.

By the time Abraham Lincoln took the oath of office of the presidency of the United States on March 4, 1861, seven states had seceded from the Union, Jefferson Davis had been elected president of the Confederacy, a Capitol had been established in Montgomery, Alabama and only a few installations in the South were left under Union control. At 4:30 in the morning of April 12, 1861, the shelling of Fort Sumpter in Charleston Harbor by Confederate forces began, and America was at war with itself.

During the first few months of war (from April to July) Congress was not in session, so Lincoln acted on his own. In April he declared a maritime blockade of the South. In May he called for more men to supplement the state militia he had already called out. He expanded the Navy and appropriated two million dollars for military expenditures, a move in clear violation of the Constitution. But most offensive to his critics were his actions regarding private citizens. Military commanders were allowed to make arrests without summonses or warrants. Private mail and telegrams were examined. People with suspect passports were detained. Thus Lincoln suffered the labels of "despot," "dictator," and "tyrant."

To raise money for the conflict, the first annual personal income tax was begun. The printing of paper money, "greenbacks," was authorized for the first time.

Lincoln saw opportunities in the states which had not immediately seceded. Through patience and negotiation, Delaware and Kentucky remained loyal, Maryland remained neutral, and West Virginia split from Virginia to form a pro-Union state in 1863.

Lincoln's initial position on the war echoed the feelings of most northerners. In a letter to Horace Greely in August of 1862 he wrote, "My paramount object in this struggle is to save the Union, and it is not either to save or destroy Slavery."

By the fall of 1862 Lincoln badly needed a Union victory to show the European powers that the South could be defeated. The Union victory at Antietam, Maryland in late summer of 1862 eliminated the fear of European intervention on the part of the South It also allowed the President to establish his place in history and make the war more than a battle for union. On September 22, 1862 he issued a preliminary proclamation which freed the slaves in areas not under control of the federal government. This was followed by the more encompassing Emancipation Proclamation on January 1, 1863, which freed all the slaves in all parts of the country.

These proclamations were Lincoln's masterstroke. The South would never voluntarily give up slavery, and so the war was now more than just a battle to re-sew the Union back together, it was about freedom for all men. It would take two more years and thousands of lives lost before the Union could claim victory.

Soon after the bloody battle of Gettysburg, Abraham Lincoln went to the battlesite to commemorate the sacrifices being made by Union soldiers all over the country. It was here that Lincoln's remarkable gift for oratory came to the fore again, when he delivered his Gettysburg Address, one of the greatest speeches ever made by a United States President. Thanks to his Emancipation Proclamation, he could rightfully state, as he looked over the gravesites of the Civil War that "these dead shall not have died in vain; that this nation...shall have a new birth of freedom."

But before Lincoln could finish the war he had to get re-elected in 1864. Though the economy in the North boomed and Union victories seemed to occur with more rapidity, the losses of life were high, and the need of the war machine for industrial goods was seen as hampering investments. Peace movements were springing up around the country and there were those opposed to the Emancipation Proclamation who wanted to see a settlement with the South rather than force its capitulation. The Democrats, whose platform advocated both of these points, nominated Union General George McClellan, who had been replaced as commander of the Union forces by Lincoln. The Republicans renominated Lincoln unanimously, and for vice-president they nominated Andrew Johnson, a Senator from Tennessee who was also a Democrat. Lincoln's victory, while overwhelming in the electoral college, was quite slim in the popular vote.

On April 9, 1865, the commander of the Confederate forces, Robert E. Lee, surrendered unconditionally to the Union forces under the command of Ulysses S. Grant. The war was over. But bigger battles now loomed, as the country debated how to treat the defeated South. Even before the conflict ended, Lincoln made clear his own policy of reconstruction, when in his second inaugural address, he spoke of "malice towards none...charity for all." As early as December, 1863, when Arkansas was about to fall into Union hands, Lincoln issued his "Proclamation of Amnesty and Reconstruction, which became known as the "10 percent plan." It offered a general amnesty to anyone who agreed to obey any acts of Congress and Presidential proclamations made during the war (including all proclamations dealing with slavery). It also allowed for a state to return to the Union once 10 percent of the electorate had sworn allegiance to the Union.

Tragically, before Lincoln could begin to deal with reconstructing a reunified nation, he was assassinated on April 14, 1865, while watching a play at Ford's Theater in Washington. Even for vanquished southerners, the news brought despair, for Lincoln seemed to be one of the few northern leaders willing to show compassion to the defeated Confederacy. For the entire country it was a loss of the highest order.

Historical Landmarks

Birthplace of Abraham Lincoln
Lincoln Birthplace National Historic Park
Hodgenville, Kentucky

This national historic site commemorates the humble beginnings of Abraham Lincoln, who was born in a crude log cabin on the Kentucky frontier. Preserved are most of the farmland that his father owned at the time of his birth, the traditional birthplace cabin and Sinking Spring, where the Lincolns obtained their water.

It was on December 12, 1808, when Thomas Lincoln bought for $200 in cash the 300-acre Sinking Spring Farm, situated a few miles south of Hodgen's Mill, now Hodgenville, Kentucky. Here, he and his wife, Nancy Hanks, and their infant daughter, Sarah, made their home in a one-room log cabin near a large limestone spring of cool water which had given its name to the place. It was in this one-room log cabin near the Sinking Spring that Abraham Lincoln was born on February 12, 1809.

The Lincolns' cabin was probably a typical frontier dwelling; about 18 by 16 feet, dirt floor, one window and one door, small fireplace, shingled roof, and low chimney made of clay, straw, and hard wood. The tiny window opening might have been covered with greased paper, animal skin or an old quilt to keep out summer insects and the cold winter wind.

The Lincolns lived about 2 1/2 years at the birthplace site, which was eventually lost to them because of a defective title.

About 1900, after an earlier attempt to commercially exploit the property, the Lincoln Farm Association was formed to preserve Lincoln's birthplace and establish a memorial to the country's 16th president. The group raised over $350,000 from more than 100,000 citizens to build a memorial shelter at the birthplace site. President Theodore Roosevelt laid the cornerstone in 1909 and two years later, the association assembled the birthplace cabin in the completed building, a huge Greek Revival structure of Connecticut pink granite and Tennessee marble. Above the six granite columns at the memorial building entrance are carved Lincoln's famous words, "With malice toward none, with charity for all." The memorial is reached by 56 steps, each representing a year in his life. President William H. Taft took part in the dedication ceremony.

The memorial and Sinking Spring Farm were established as a national park in 1916 and designated Abraham Lincoln Birthplace National Historic Site in 1959. It comprises 116 1/2 acres of land, which include nearly 100 acres of the original Thomas Lincoln farm, and is operated by the National Park Service.

Visitor's Information

A Visitor Center features a diorama of the farm, exhibits about the family and a movie, "Lincoln: The Kentucky Years."

Open daily 8:00 a.m.-6:45 p.m., mid-June through Labor Day; 8:00 a.m.-5:45 p.m., April 1 through mid-June and day after Labor Day; 8:00 a.m.- 4:45 p.m., rest of year. Closed December 25.
Admission: Free. Telephone: (502) 358-3874.

The Abraham Lincoln Birthplace National Historic Park is located 3 miles south of Hodgenville, Kentucky on U.S. 31E and KY 61. Hodgenville is about 60 miles south of Louisville.

Knob Creek Farm, Lincoln's Boyhood Home, 1811-1816
U.S. 31E
Hodgenville, Kentucky

When Thomas Lincoln lost title to his Kentucky farm in 1811, the family moved 10 miles east to a farm on Knob Creek, where the soil was richer. The family lived on the 228-acre

Knob Creek Farm from the time "Abe" was two until he was almost eight years old. Here he learned to talk and soon grew big enough to run errands such as carrying water, and gathering wood for the fires. Later in life he wrote, "My earliest recollection is of the Knob Creek place." It was here that Abraham Lincoln first saw slave dealers on horseback, whip in hand, driving Negroes along the old road to be sold down South.

The original log cabin was torn down in 1870. It had been used as a corn crib until that time. It was rebuilt in 1931 and stands on the original site. The cabin is furnished with pioneer relics donated by the descendants of early settlers on Knob Creek.

Visitor's Information

Open daily, 9:00 a.m.-5:00 p.m., April 1-November 1; 9:00 a.m.-7:00 p.m., Memorial Day-Labor Day.

Admission: Adults $1.00; ages 6-12, $.50

Abraham Lincoln's Boyhood Home on Knob Creek is on U.S. 31E between Hodgenville and Bardstown, Kentucky.

Lincoln Boyhood National Memorial
IN 162
Leavenworth, Indiana

This national memorial preserves the site of the farm where Abraham Lincoln grew to manhood and the traditional gravesite of his mother, Nancy Hanks Lincoln, who died in 1818 when Lincoln was nine years old.

Early in the winter of 1816, Thomas Lincoln was again embroiled in a land title dispute and decided to move to Indiana to make a fresh start. With his wife, Nancy Hanks, his nine year old daughter Sarah, and his seven year old son, Abraham, they crossed the Ohio River, followed the Troy-Vincennes Road north about 12 miles, and then turned west a short distance to a tiny settlement along Little Pidgeon Creek. Aided by neighbors the

166

family soon completed a small log cabin and settled down to the slow and painstaking task of converting the surrounding forest to farmland.

During the 14 years in Indiana, Abraham Lincoln grew to manhood and during his last few years in Indiana, whenever possible, he traveled to the county courthouse at Rockport to hear lawyers pleading their cases.

Sometime in 1830, the Lincolns, spurred by glowing reports from a relative who had settled in Illinois, decided to move west once again.

With the passage of time, the Lincoln sites in Indiana disappeared. In 1879, a private citizen, using tradition as a guide, marked the probable site of Nancy Hanks Lincoln's grave, and the owners donated the site to the county. Subsequently, the state acquired the site, purchased additional acreage, including part of Thomas Lincoln's landholdings, and marked the approximate location of the Lincoln cabin. A memorial building was constructed and in 1962 Congress authorized establishment of Lincoln Boyhood National Memorial, which is administered by the National Park Service.

The memorial building consists of two wings connected by a semicircular cloister and features a central courtyard. The west wing, Abraham Lincoln Hall, serves as a small chapel; the east wing, Nancy Hanks Lincoln Hall, designed and furnished to represent a frontier dwelling, is used as a meeting room and exhibit area. Five relief panels symbolizing events in Lincoln's life adorn the walls of the cloister facing the courtyard. North of the memorial structure lies a grassy plaza and parking lot. From the latter, a mall extends through the woods to the gravesite, beyond which a trail leads to the cabin site and the Living Historical Farm planted with crops of the period. This area includes part of the original Thomas Lincoln farm, and recreates the rural environment where Lincoln grew to manhood.

The Visitor Center, which is in the memorial building, has a film and museum based on Lincoln's 14 years in the state.

Visitor's Information

Open daily, 8:00 a.m.-5:00 p.m. Closed January 1 and December 25. The Farm is open from Mid-April-October. Telephone: (812) 937-4541.

Admission: Adults $1.00, under 17 and over 62, free.

The Lincoln Boyhood National Memorial is on Indiana State Route 162, 2 miles east of Gentryville, 4 miles south of Dale, and 4 miles west of Santa Claus, Indiana. Exit I-64 at Dale (Exit 57) south on U.S. 231 to IN 162 east, or Santa Claus (Exit 63) to IN 162 west.

Lincoln's New Salem State Historic Site
State Route 97
Petersburg, Illinois

When Thomas Lincoln moved his family to Illinois in 1830, they settled near Decatur. Abraham was 21 and he remained with his family for one more year before striking out on his own. He decided to live in the village of New Salem, Illinois, after stopping off there while co-piloting a flatboat down the Sangamon, Illinois and Mississippi waterways.

The six years Lincoln spent in New Salem almost completely encompass the town's brief history. The community was growing and thriving when Lincoln settled in 1831, but in 1839, just two years after he left New Salem for Springfield to practice law, the county seat was established at nearby Petersburg. Thereafter, New Salem declined rapidly. Interest in the village was maintained and restoration efforts began about 1920. The park covers 600 acres and twelve timber houses, the Rutledge tavern, ten workshops, stores, and mills, and a school where church services were held have been reproduced and furnished as they were in the 1830s. A museum exhibits artifacts associated with Lincoln and other early residents. Interpreters in period dress go about the daily work of blacksmithing, cooking, carding wool and farming.

Visitor's Information

The Talisman Riverboat, a replica of the only steamboat to successfully navigate the Sangamon River, operates 45 minute scenic rides, and a summer stock theatrical group presents "Your Obedient Servant, A. Lincoln," which portrays the 16th President through his speeches, letters and those who knew him.

The Park is open daily, 9:00 a.m.-5:00 p.m., late April-late October; 8:00 a.m.-4:00 p.m., late October-late April. Closed January 1, Thanksgiving, and December 25.
Telephone: (217) 632-7953.

The Talisman operates hourly everyday, 10:00 a.m.-5:00 p.m., May 1-Labor Day, water level permitting; weekends, rest of year.
Telephone: (217) 632-7953.

Show performances Tuesday-Sunday, at 8:00 p.m., June 16-August 18.
Telephone: (217)367-1900.

Admission: Lincoln's New Salem State Park, Free.
Talisman cruise, $1.50; ages 4-12, $1.00.
Show performance, Adults $7.00; over 65 and ages 7-18, $6.00; family rate $20.00.

Lincoln's New Salem is located on State Route 97, twenty miles northwest of Springfield and two miles south of Petersburg, Illinois.

Lincoln Home National Historic Site
8th and Jackson Streets
Springfield, Illinois

This national historic site preserves the only home Abraham Lincoln ever owned, as well as the surrounding 4 blocks, which contain several structures from his era. He lived in the residence for most of the period 1844-1861, during which time he advanced from small town lawyer and local politician to President of the United States.

In 1839, Rev. Charles Dressler, rector of St. Paul's Episcopal Church in Springfield, erected a modest 1 1/2-story, frame residence on the northeast corner of Eighth and Jackson Streets. Lincoln, who in 1837 had moved to Springfield from New Salem, and was living in rented quarters, purchased it in 1844, two years after his marriage to Mary Todd and less than a year after the birth of his first son, Robert Todd. Mrs. Lincoln gave birth to three more sons in the house.

169

In 1849-1850, Lincoln had the house repainted, remodeled, and repaired. In 1856, he enlarged it to two full stories, containing 12 rooms. On May 19, 1860, in his parlor, Lincoln received official notification of his Presidential nomination from a committee of Republican officials. He conducted the campaign from his residence, leaving the traveling, speechmaking and writing to others.

In 1887, Lincoln's son, Robert Todd, donated the house to the state and it eventually became a national historic site administered by the National Park Service. The house has been restored as nearly as possible to its appearance at the time of Lincoln's occupancy. Although most of the Lincoln's household belongings were sold before they left for Washington, many have since been recovered and are displayed throughout the house.

Visitor's Information

Tours are conducted by park service representatives and those who wish to tour the home must obtain a ticket at the Visitor Center, 426 S. 7th Street, . Each ticket indicates a specific time for a scheduled tour and they are given out on a first come, first served basis.

Open daily, 8:30 a.m.-5:00 p.m. Closed January 1, Thanksgiving, December 25. Telephone: (217) 492-4150.

Admission: Free.

The Lincoln Home is at 8th and Jackson Streets in downtown Springfield, Illinois. The Visitor Center is 426 S. 7th Street, one block west of the Lincoln Home.

Lincoln-Herndon Law Offices State Historic Site
209 S. Sixth Street
Springfield, Illinois

Constructed in 1840, this site is the only surviving structure in which Lincoln maintained working law offices. Mr. Lincoln practiced law here from 1843 to 1852, first with Stephen T. Logan, and later with William H. Herndon. Visitors learn about Lincoln's professional life and the importance of law in a rapidly expanding state, as well as the differences between home and workplace in the nineteenth century. The Court located one floor below Lincoln's office is restored to the time period when it was the only Federal Court in Illinois.

Visitor's Information

Open daily 9:00 a.m.-5:00 p.m. Closed January 1, Thanksgiving, December 25. Telephone: (217) 785-7289.

Admission: Free.

The Lincoln-Herndon Law Offices are located at the corner of Sixth and Adams Streets in downtown Springfield, one half-block east of the Old State Capitol. From I-55, exit State Route 29 north (South Grand Avenue) to Sixth Street, north to Old State Capitol Plaza.

Lincoln and The Eighth Judicial Circuit

The Lincolns lived on a tight budget after buying their home in Springfield. Lincoln himself chopped the wood, carried the water, milked the cow, and did the rest of the chores men did in those days. And, to keep the money coming in, Lincoln had to go out and travel the judicial circuit. The Eighth Circuit, in which he practiced, covered 11,000 square miles and was sparsely settled with county seats far apart. Lincoln labored on the Eighth Circuit full time for a dozen years and on a part time basis for several more. He made a name for himself on the circuit and in 1846 won election to the U.S. House of Representatives. Except for the two years he served in Congress, he devoted at least half the year to circuit traveling until he became president.

Some of the courthouses on his circuit have been restored and preserved as historic sites.

Lincoln Log Cabin Courthouse
Fairview Park
Jct. U.S. 36 & IL 48
Decatur, Illinois

A reconstruction of the first courthouse in Macon County where Lincoln practiced law. It was originally located in the heart of the city, constructed of hewn oak logs in 1829-1830. Lincoln's first big case was here in 1838, which he won. The opposing lawyer was Stephen A. Douglas.

Visitor's Information

Fairview Park is open daily. The interior of the Lincoln Log Cabin Courthouse is not furnished, exterior viewable at all times.

Admission: Free.

Fairview Park is on West Eldorado Street, at the junction of U.S. 36 and Illinois State Route 48 in downtown Decatur, Illinois.

Mount Pulaski Courthouse State Historic Site
City Square
Mount Pulaski, Illinois

Mount Pulaski Courthouse is one of only two surviving Eighth Judicial Circuit courthouses in Illinois. From 1848 to 1855 the Courthouse served as the second Logan County Courthouse. The first floor contains six offices used by county officials and the second floor has the courtroom in which Abraham Lincoln, as a lawyer, visited when court was in session. The Courthouse has been restored and furnished to its original 1850s appearance.

Abraham Lincoln

Visitor's Information

Open daily 9:00 a.m.-5:00 p.m.. Closed January 1, Thanksgiving, December 25. Telephone: (217) 792-3919.

Admission: Free.

Mount Pulaski Courthouse is located on the City Square in Mount Pulaski, Illinois. From State Route 54, Exit right on State Route 121, to historical marker at DeKalb Street, left on DeKalb four blocks to Vine Street, turn left two blocks to Jefferson, turn right and travel two blocks to City Square.

Postville Courthouse State Historic Site
5th Street
Lincoln, Illinois

Postville Courthouse is a reproduction of the first Logan County Courthouse which was in use from 1840 to 1847. During this period Abraham Lincoln served as lawyer on the Eighth Judicial Circuit which held semi-annual sessions at the courthouse. The main floor of the Courthouse includes an exhibit which introduces visitors to the Eighth Judicial Circuit. The second floor contains a courtroom and county office furnished in the 1840s period. (In 1865, the growing city of Lincoln absorbed Postville completely within its municipal boundaries.)

The original Logan County Courthouse was purchased by Henry Ford and moved to his Greenfield Village at Dearborn, Michigan, despite protests by some of Logan County's leading citizens. In the courtroom are several pieces of Lincoln furniture, the original corner cupboard fashioned by young "Abe" and his father, Lincoln's wardrobe, the table from a law office where he once practiced, and a number of chairs and other pieces from his Springfield home. Also in the courtroom is the chair on which he was seated in the Washington theatre on the night of his assassination.

Abraham Lincoln

Visitor's Information

Open daily 9:00 a.m.-5:00 p.m. Closed January 1, Thanksgiving, December 25. Telephone: (217) 732-8930.

Admission: Free.

Postville Courthouse is located on 5th Street in Lincoln, Illinois. From I-55, take Lincoln Exit 126 (State Route 10), at first stoplight turn south, to next stoplight (Fifth Street) turn east, and proceed five blocks to site.

Greenfield Village is a 240-acre historical site with many homes and shops and the Logan County Courthouse moved here from all parts of the nation.

Open daily 9:00 a.m.-5:00 p.m. Closed Thanksgiving, December 25. Building interiors closed January 2-March 16.
Telephone: (313) 271-1620.

Admission: Adults $10.50; over 62, $9.50; ages 5-12, $5.25.

Greenfield Village is located at Village Road and Oakwood Boulevard in Dearborn, Michigan.

Old State Capitol State Historic Site
5th and Adams Street
Springfield, Illinois

The Old State Capitol, the center of Illinois government from 1839 to 1876, is among the most important nineteenth century buildings in the United States. Here Abraham Lincoln served as a state legislator, pleaded cases before the Supreme Court, and delivered his famous "House Divided" speech on June 16, 1858. After his assassination in 1865, his body lay in state in the House of Representatives. Period furnishings and artifacts recreate the period of Lincoln's legislative years and where his political fortunes were molded. Living history tours which feature authentically costumed characters from the 1850s are offered on most Fridays and Saturdays. An original copy of the Gettysburg Address written in Lincoln's own hand is on permanent exhibit in the lobby.

Visitor's Information

Open daily 9:00 a.m.-5:00 p.m. Closed January 1, Thanksgiving, December 25. Telephone: (217) 785-7960.

Friday and Saturday tours, "Mr. Lincoln's World"; 10:00 a.m.-noon and 1:00 p.m.-4:00 p.m., except May.

Admission: Free.

The Old State Capitol is located in downtown Springfield on the Old State Capitol Plaza, one half-block west of the Lincoln-Herndon Law Offices. From I-55, exit State Route 29 north (South Grand Avenue) to Sixth Street, north to Old State Capitol Plaza.

Lincoln Depot
Monroe Street between 9th & 10th Streets
Springfield, Illinois

It was from this Depot that President-elect Lincoln bade farewell to the Springfield he loved and boarded a train for Washington, D.C. and his inauguration as President. The Depot contains restored waiting rooms, an exhibit area, and a 20-minute multi-media presentation describing Lincoln's trip across the country to assume the presidency. Also, on the balcony, is a replica of the famous Lincoln farewell speech, a moving tribute to his friends and neighbors, given on February 11, 1861, which was the day he left Springfield for Washington. He never returned alive.

Visitor's Information

Open daily 10:00 a.m.-4:00 p.m., April-August. Telephone: (217) 544-8695.

Admission: Free.

The Depot is located in Downtown Springfield on Monroe Street about one block from the Lincoln Home National Historic Site.

Ford's Theatre National Historic Site
Ford's Theatre, 511 10th Street NW
Petersen House, 516 10th Street NW
Washington, DC

This national historic site consists of two units: Ford's Theatre, the scene of the assassination of President Abraham Lincoln; and the Petersen House, also known as the House Where Lincoln Died. Ford's Theatre now offers regularly scheduled theatrical performances and serves as a museum and shrine to Lincoln. Complementing it across the street is the Petersen House, whose historical appearance has also been restored.

After the assassination, the theatre was sold to the Federal Government and converted to an office building. In 1932, the building became the Lincoln Museum, depository of the Lincoln Collection of Osborn H. Oldroyd, a private citizen who had acquired more than 3,000 items of Lincolniana over a period of 60 years. He sold the collection to the Government in 1926. Congress authorized a total restoration which was completed by the National Park Service in 1968.

When plays are not in progress, visitors may tour the theatre and witness a program given hourly which recreates the atmosphere of the Civil War era in Washington, relates the history of the theatre, and recounts the story of the assassination. The interior of the theatre is furnished with period pieces and authentic reproductions; the Presidential box appears exactly as it did on the night of April 14, 1865; and the stage is set for the scene in *Our American Cousin* during which the fatal shot was fired.

In the basement is the Lincoln Museum, the nucleus of which was the Oldroyd Collection. Display areas contain objects connected with different phases of Lincoln's life. One alcove is devoted exclusively to items associated with the assassination.

The Petersen House across the street was built in 1849 by William Petersen. It has been restored to its 1860s appearance. A semicircular stairway with a wrought iron railing leads to the entrance on the first floor, the only section of the house open to the public. The first room to the left of the entrance hall is the front parlor, where Mary Todd Lincoln spent the night of April 14-15 with her son, Robert and friends. From this room, a double doorway leads to the back parlor, which features the marble top center table that Secretary of War Edwin Stanton used as he began his investigation of the events surrounding Lincoln's assassination. In announcing Lincoln's death from this house, Stanton uttered the memorable words, "Now he belongs to the ages." At the rear of the house and at the end of the hallway is the room where Lincoln died. Its furnishings approximate those of April 14-15, 1865, including replicas of the pictures hanging on the walls and similar wallpaper. The pillow and the bloodstained pillow cases are some of the ones used for Lincoln that night.

Visitor's Information

Open daily 9:30 a.m.-4:30 p.m. except December 25. The theatre is closed to tours when rehearsals or matinees are in progress, generally held on Thursday, Saturday and Sunday. However, the Lincoln Museum in the theatre's basement and the House Where Lincoln Died remain open. Telephone: (202) 426-6924.

Admission: Free.

Ford's Theatre and Petersen House are located at 10th Street between E and F Streets, in the heart of downtown Washington, D.C. The site is easily available with the Metro Center subway (1 1/2 blocks from the 11th Street exit) and other public transportation.

Burial Site
Oak Ridge Cemetery
1500 N. Monumnet Avenue
Springfield, Illinois

Lincoln was buried in Oak Ridge Cemetery in Springfield on May 4, 1865. The tomb, dedicated in 1874, was built with public contributions at a cost of $18,000. The remains of President Lincoln and sons Edward and William, who had preceded their father in death, had been placed in crypts in the inner wall of the uncompleted tomb in 1871. Eventually, Mary Lincoln was also buried here. A few days before the formal dedication, Lincoln's coffin was placed in a white marble sarcophagus on the floor in the center of the burial chamber. Years later, following reconstruction, Lincoln's body was placed in a steel and concrete vault beneath the floor of the chamber. The tomb is enhanced by an impressive collection of Lincoln and Civil War sculpture. At the entrance to the Tomb a bust of Lincoln stands, the nose rubbed shiny by thousands of visitors who hope they will experience good luck, a tradition passed down through the years.

Visitor's Information

Monument open daily, 9:00 a.m.-5:00 p.m.
Cemetery open daily, 7:00 a.m.-8:00 p.m., May-September; 7:00 a.m.-6:00 p.m., October-April. Telephone:(217) 782-2717.

Admission: Free.

Oak Ridge Cemetery can be entered at 1500 N. Monument Avenue or at North Walnut Street (SR 29), Springfield, Illinois.

Abraham Lincoln Museum
Lincoln Memorial University
Cumberland Gap Parkway
Harrogate, Tennessee

The Abraham Lincoln Museum at Lincoln Memorial University houses one of the most complete collections of Abraham Lincoln and Civil War history in the United States. The collection contains books, manuscripts,photographs, prints, medallions, coins, musical scores, oil paintings, sculptures, artifacts, period documents and memorabilia. Among its many high quality unique items is the cane Lincoln carried to Ford's theatre on the night he was assassinated, a large Lincoln bust by Gutzon Borglum, whose most famous work is South Dakota's Mount Rushmore, and the only known photograph of Thomas Lincoln, the president's father.

Abraham Lincoln

Visitor's Information

Open Monday-Friday, 9:00 a.m.-4:00 p.m.; Saturday, 11:00 a.m.-4:00 p.m.; Sunday, 1:00 p.m.-4:00 p.m. Closed January 1, Easter, weekends in June, Thanksgiving, December 25. Telephone:(615) 869-6237.

Admission: adults $2.00; over 60, $1.50; ages 6-12, $1.00; under 6, free.

The Abraham Lincoln Museum is located on the campus of Lincoln Memorial University in Harrogate, Tennessee. The Museum is a short drive south of Middlesboro, Kentucky on U.S. 25E.

Chicago Historical Society Museum
Clark Street at North Avenue
Chicago, Illinois

It has been said that after Lincoln's home, The Chicago Historical Society's Museum contains the nation's most significant Lincoln display. Original items in its collection include the bed from the Petersen bedroom on which President Lincoln died on April 15, 1865, the mahogany table in the White House on which Lincoln drafted the Emancipation Proclamation, a White House piano bought by Mary Lincoln, the table from the McLean house at Appomattox Court House, Virginia, on which General Robert E. Lee signed the terms of surrender which ended the Civil War, plus numerous other items.

Visitor's Information

Open Monday-Saturday, 9:30 a.m.-4:30 p.m.; Sunday, 12:00 noon-5:00 p.m. Closed January 1, Thanksgiving, December 25. Telephone: (312) 642-4600.

Admission: adults $3.00; 65 and older and students 17-22 with school ID, $2.00; ages 6-17, $1.00; under 6, free.

The Museum is located at the south end of Lincoln Park, Clark Street at North Avenue in Chicago. CTA bus numbers 11, 22, 36, 72, 151 and 156 stop nearby.

Abraham Lincoln

The Civil War Library and Museum
1805 Pine Street
Philadelphia, Pennsylvania

The Civil War Library and Museum was founded in 1888 as part of The Military Order of the Loyal Legion of the United States. Its first president was Colonel Rutherford B. Hayes, the nineteenth president of the United States. The organization has devoted over 100 years to acquiring, conserving and displaying a comprehensive range of artifacts and documentary material on the Civil War period. The Lincoln Room contains important artifacts and portraits of Lincoln, lifemasks, a cast of his hands, original paper items connected with his assassination such as a playbill for *Our American Cousin,* the play being performed when Lincoln was shot, a reward poster for Lincoln's assassins, John Wilkes Booth, Davy Herold and John Surratt, and many other items.

Visitor's Information

Open 10:00 a.m.-4:00 p.m., Monday-Saturday. Closed holidays. Telephone: (215) 735-8196.

Admission: Adults $3.00, senior citizens $2.00, under 12 free.

The Civil War Library and Museum is located at 1805 Pine Street in downtown Philadelphia near the Schuylkill Expressway and I-95.

Lincoln College Museum
300 Keokuk
Lincoln, Illinois

The Lincoln College Museum in the McKinstry Memorial Library houses and displays more than 2,000 Lincoln volumes, numerous pamphlets, art, objects d'art and assorted items of historical significance. Notable in the collection is the original Power of Attorney which was drawn up in Lincoln's office and used to found the town of Lincoln, Illinois, and a campaign poster carried in a torch light parade in Lincoln and later in the 1860 nomination parade in Springfield where it won a prize and was reproduced in *Leslie's*

Magazine. On display are several signatures of Abraham Lincoln, the table of Mentor Graham upon which Lincoln studied, and the desk used by Lincoln in the Illinois State Legislature at Springfield.

Visitor's Information

Open Monday-Friday 10:00 a.m.-noon, 1:00 p.m.-4:30 p.m.; Saturday-Sunday 1:00 p.m.-4:30 p.m.

Admission: Free.

The Museum is located on the intersection of State Routes 10 and 121.

Lincoln Memorial
West Potomac Park
Washington, D.C.

This memorial ranks with the Washington Monument and the Jefferson Memorial as one of the most beloved shrines in the nation. It is also one of the most impressive examples of classical architecture in the United States.

A national Lincoln memorial had been urged since 1867, but not until 1911 did Congress provide legislation for it. The cornerstone was laid on February 12, 1915 and dedicated on Memorial Day, May 30, 1922. It is administered by the National Park Service.

The memorial, constructed primarily of white Colorado-Yule marble, is of classical design and resembles the Parthenon in Athens, Greece. The basic structure, rectangular in shape, is surrounded on all four sides by a colonnade of 36 Doric columns, one for each state at the time of Lincoln's death. Their names are carved into the frieze above the colonnade. Inscribed on the walls over the frieze are the names of the 48 states at the time of the dedication.

Within the memorial chamber are three commemorative features, a colossal seated statue of Lincoln and two huge inscribed tablets. The marble statue of Lincoln occupies the place of honor. It is centrally located near the back of the chamber and faces the Washington Monument and the Capitol. The statue from head to foot is 19 feet high. The scale is such that if Lincoln was standing he would be 28 feet tall. On the north wall inscribed in stone is Lincoln's Second Inaugural Address; on the south wall, similarly inscribed, is the Gettysburg Address. Above each of these tablets are murals, 60 feet long and 12 feet high, which allegorically depict principles espoused by Lincoln.

Visitor's Information

The memorial is always open. A ranger is in attendance 8:00 a.m.-midnight except on December 25. Telephone: (202) 619-7222.

Admission: Free.

The memorial is in downtown Washington at the beginning of 23rd Street NW, between Constitution and Independence Avenues. From Virginia, follow Route 50 west to Washington and turn right on 23rd Street or take George Washington Parkway to Memorial Bridge.

Lincoln Memorial Shrine
125 West Vine Street
Redlands, California

Robert Watchorn, an easterner who early in his life became fascinated with Lincoln and the Civil War period, began to collect Lincolniana. In 1931, he and his wife started to formulate plans for the construction of a memorial to Lincoln and a repository for their Lincoln collection. Choosing their winter home in Redlands, California, the Watchorns presented to the city a memorial to Lincoln, the only one in existence west of the Mississippi River, monument, museum, library and archives.

The Lincoln Memorial building was designed in an octagon shape with construction of reinforced concrete faced with Bedford Indiana limestone plates upon which are incised excerpts from Lincoln's addresses. The Shrine houses the famous Carrara bust of Lincoln by the noted sculptor George Gray Barnard. Ceiling murals were painted on canvas by a New York artist, as were the lunettes, each depicting Lincoln's character and deeds through allegorical symbols.

The Shrine library contains thousands of volumes on Lincoln and the Civil War. The manuscript collection includes a number of letters and documents from Lincoln, as well as many from his family and cabinet members. There are also thousands of rare pamphlets, newspapers, photographs, diaries and relics of Lincoln and the Civil War period.

Visitor's Information

Open 1:00 p.m.-5:00 p.m., Tuesday-Saturday, closed Sunday, Monday and holidays, except Lincoln's birthday. Telephone: Morning, (714) 798-7632; afternoon, (714) 798-7636.

Admission: Free.

The Lincoln Memorial Shrine is located in Smiley Park at the rear of the A.K. Smiley Public Library.

Lincoln Monument
Sherman Hill
Laramie, Wyoming

This bronze bust, believed to be the largest free standing bust of Lincoln in the world, is twelve and a half feet high and weighs three and a half tons. It rests on a thirty foot stone base made of native granite on the summit of Sherman Hill, the highest point on the transcontinental highway once known as Lincoln Highway but now designated as Interstate 80.

Dr. Robert I. Russin, well-known sculptor and Professor of art at the University of Wyoming, created the bronze bust. It was cast in Mexico City and transported the 2,000 miles from there to Wyoming by railroad.

The monument was dedicated in 1959 as part of the 150th anniversary of Lincoln's birth. A bronze plaque near the base of the monument quotes these words from Lincoln: "We must think anew and act anew."

Visitor's Information

The Lincoln Monument is nine miles east of Laramie on I-80 at the edge of a rest area. It is always viewable at no charge.

The Lincoln Museum
66 Lincoln Square
Hodgenville, Kentucky

The first level of the Lincoln Museum contains twelve scenes of great importance in Lincoln's life and our nation's history. These are: The Cabin Years, 1809-1816; The Berry-Lincoln Store, 1831; The Railsplitter, 1825; The Mary Todd Home, 1849; Lincoln Visits Farmington, 1841; The Lincoln-Douglas Debates, 1858; Emancipation Proclamation, 1862; The Mathew Brady Studio, February, 1864; The Second Inauguration, March 4, 1865; The Gettysburg Address, November 19, 1963; Surrender, April 9, 1865; and Ford's Theatre, April 14, 1865. On the second level are exhibits, memorabilia, and the Lincoln Days Art Collection.

Visitor's Information

Open Monday-Saturday 9:00 a.m.-6:00 p.m., Sunday, 1:00 p.m.-6:00 p.m.

Admission: adults $3.00; senior citizen, $2.50; ages 5-12, $1.50.

The museum is located on the town square near the original bronze statue of Lincoln by A. A. Weinmann

Abraham Lincoln

The Lincoln Museum
1300 South Clinton Street
Fort Wayne, Indiana

Since 1928, The Lincoln Museum has collected material from the life and times of one of America's greatest Presidents. Today, it has the world's largest private collection of Lincolniana.

The collection is funded by Lincoln National Corporation, which has taken special interest in Abraham Lincoln's life since the company began in 1905. At that time, Robert Todd Lincoln, the president's sole surviving son, gave the fledgling insurance company permission to use the Lincoln name and sent a portrait by Civil War photographer Mathew Brady for use on the company's first letterhead.

The museum contains 60 chronological and thematic exhibits that depict Lincoln's life. They begin with his birth in a Kentucky log cabin and end with his assassination in 1865 and his historic 16-day funeral. Important moments in his life are dramatized in displays of manuscripts written by Lincoln, personal family belongings, and other artifacts including a flag that draped the president's box on the fateful night at Ford's theatre. Vintage campaign buttons, posters, flags, and torches provide vivid reminders of his political campaigns. The library's files contain 200,000 newspaper clippings and magazine articles on Lincoln, 20,000 volumes, half of them on Lincoln, and more than 5,000 original photographs, including those from Lincoln's own family album and dozens of rare portraits of Lincoln himself.

Visitor's Information

Posters and free literature related to Abraham Lincoln's life are provided to visitors.

Open: Memorial Day-Labor Day, 8:00 a.m.-4:30 p.m., Monday-Friday, 10:00 a.m.-4:30 p.m. Saturday; rest of the year, 8:00 a.m.-4:30 p.m., Monday-Thursday, 8:00 a.m.-12:30 p.m., Friday. Closed holidays. Telephone: (219) 427-3864.

Admission: Free.

The Lincoln Museum is located at 1300 S. Clinton Street in downtown Fort Wayne, Indiana.

The Lincoln Room Museum
12 Lincoln Square
Gettysburg, Pennsylvania

This museum is in the Wills house. Constructed about 1818, this brick three-story house became famous for being the place where Lincoln stayed overnight on November 18, 1863, and worked on the speech he was giving at the dedication of the Gettysburg Cemetery the next day. The story of Lincoln's stay at this house and the writing of the last copy of the Gettysburg Address and his stirring address are presented in a light and sound show. The house has original furnishings and there are two rooms of artifacts of Lincoln and the Wills family.

Visitor's Information

Open daily 9:00 a.m.-7:00 p.m., Memorial Day-Labor Day; reduced hours the rest of the year. Telephone: (717) 334-8188.

Admission: adults $3.00; over 60, $2.50; ages 8-18, $1.50.

The Lincoln Room Museum, in the Wiils House is located in Lincoln Square in the middle of Gettysburg at U.S. 15 business route and U.S. 30.

Union Pacific Historical Museum
1416 Dodge Street
Omaha, Nebraska

The museum was founded in 1921 and tells the story of Union Pacific's colorful history and its contributions to settling and building the west.

In 1866, Union Pacific purchased President Lincoln's funeral car at auction from the federal government and used it as a private car for its directors. The model in the museum has many of its original furnishings including the desk, bookcase, reclining chair, mirrors, davenports and silver hollowware. One of the davenports is extra long for President Lincoln. The car symbolizes Union Pacific's ties to Lincoln. He signed the Pacific Railroad Acts of 1862 and 1864 which created Union Pacific. He also chose the Omaha-Council Bluffs area as the transcontinental railroad's eastern terminus.

In Council Bluffs, Iowa, a Lincoln Monument erected July, 1911, marks the spot where Lincoln stood with Union Pacific's chief engineer, Grenville Dodge, in 1859, when he visited the city and viewed the Missouri River panorama from a bluffs hillside. In 1863, after becoming president, he proclaimed Council Bluffs the eastern terminus of the future transcontinental railroad.

Visitor's Information

Open 9:00 a.m.-5:00 p.m., Monday-Friday; 9:00 a.m.-1:00 p.m. Saturday. Closed holidays. Telephone: (402) 271-5457.

Admission: Free.

The Union Pacific Historical Museum is at 1416 Dodge Street in downtown Omaha, Nebraska.

Across the Missouri River from Omaha, in Council Bluffs, Iowa, the Lincoln Monument is located at Lafayette Avenue and Oakland Avenue and available for viewing year round.

Andrew Johnson, 17th President, 1865-1869

Birthplace of Andrew Johnson

Rear view of the 1830's Andrew Johnson House showing the unrestored altered ell

Andrew Johnson's Tailor Shop

Andrew Johnson's Burial Site

Andrew Johnson

Seventeenth President
1865 - 1869
Democrat / Republican

Andrew Johnson was born to a poor sexton and his wife on December 29, 1808 in Raleigh, North Carolina. What makes his rise to the Presidency remarkable is that he was the only president who never attended a day of school in his life. His father died when he was five, and at ten he was apprenticed to a tailor, our only president to hold that job. When he and his mother moved to Greeneville, Tennessee, he opened his own shop. While setting up his business he met Eliza McCardle (a seamstress herself), who became his teacher and soon his fiancee.

Johnson learned to read and write, and soon was involved in debates and giving speeches. He was elected city alderman at the age of 20, mayor at 22 (our first president to have held this office), a Tennessee legislator at 25, and at 33 a State Senator. He was then elected to the United States Congress for ten years before serving, from 1853 to 1857, as Governor of Tennessee. In 1857 he was elected to the Senate, where he was the only southern Senator among twenty two who fought against secession. When the Confederacy formed he was exiled, and his property seized by the government. In 1862 Abraham Lincoln appointed him military governor of Tennessee. Meanwhile, his home in Greenville first became a Confederate hospital and then barracks, and was later almost demolished by the rebels before the area was captured by the Union.

Though he was a Democrat, Andrew Johnson was nominated for the vice presidency in 1864. On April 15, 1865, he ascended to the presidency after the assassaination of Abraham Lincoln. The Radical Republicans (who advocated punishment of the South for the war) and their political allies expected he would take a strong, punitive approach towards the conquered Confederacy. Johnson had spoken out frequently against the rich plantation owners. But this dislike of the slaveowner stemmed from his own poor southern background, not from his agreement with the Radicals on such issues as racial equality and the re-admittance of the seceded states. In fact, Johnson was not opposed to slavery and did not believe in giving the vote to the blacks.

With Congress out of session in the spring of 1865, Johnson set out on his own program of reconstruction, (one which closely followed Lincoln's), which recognized new governments in four states. On May 29, 1865 he issued a Proclamation of Amnesty which said that if a state abolished slavery and repudiated any war debts it could return to the Union. An interesting part to this Proclamation was the provision that owners of property worth more than twenty thousand dollars had to personally petition the president for full citizenship in the Union. Andrew Johnson, the dirt-poor farm boy from Tennessee now had the rich land owners coming to him for forgiveness.

When Congress reconvened in December Johnson asked for the re-admittance of all but one of the former members of the Confederacy. Congress refused to accept Johnson's version of reconstruction, partly out of their anger over his selection of former Confederate officials as Congressmen and for the South's apparent determination to keep the newly freed blacks from making any economic or social gains, under what was called the Black Codes. They proceded to create their own version of Reconstruction, which included a demand that former Confederate states had to ratify the Thirteenth Amendment (which did not, at that time, require the state to give blacks the vote).

Though the amendment was fairly palatable to the South, (it did not require giving blacks the vote) Johnson refused to side with the Radical Republicans, and he made the 1866 mid-term elections a mandate on the Fourteenth Amendment. He made a nationwide tour of the country which he called a "Swing Around the Circle," making speeches and appearances at every opportunity. The trip was a disaster, and Johnson suceeded only in producing a Republican victory in both houses of Congrees which gave them more than the two-thirds majority they needed to override his vetos.

In March of 1867 Congress passed two bills intended to reduce the power of Johnson's presidency. The President, according these laws, could no longer remove his own Cabinet members or army officers under his command. On February 21, 1868, Johnson, determined to test the constitutionality of the Tenure of Office Act, removed Edwin M. Stanton (the Secretary of War and a Republican Radical) from the Cabinet. The next day, for the first time in United States history, Congress voted for the impeachment of the President. It should be noted that the grounds for impeachment were shaky...Johnson was never charged, as the Constitution requires, of "treason, bribery, or high crimes and mistemeanors," and after a two month trial, he was acquitted - by a one vote margin.

One non-Reconstruction related action which Johnson took was the purchase of Alaska from Russia for a little over seven million dollars. It was the object of much derision in 1867 (some called it Seward's Folly), but proved to be one of his administration's most lasting contributions to America. Not only did it remove the last vestige of Russian control from North America, but gave America sole ownership of vast oil deposits.

During Johnson's term the Midway Islands were also purchased as well as treaties signed with Columbia and Nicaragua which paved the way for an isthmus canal.

Johnson sought the nomination of his party for re-election in 1868, but the Democrats settled on a less controversial man, Horatio Seymour. Johnson did not retire from politics, however, trying several times for a seat in Congress. In 1874 he won perhaps his greatest political victory (short of the impeachment vote) when he was elected to the Senate from Tennessee, becoming the only president to serve in that body after leaving the White House. Sadly, he barely had time to settle into those duties when he died on July 31, 1876, in Tennessee.

Historical Landmarks

Birthplace of Andrew Johnson
Mordecai Historic Park
1 Mimosa Street
Raleigh, North Carolina

In 1808, Raleigh, North Carolina, was a small town of fewer than a thousand people, and though it was the capital of the state, it was still only a country village. Just south of the State House, on Fayetteville Street, was a rambling frame building known as Casso's Inn, which was a noted hostelry in its day. In the yard of the Inn was a tiny gambrel-roofed house built about 1795. Jacob Johnson, Andrew's father and his mother, Mary McDonough Johnson, lived in this small house. Jacob was hostler at the inn and janitor of the State House. His wife did weaving for the inn and was known as "Polly the Weaver." It was in this environment that Andrew Johnson, seventeenth President of the United States, was born on December 29, 1808.

Visitor's Information

The birthplace house has been restored to its appearance in the late 1790s with furnishings of the same period. The house has been moved to Mordecai Historic Park where it stands with other 18th-century restorations.

Open Tuesday-Friday 10:00 a.m.-4:00 p.m., Saturday-Sunday 1:30 p.m.-4:30 p.m. Closed holidays. Telephone: (919) 834-4844.

Admission: adults $3.00,; ages 7-17, $1.00.

Mordecai Historic Park is located at 1 Mimosa Street, Raleigh, North Carolina.

Andrew Johnson National Historic Site
Depot and College Streets
Greeneville, Tennessee

Andrew Johnson National Historic Site, operated by the National Park Service, dramatically illustrates Johnson's rise from very humble beginnings to the presidency. Three structures, at separate but nearby locations, represent nearly 45 years of his life: the tailor shop he owned for many years and two of his residences. The cemetery in which Johnson is buried is also in the national historic site.

The tailor shop which Johnson acquired in 1831 was a small one-room frame building with a high ceiling and steep roof covered with shingles. The exterior walls have yellow poplar weatherboarding. The interior walls and floor are of pine, and a large fireplace occupies one end of the room. The shop is furnished with items Johnson used including a tailoring bench, heating stove, iron, pair of candle molds, and water pitcher. The State which had purchased the shop from the family in 1921, enclosed the structure in a brick shelter and administered it as a historic shrine until the federal government acquired it in 1941. Today the building also houses the Visitor Center for the site which includes a museum with exhibits on the life and career of this self-made man.

Johnson's first Greeneville house has not survived. The 1831-1851 residence, also known as the Kerbaugh House, was a two-story brick structure, probably constructed in the 1820s. It originally had four rooms: living room and kitchen/dining room on the first floor and two bedrooms on the second. Additions include an ell on a slightly lower level adjoining the east end of the house, a porch along the south end and a portico at the Water Street entrance. (This house is not open to the public.)

Andrew Johnson

The 1851-75 Homestead, built not long before Johnson purchased it, had undergone considerable alteration but it is now restored to its 1869-1875 appearance. It is a two-story, brick main house and a two-story, brick ell at the rear. A double veranda extends along the rear of the main section and the northeast side and end of the ell; the exposed basement level gives the effect of three stories on this side. The structure contains ten rooms: kitchen and storeroom (also the servant's quarters) in the basement; parlor, dining room, and two bedrooms on the first floor, and four bedrooms on the second. The family's simple furnishings and possessions are displayed in the Homestead.

Visitor's Information

Open everyday 9:00 a.m.-5:00 p.m., except December 25.

Admission: for Homestead, adults $1.00, under 17 free.

The Visitor Center is at the corner of Depot and College Streets and one block east of Main Street in Greeneville, Tennessee. In approaching Greeneville by highway, orientation signs direct visitors to the Visitor Center

Burial Site
Andrew Johnson Cemetery
End of Monument Avenue
Greeneville, Tennessee

Andrew Johnson had gone on a visit to his daughter but soon after his arrival he suffered a paralytic stroke and died a few days later on July 31, 1875. He is buried in the cemetery which is part of the Andrew Johnson National Historic Site. In 1906, the cemetery, now known as the Andrew Johnson National Cemetery, was donated to the federal government by the Johnson heirs. Besides Johnson, it includes the burial site of his wife, children and other descendants.

As he had requested, Johnson's remains were put to rest with a copy of the constitution as a pillow and the American flag as a blanket. The 26-foot high monument over his grave memorializes two great fundamentals that dominated his career. A scroll represents the Constitution and below is a hand placed on a bible as in taking an oath. His constant adherence to democracy is commemorated by these words, "His faith in the people never wavered."

Visitor's Information

Open every day 9:00 a.m.-5:00 p.m., except December 25.

Admission: Free.

Andrew Johnson Cemetery is at the end of Monument Avenue and one block south of West Main Street in the Andrew Johnson National Historic Site in downtown Greeneville, Tennessee.

Ulysses Simpson Grant, 18th President, 1869-1877

ULYSSES S. GRANT BIRTHPLACE

Ulysses S. Grant Birthplace

Ulysses S. Grant Boyhood Home

U. S. Grant Home

Grant Cottage

General Grant National Memorial

Ulysses S. Grant

Eighteenth President
1869 - 1877
Republican

Born on April 27, 1822, in Point Pleasant, Ohio, Hiram Ulysses Grant's first choice for a career was to follow in his father's footsteps and became a tanner. But this young boy's grandfather had fought in the Revolution at Bunker Hill and at Yorktown, so he jumped when the chance arose to leave the leather business and enter West Point. Soon after receiving his commission Grant saw action in the Mexican War, serving under Winfield Scott and future President Zachary Taylor. (Graduating from West Point an error in registration caused his name to be changed to Ulysses Simpson Grant.) After the war he spent some time as a captain in a garrison in Oregon.

It was while serving in the Mexican War that he was introduced to a West Point classmate's sister, Julia Dent. After the war ended, they were married, much to her father's dismay, as he did not think much of the young man's prospects. For a while it looked like the father was right.

The boredom in Oregon apparently got to Grant, who had begun to drink heavily. He resigned his post and returned to Ohio to try his hand at farming. The farm failed. He tried opening a business. That failed, too. When the Civil War broke out he was working as a junior clerk in his brothers' leather store in Galena, Ohio. Grant volunteered and, thanks to his West Point experience, was appointed a brigadier general and given a command.

Grant's victory over the rebels at Fort Donelson was the Union's first major victory. His message to his Confederate opponent, Simon Buckner, became famous: "No terms except an unconditional and immediate surrender can be accepted. I propose to move immediately upon your works." Later, his victories at Vicksburg and Shiloh led his men to anoint him with a nickname: Unconditional Surrender Grant. In March of 1864 he was named supreme commander of all the Union Armies. On April 9, 1865, after a bloody Virginia campaign that lasted almost a year and cost many tens of thousands of lives, Grant accepted the surrender of the Confederate forces from their commander, Robert E. Lee, at the Appomattox Court House.

Grant, now a nationally revered hero, remained in the army this time, returning to Galena for a short while. He then moved first to Philadelphia and then Washington.

Although Grant was known to have voted for Democrats James Buchanan and Stephen Douglas, the Republicans nominated him to run for the presidency in 1868. The Republicans won easily, running the popular war hero while at the same time employing a campaign strategy known as "waving the bloody shirt," (where they portrayed the Democrats as the party of rebellion and themselves as the party that saved the Union). Grant became the first president to come from Ohio.

Grant presided over the period of American history known as Reconstruction, when the southern states were brought back into the Union and began the process of rebuilding their economy and social order. Reconstruction was difficult on the South as the former belligerents attempted to repair and rebuild roads, hospitals, schools, and businesses. Corruption and graft following the war were rampant not just in the South but in the North as well, and while Grant was a brilliant military strategist, he was no match for Washington's spoils system.

His political philosophy was a throwback to the days when it was believed that presidents should exercise the will of Congress, not lead it. His choice of cabinet officers were, with the exception of Secretary of State Hamilton Fish, less than exemplary appointments. Jobs were given to friends, family members, and political hangers-on. Corruption, though perhaps no more abundant during the Grant administration than before, became more public. Although Grant was never a participant, merely an unwitting accomplice, his administration has become known as one of the country's most corrupt.

During Grant's first term, two speculators named Jim Fisk and Jay Gould, using the President's unwitting brother-in-law, convinced Grant to hold back on the government's supply of gold, thereby driving up the price. On September 24, 1869 there was a panic at the stock exchange, forcing Grant to release gold bullion from federal reserves. Many businesses were adversely affected, and the day became known as Black Friday.

Other scandals included Grant's Secretary of Treasury hiring a private citizen to collect back taxes, only to have the collector keep more than his agreed share. The War Department suffered too, when it was discovered that Secretary of War William Belknap accepted bribes in exchange for an exclusive trading concession. When the House voted to impeach Belknap, he quickly resigned. Later, it was discovered that the Secretary of the Navy had accepted influence money for ship contracts, and the Secretary of the Interior had done the same with land speculators.

In 1872, as the campaign for the presidency began heating up, the New York Sun published the story of how stocks in Credit Mobilier (a construction company formed by investors in the Union Pacific Railroad) were given to congressmen who had helped the company gain the contract to build the first trans-continental railroad and to keep them from investigating other improprieties. Congress was forced to investigate and before they were done (after Grant's re-election) they found that Schuyler Colfax, Grant's vice-president during his first term and Henry Wilson, his current vice-president, were involved.

Despite the public attacks on Grant and the scandals in his administration Grant was re-elected to the presidency by an even bigger margin in 1872 than in 1868.

Then, just as his second term began, another scandal came to light involving the Secretary of Treasury and a ring of whisky distillers who had been evading federal taxes to the tune of over a million dollars annually. Even Grant's own private secretary had been involved.

But larger troubles than the scandals were coming. The country's growth, along with the accelerated war economy (which had fed the Western and Northern economies for the previous forty years), slowed in the early 1870s. There was also a large unfavorable balance of trade and credit had been over-extended to many people who could no longer pay their debts. Banks began to fail and in September of 1873, the country fell into a terrible depression, which Grant was unable to curb.

Ulysses Grant's administration had its successes. His Secretary of State, Hamilton Fish, negotiated a settlement with Britain over the Alabama claims. This treaty not only helped foster stronger British-American ties, but helped set up America as a player on the world stage. Grant also sought to end the mistreatment of the Native Americans with his Peace Policy. He was quick to abolish the wartime income tax and most of the wartime excise duties. Grant also required that the paper currency printed during the Civil War be redeemable in gold, a compromise which satisfied the Western farmers and Eastern bankers.

Grant chose not to run again in 1876, and took off on trip around the world, during which he was greeted by thousands of admirers. Upon his return to America, bored with retirement, he attempted to gain the nomination for the presidency in 1880, but failed. He then entered into partnership in a Wall Street bank, but when the institution went bankrupt (it turned out to be, unbeknownst to Grant, a swindling organization), he lost practically everything he owned.

Offered a large sum of money by Samuel Clemens (Mark Twain) to write his memoirs, Grant spent the last year of his life writing. Just a few days before his death, on July 23, 1885, he completed the task.

Historical Landmarks

Birthplace of Ulysses S. Grant
Intersection of State Routes 52 and 232
Point Pleasant, Ohio

Jesse Grant arrived in the village of Point Pleasant, Ohio, about twenty-six miles from Cincinnati, in 1820, to work in a tannery. The following year, in June, he married Hannah Simpson and they lived in a little frame cottage near the Ohio River. Some ten months later, on April 27, 1822, Ulysses S. Grant was born.

Their home was a one-story building of two very small rooms, with an outside chimney at one end in the manner of Southern cottages. In one room the family lived in daytime, cooking at the big fireplace, and eating at a pine table. In the other room they slept.

Within a year after Ulysses' birth, Jesse Grant had saved enough money to build his own tannery in Georgetown, the county seat of Brown County, twenty miles east of Point Pleasant, where they moved.

Visitor's Information

The Grant birthplace cottage has been restored and furnished with period items in the living. dining, and kitchen areas.

Open April-October, Wednesday-Saturday, 9:30 a.m.-noon and 1:00 p.m.-5:00 p.m.; Sunday, noon-5:00 p.m. Closed January 1, Thanksgiving, December 25.

Admission: adults $1.00; senior citizens, $.75; ages 6-12, $.50.

Grant's birthplace is located in the Clermont County village of Point Pleasant, Ohio, near the intersection of State Routes 52 and 232.

Ulysses S. Grant

Grant Boyhood Home
219 E. Grant Avenue
Georgetown, Ohio

During 1823, after the move from Point Pleasant to Georgetown, Jesse Grant built a two-room, two-story brick house just 300 feet east of the town square. As his family grew and his business prospered, Jesse added an 1824 kitchen and 1828 parlor, two bedroom addition. Ulysses lived in the homestead longer than any other of his residences.

The house is listed on the National Register of Historic Places and is a National Landmark. Except for the restored kitchen the house is as it was in 1839 when Grant left for West Point and it contains exhibits and memorabilia of the Grant family.

Visitor's Information

Open Tuesday-Saturday, 9:00 a.m.-1:00 p.m. and 2:00 p.m.-5:00 p.m. Closed January 1, Thanksgiving, December 25. Telephone: (513) 381-0800.

Admission: Free.

The house is located at the corner of east Grant and North Water Streets in downtown Georgetown, Ohio.

U.S. Grant House, 1849-1851
Michigan State Fair Grounds
State Fair and Woodward Avenues
Detroit, Michigan

On his return from duty in the Mexican War, General Ulysses S. Grant came to Detroit in the spring of 1849 with the 4th Infantry Regiment. His residence, then located at 1369 (old number 253) E. Fort Street, a two-story pine cottage with a white picket fence. The house was described by Grant as "a neat little house [with] a double parlor, a dining room, one small bedroom and kitchen in the lower level. There is a nice upstairs and a garden filled with the best kind of fruit."

Grant served as Company Officer and Quartermaster of the Detroit Barracks until June, 1851 before moving West. In succeeding years the house had many owners and existed in obscurity. In 1936, when the house was threatened with demolishment if not sold, it was purchased by the Michigan Mutual Liability Company, refurbished and presented to the State of Michigan with the understanding that it would be moved to the Michigan State Fair Grounds and used as a historical museum.

Visitor's Information

The Grant House is on the Michigan State Fair Grounds and can be seen during the Fair which is traditionally held the week before Labor Day. The house is no longer open to visitors but can be viewed from the outside. Fair hours are from 10:00 a.m.-10:00 p.m.

Admission to Fair: $5.00, children under 12 free.

The Michigan State Fair Grounds are at Woodward and State Fair Avenues. From I-75 take the 8 Mile Road Exit one mile west to the grounds. The Grant House, located on the Fair Grounds, is at the edge of the Picnic Grove near Avenue "B." Telephone: (313) 368-1000.

Grant's Farm,"Hardscrabble"
10501 Gravois Road
St. Louis, Missouri

After resigning from the army in July, 1854, Grant and his family returned to St. Louis and, living on his father-in-law's estate of White Haven, began to farm a 100-acre parcel of land which had been a gift to his wife, Julia, from her father, Colonel Frederick Dent. White Haven, however, was a great distance from Julia's land so, in 1855, Grant decided to build a home of his own, which would be christened Hardscrabble to reflect the difficulty of the times.

Ulysses S. Grant

In the autumn of 1855, Grant cut, shaped and notched the oak and elm logs for his house. He split shingles and hauled stones for the cellar and foundation. And in pioneer tradition, he invited his neighbors to gather for a cabin-raising. Grant did much of the remaining work himself: shingling the roof, building the stairs, laying the floors. Experienced carpenters finished the white-painted window frames, sashes and doors by hand, making the house ready for the Grant family, which by then had included two sons and a daughter.

The Grants resided at Hardscrabble until Julia's mother died and the family returned to White Haven to assist Colonel Dent. The cabin, along with the farm, was later leased to tenant farmers but remained in Grant's possession until 1884 when it was lost to a mortgage holder. It passed though several hands; one buyer disassembled the structure and had it reconstructed on his property; another moved it to St. Louis as an attraction during the city's 1904 World's Fair.

Following the fair, the cabin was purchased by Adolphus Busch, founder of Anheuser-Busch, Inc., who coincidentally had recently purchased a suburban estate which included acreage from White Haven. Busch had the cabin moved about a mile from its original location. In 1977, because serious deterioration was observed in sections of Hardscrabble, it was disassembled totally one more time; all deteriorating sections replaced, the interior restored authentically, and the environs of the home, the outbuilding, kitchen garden and other outdoor elements constructed to make the cabin appear just as it did when Ulysses and Julia were in residence. Finally, a national search was launched to locate and acquire authentic furnishings which, if not those which originally graced the house, were at least typical of the era and corresponded as closely as possible to descriptions of Julia Grant's home.

Visitor's Information

The cabin is on a 281-acre tract, named Grant's Farm in honor of Ulysses S. Grant. It is operated by Anheuser-Busch Co., Inc. and in addition to the Grant home it includes a Clydesdale stallion stable and padlock, carriage collection, miniature zoo, trophy room, animal feeding area, deer park, and elephant and bird shows.

Open Tuesday-Sunday, June-August; Thursday-Sunday, April 15-May 31 and September 1-October 15, complimentary trackless train tours available at 9:00 a.m., 10:00 a.m., 11:00

a.m., 1:00 p.m., 2:00 p.m., and 3:00 p.m. Advance reservations are necessary. Telephone: (314) 843-1700.

Admission: Free.

Grant's Farm is on 10501 Gravois Road, St. Louis, Missouri. Both I-70 and I-270 intersect Gravois Road. From I-70 turn east and from I-270, turn west to Grant's Farm.

Grant's Home at White Haven
7400 Grant Road
St. Louis, Missouri

White Haven was the family home of Ulysses S. Grant's father-in-law, Colonel Frederick Dent whose son was a roommate of Grant's at West Point. When Grant was assigned to nearby Jefferson Barracks and visited White Haven, he met his future wife, Julia Dent. They were married at White Haven, lived there briefly before transferring to other army posts, and Julia gave birth to their first child there. When Grant resigned from the army in 1854, he returned to White Haven. They lived in the main house for a while, then occupied Julia's brother Louis' house, Wish-ton-Wish, on the plantation while Grant farmed 100-acres given to Julia by her father and built a log home known as Hard-scrabble on White Haven land. They lived at Hardscrabble only a few months before returning to White Haven. Their third child, Nellie, was born in 1855, probably at Wishton-Wish; their youngest child, Jesse, was born in 1858, apparently in the main house.

During the Civil War and his presidency, Ulysses Grant bought the property from the Dent family and planned to retire at White Haven and raise horses. Unknown circumstances cause him to abandon those retirement plans but he held the property until he lost it in payment of a debt months before his death.

In 1990, Congress authorized establishment of Grant's Home, White Haven, as Ulysses S. Grant National Historic Site and the National Park Service assumed management of the location. The 9.65-acre site includes a two-story residence, a barn, a chicken coop, a smoke and ice house, and a stone building believed to have housed Grant's father-in-law's slaves. Architecturally, the southwest wing of the main house is regionally significant because it is one of the nation's few surviving examples of French colonial vertical log construction.

Visitor's Information

The National Park Service is currently conducting research on the history of the property, its structures, and its connections with the Dent and Grant families. When sufficient information is available, the structures will be restored and the site, located in an unincorporated portion of south St. Louis County, Missouri, open to the public.

Limited access is now available for groups by appointment only. Telephone: (314) 425-4468.

City Point Unit
Petersburg National Battlefield
Pecan Avenue and Cedar Lane
Hopewell, Virginia

On June 14, 1864, Ulysses S. Grant, General in Chief of the Union Army, launched an attack on General Robert E. Lee's forces in Petersburg, Virginia. After the failure of his initial strike, a siege lasting ten months began, which culminated in the surrender of Lee and his Army of Northern Virginia on April 9, 1865, in the Appomattox Court House, Appomattox, Virginia.

Headquarters and home for Grant during the Battle of Petersburg was a two-room log cabin built for him on the grounds of Appomattox Manor in City Point, now Hopewell, Virginia. Appomattox Manor, also known as the Eppes House, a 1 1/2-story frame house, part of which was built before the Revolutionary War, was the ancestral home of the Eppes family and owned by Dr. Richard Eppes.

In 1968, Grant's cabin was moved from City Point to Philadelphia where it was exhibited for over a century in that city's Fairmount Park. In 1981, it was returned in very poor condition and the following year it was reconstructed on its original site in the City Point Unit of Petersburg National Battlefield.

Visitor's Information

The City Point Unit, operated by the National Park Service, is seven miles from the Petersburg National Battlefield and approximately 90 miles from the Appomattox Court House.

Open daily 8:00 a.m.-5:0 p.m.; closed January 1, December 25. Telephone: (804) 732-3531.

Admission: free.

Hopewell can be reached from I-95 by exiting at Route 10, Hopewell; continue on Route 10 to Appomattox Street, turn left and continue to Cedar Lane, turn left and proceed to City Point Unit.

U.S. Grant Home
500 Bouthillier Street
Galena, Illinois

On August 18, 1865, Galena, Illinois celebrated the return of its Civil War hero, General Ulysses S. Grant. Following a jubilant procession, much flag waving and speeches, a group of Galena Citizens presented the General with a handsome furnished house on Bouthillier Street which overlooked the Galena River and afforded a commanding view of the city.

A two-story, Italianate structure of brick, it had been built in 1859-60 by Galena's former city clerk Alexander J. Jackson. The house featured wide overhanging eaves supported by large wooden brackets, a low-pitched roof, white wood trim, and green shutters. A columned and balconied piazza adorned the main entrance at the southeast corner. The kitchen was in a one-story rear wing.

Grant spent little time in the Galena house. Following his election as president in 1868 he visited only occasionally. In 1904, Grant's children gave the house to the City of Galena "with the understanding that this property is to be kept as a memorial to the late General Ulysses S. Grant, and for no other purpose." It was also "to be kept as nearly as possible as it was when General Grant resided in it, with his pictures and furniture placed as then."

In 1931 the City deeded the house to the State of Illinois. A thorough restoration project was undertaken in 1955 to return the house to its 1870s appearance. The home is furnished with much of the furniture used by Grant and his family and other Grant items such as china and silver used in the White House, military trophies, and souvenirs acquired on his world tour.

Visitor's Information

Open 9:00 a.m.-5:00 p.m. daily, except January 1, Thanksgiving, December 25. Telephone: (815) 777-0248.

Admission: Free.

The Ulysses S. Grant Home is located in Galena, Illinois, which is 160 miles from Chicago, 85 miles from Moline and 95 miles from Madison, Wisconsin. Galena is located on U.S. 20 and State Route 84. Follow the directional signs conveniently placed throughout the city.

Grant Cottage State Historic Site
Mount McGregor
Wilton, New York

In June, 1885, Grant and his family moved into a summer cottage located on top of Mount McGregor, just eight miles from Saratoga Springs. For six weeks during the summer of 1885, the man who commanded the Union Armies during the Civil War fought his last battle here. This time rather than bullets and swords, Grant faced disease.

Only a year earlier in 1884, Grant had learned that he had throat cancer and that it would likely prove fatal.

In addition to his health problems, Grant faced financial ruin because of a partner in a brokerage and banking firm who swindled him and others out of their investments. Concerned about his family's future, Grant raced to complete his memoirs on the Civil War, which he hoped would provide financial security for his family. Despite being weakened by the cancer, he spent countless hours perfecting his memoirs. Grant spent his days working on the porch of the cottage, making occasional trips in a wheelchair to enjoy the panoramic view that Mount McGregor offered.

On July 16, 1885 Grant, unable to speak, wrote a note to his doctor indicating that he had completed his work and could at last rest. Six days later, Grant asked to be moved from the two armchairs where he slept to a bed. At 8:08 the next morning, July 23, 1885, Ulysses S. Grant died, but even in his last battle Grant achieved a victory. Mark Twain, a close friend, published and sold the memoirs earning for the Grant family almost half a million dollars.

The cottage has been preserved as Grant had left it. The furnishings, decorations, and personal effects all remain where they stood in 1885 due to efforts of friends, family and admirers, and the assistance of the Grand Army of the Republic. Grant Cottage opened to the public for the first time in 1890 and is operated today by the Saratoga County Historical Society in cooperation with the New York State Office of Parks, Recreation and Historic Preservation.

Visitor's Information

Open Memorial Day-Labor Day, Wednesday-Sunday, 10:00 a.m.-4:00 p.m., and on holidays during the season. Telephone: (518) 587-8277.

Admission: adults $2.00; ages 3-12, $1.00.

Grant's Cottage is located in Wilton, New York. From the Northway (I-87) take Exit 16 West on Ballard Road to intersection at Route 9 and follow Historic Site markers. Entrance to Grant Cottage is through the gates of the Wilton Correctional Facility.

Ulysses S. Grant

Burial Site
General Grant National Memorial
Riverside Drive and West 122nd Street
New York, New York

On August 4, 1885, a special funeral train left Mount McGregor to bring the General to New York City which the family chose as the burial site. The funeral was held on August 8, 1885, and was one of the most spectacular processions ever staged in America. Buildings all over the city were draped in black, with the most elaborate displays along Broadway, the route of the funeral march. An estimated one million people watched the procession which included 60,000 marchers, stretched seven miles, and took up to five hours to pass. President Grover Cleveland, his cabinet, the Justices of the Supreme Court, and virtually the entire Congress took part in the parade.

His remains were placed in a temporary vault in Riverside Park and a fund-raising campaign, supported by more than 90,000 donors, was organized to create a permanent memorial. The completed monument was dedicated on April 27, 1897, the 75th anniversary of Grant's birth. When Mrs. Grant died in 1902, her body was placed in a sarcophagus adjoining that of her husband.

Popularly known as Grant's Tomb, the memorial to General Grant is the largest mausoleum in America, rising to an imposing 150 feet from a bluff overlooking the Hudson River. Several styles and motifs of classical architecture are combined in the monument. The base is 90 feet square and 72 feet high. A portico supported by 10 fluted Doric columns, projects from its southern facade and provides access to the interior. Rising from the base is a rotunda surrounded by Ionic columns and topped by a conical dome with a 5-ton capstone. Dominating the white-marble-lined interior is the open crypt containing the sarcophagi of Grant and his wife. Two trophy rooms at the rear of the crypt exhibit Union Army battle flags and mural maps outlining Civil War campaigns. Between the arches of the rotunda are allegorical figures representing phases of Grant's life. In niches around the walls of the crypt are heroic bronze busts of five of his comrades-in-arms: Generals William T. Sherman, Philip H. Sheridan, George H. Thomas, Edward O.C. Ord, and James B. McPherson.

Ulysses S. Grant

Visitor's Information

Open 9:00 a.m.-5:00 p.m., Wednesday-Sunday. Closed on national holidays. Telephone: (212) 666-1640.

Admission: Free.

General Grant National Memorial, administered by the National Park Service, is located near the intersection of Riverside Drive and West 122nd Street in New York City and can be reached by bus or subway. Riverside Drive is also accessible from the Henry Hudson Parkway at several points.

Rutherford Birchard Hayes, 19th President, 1877-1881

Spiegel Grove

Rutherford B. Hayes Burial Site

Rutherford B. Hayes Memorial Library and Museum

Rutherford B. Hayes

Nineteenth President
1877 - 1881
Republican

Rutherford Birchard Hayes was born on October 4, 1822 in Delaware, Ohio, soon after his father had died. Thanks to an uncle, he got a good education, and after attending Kenyon College, (where he was class valedictorian), he was admitted to Harvard Law School, where he graduated in 1845.

Hayes was admitted to the bar and began practicing law in Lower Sandusky (later Fremont), Ohio. In 1852, two years after he moved to Cincinnatti, Hayes married Lucy Webb, who had just graduated from Wesleyan Female College. Lucy Hayes would become the first president's wife to be a college graduate.

Appointed a major in the Ohio Volunteers, Hayes took part in several battles of the Civil War, was wounded during one skirmish, and earned the rank of brigadier general. A sergeant in his regiment, future president William McKinley, called him "intense and ferocious" in battle.

In 1864 he began his political career with the first of two elections to the United States House of Representatives. He was then elected governor of Ohio for two terms. Beaten at an attempt for a third term in Congress in 1872, he returned to the governor's office for the third time in 1875.

"Grantism," as the widespread political corruption of the past eight years had come to be known, had left a bad taste in the public's mouth by 1876. So it was that the honest but unknown Rutherford B. Hayes of Ohio became the Republican party's presidential nominee. His opponent was New York Governor Samual B. Tilden, who had broken the Tweed ring and exposed a fraud surrounding New York's canal system. Since both candidates were anti-corruption, the Republicans "waved the bloody shirt" again, trying to place the blame for the Civil War on the Democrats. The Democrats, in turn, described the Republicans as the party of corruption. When the votes were counted, Tilden had a majority of the popular vote, and was ahead in the electoral college by twenty votes.

However, the returns from Florida, Louisiana, and South Carolina were in question, as was an electoral vote in Oregon. Tilden needed just one electoral vote to win while Hayes needed all twenty from the four states. What happened next is the subject of some debate, but this much is known; a deal was struck between Democratic and Republican leaders which gave the presidency to Hayes in exchange for Republican concessions to the South. Rutherford B. Hayes became our nation's 19th president even though, in all likelihood, he actually lost *both* the popular and electoral vote.

Hayes and his wife both held strong to their religious and moral beliefs. When his wife Lucy banned alcohol from the White House for the first time in history, she gained the nickname "Lemonade Lucy." Lucy Hayes also began the tradition of holding the annual Easter egg rolling party for children on the White House lawn.

One of Hayes's first acts was to withdraw Federal troops from the last two occupied states in the South, Louisiana and South Carolina. The federal government also removed itself from the enforcement of civil rights in the South, with the unfortunate side effect that white supremacy swept the region.

Hayes fought hard for reform in government, advocating the replacement of the spoils system with the merit system. For this stand he gained the enmity of many political leaders. This did not deter Hayes from appointing a talented group of reformers to his Cabinet, among them Carl Shurz to be Secretary of the Interior. Hayes' appointment of a former Confederate, Donald Key, to head the Post Office, was met with great rancor by the Senate, which attempted to invoke Senatorial Privilege to block the nomination. Public reaction against the Senate's move was so strong, however, that Hayes got his man.

Hayes spent a great deal of his time trying to initiate reforms within government, with mixed results. His attempts to clean up corruption at the New York Customs House pitted him against New York boss Roscoe Conklin who, referring to the disputed presidential election results, called Hayes "His Fraudulency." Hayes managed to secure the resignations of two Conklin appointees, (one of whom was future president Chaster A. Arthur), but the spoils system remained well entrenched in New York and most of the country. Hayes also lost much of his own party's support, and for most of his administration found himself at odds with a spoils-entrenched Congress.

The depression of 1873 still gripped the country when Hayes took office in 1877. The Specie Resumption Act, which had been passed before Hayes took office, returned the country to the gold standard in 1879. Hayes supported this "sound money" policy believing it would strengthen the dollar.

Hayes was the first president who had to respond to a large scale labor strike when, in July 1877, America's railroad workers walked off their jobs in protest over a ten percent wage cut. Hayes, in a move repeated by succeeding presidents, sent Federal troops into several states to quell rioting. The strike was broken, but not without the loss of some lives and several million dollars in property. Hayes' problems with labor continued over the question of Chinese immigration. Laborers in the west protested against the employment of low-wage Chinese workers, which ultimately caused Congress to pass a law restricting immigration. Hayes' veto of the bill, which he felt was a violation of the Burlingame Treaty, stood.

Hayes became the first president to travel across the continent and the first to use a telephone. He and Lucy were the first President and First Lady to celebrate a golden wedding anniversary in the White House.

As the 1880s began and the depression lifted, Hayes' popularity began to rise. Choosing not to run for re-election, he retired from the presidency and took up philanthropy, making the issues of prison reform and education for blacks his own. Rutherford Hayes died in Fremont, Ohio on January 17, 1893, at the age of 70.

Historical Landmarks

Birthplace of Rutherford B. Hayes
East William and Winter Streets
Delaware, Ohio

Rutherford Birchard Hayes, the youngest of five children, was born on October 4, 1822, in a brick house on East William Street in Delaware, Ohio. His father and mother, Rutherford Hayes, Jr. and Sophia Birchard Hayes and their children had migrated to Ohio from West Dummerston, Vermont, in 1817. Hayes' father, a storekeeper and farmer, died two months before Hayes was born. A bachelor uncle, Sardis Birchard became the children's guardian.

The future nineteenth President of the United States lived in this house until 1836.

Visitor's Information

Hayes's birthplace was torn down in 1928. A bronze tablet marks the site of the house.

Rutherford B. Hayes

The birthplace home of Rutherford B. Hayes was located at the northeast corner of East William and Winter Streets in Delaware, Ohio. Delaware, about 25 miles north of Columbus, is on U.S. 23, west of I-71.

Spiegel Grove National Historic Landmark
Rutherford B. Hayes Presidential Center
1337 Hayes Avenue
Fremont, Ohio

About 1846, Sardis Birchard, uncle-guardian of Hayes, acquired a 25-acre estate in Lower Sandusky, as Fremont was called then, as a prospective home for himself and his nephew. He called the estate "Spiegel Grove" using the German word for mirror because the reflection of the trees and lush vegetation in pools of water after a rain reminded Birchard of German fairy tales he heard in his youth. In 1859-1863, he constructed a 2 1/2-story brick residence with a veranda. Hayes moved to the house in 1873, after completing two terms as Governor of Ohio. He enlarged the house with a one-story frame addition which extended the veranda and provided an office-library, drawing room, a new kitchen, wood house, and privy.

After his uncle's death, Hayes inherited the estate. In 1880, while serving as President of the United States, he erected a major brick addition on the north side which duplicated the gabled front of the original portion of the structure and more than doubled its size. Also completely remodeling the interior, Hayes extended the master bedroom on the first floor, enlarged certain other rooms by constructing a three-story projecting bay, and built a cupola on the fourth level.

The rambling mansion with some 33 rooms, epitomizes 19th century Victorian architecture. Its broad veranda, now screened, stretches along the double-gabled facade. The six entrance ways to the estate consist of impressive iron gates that were once at the White House.

Original furnishings and family possessions are displayed in the house.

Also on the grounds, constructed between 1916 and 1922, and enlarged in 1967, is the Rutherford B. Hayes Memorial Library and Museum. This was the first presidential library in the United States. It contains books, correspondence, diaries, pictures and photographs, scrapbooks, and other possessions of the Hayes family which form the nucleus of the voluminous collections.

The museum contains more than 10,000 objects that belonged to the President, his family and his administration, including the White House carriage used by President Hayes. Two floors of exhibits tell about the president and life before and after the turn of the century.

Visitor's Information

Open Monday-Saturday, 9:00 a.m.-5:00 p.m.; Sunday and holidays, noon-5:00 p.m. Closed January 1, Thanksgiving, December 25. The Library is also closed on Sundays and holidays. The telephone number is (419) 332-2081.

	Residence	Museum
Admission: adults	$3.00	$3.00
ages 7-12	$1.00	$1.00

The Library is open for reading and research without charge.

The Rutherford B. Hayes Presidential Center, which includes the Residence, Library, Museum and burial site of Hayes and his wife, is located at 1337 Hayes Avenue at Buckland Avenue, Fremont, Ohio. Fremont, southeast of Toledo, is a few miles south of the Ohio Turnpike, I-80-90. Within the city, follow the Hayes Center signs.

Burial Site
Spiegel Grove National Historic Site
1337 Hayes Avenue
Fremont, Ohio

Hayes became ill while visiting friends in Cleveland in January 1893. His friends urged him to remain in bed. Hayes, however, insisted on returning home, saying, "I would rather die at Spiegel Grove than to live anywhere else." He died on January 17, 1893. His last words were, "I know I am going where Lucy is." His wife, Lucy Webb Hayes had died June 25, 1889.

Hayes and his wife are buried on a wooded knoll, not far from the mansion and museum, near a section of the Sandusky-Scioto trail, an Indian trail which winds for a half-mile through Spiegel Grove.

After the death of his wife in 1889, President Hayes had designed a monument of Vermont granite which had been brought from the farm in West Dummerston, Vermont, from which his parents had migrated to Delaware, Ohio in 1817. After his own death, the caskets of both were placed in a granite block twelve by twenty feet, which was then sealed. The monument was brought from the Oakwood cemetery, where his wife had previously been laid to rest, and placed on this new granite base on the knoll in Spiegel Grove, in April, 1915.

Visitor's Information

See details above for Spiegel Grove National Historic Landmark.

James A. Garfield, 20th President, 1881-1881

Lawnfield, Home of James A. Garfield

Tomb of James A. Garfield

James A. Garfield

Twentieth President
1881
Republican

America's last log cabin President was James Abram Garfield, who was born in Orange, Ohio, on November 19, 1831. He lost his father when he was two, and at an early age began working to support his family, first as a mule driver, then a bargeman, carpenter, and farmer. James had learned the alphabet when he was three, and worked so hard in school that he graduated first in his classes at the Geauga Acadamy, Western Reserve Eclectic Institute (Hiram College), and Williams College in Massachusetts.

Garfield returned to Ohio to teach Latin and Greek at Hiram College. In 1858 he married Lucretia Rudolph, a former classmate at the Hiram Institute to whom he had been engaged for several years. They lived on the campus while Garfield taught and then became the school president.

He studied law, was admitted to the bar, and soon ran for and won a seat in the Ohio Senate. When the Civil War broke out, he helped organize a regiment of infantry and became the youngest brigadier general in the Union army when he was promoted for his bravery during the battle of Chickamauga.

James Garfield resigned from the army in 1863 and was elected to Congress, where he served for seventeen years. At the Republican convention in 1880 his name was placed in nomination after the two factions of the Republican Party battled for thirty-five ballots to a draw. In the general election Garfield faced off against Union General Winfield Hancock, who was nominated by a Democratic party that wanted be assured of not having the "bloody shirt" waved before the public again. Garfield won the presidency in a close election, thus becoming the first man to go directly from the House of Representatives to the White House. His was also the first of the "front porch" campaigners.

Garfield began his administration making a series of appointments which angered members of his own party. James Blaine, one of his foes for the Republican nomination was made Secretary of State. This and other incidents raised the level of political tension in the country, and charges against Garfield were rampant in the press. On July 2, 1881, while in the railroad station in Washington, James Garfield was shot in the back by a man who had been turned down for a job by James Blaine. When he was seized, assassin Charles Guiteau declared "I am a Stalwart and Arthur is President now!"

Garfield was not killed instantly, and was taken to a seashore resort in New Jersey to recuperate. He suffered for most of the summer, succumbing to his wound on September 19, 1881.

Historical Landmarks

Birthplace of James A. Garfield
Abram Garfield Farm Site Park
S.O.M. Center and Jackson Roads
Moreland Hills, Ohio

James Garfield was born on November 19, 1831 at Orange Township, now Moreland Hills, in Cayahoga County, Ohio. The youngest of four children, he was only 18-months old when his father Abram died from the effects of fighting a forest fire that threatened their cabin. The family was poor and Garfield's mother, Eliza, had to sell part of the farm to pay the mortgage.

The cabin was replaced by a new frame house in 1843; his mother sold the property around 1853.

Visitor's Information

The house has long disappeared and no trace of the farmstead, which was Garfield's home until about 1850, remains. A marker identifies Abram Garfield Farm Site Park at the southwest corner of S.O.M. Center and Jackson Roads in Moreland Hills, Ohio. Moreland Hills, is 23 miles southwest of Mentor, Ohio and south of Cleveland.

James A. Garfield

Garfield House
6825 Hinsdale Street
Hiram, Ohio

During his early congressional career Garfield lived in Hiram where he bought a two-story frame house in 1863. The Garfields later enlarged the original 1852 dwelling and lived there until 1872 when they sold the property to Hiram College President Burke Hinsdale. Hinsdale owned the house for ten years before selling it to the great-grandmother of one of the present owners, John and Phoebe Zimmerman. A window in one room has the clearly etched initials, JAG.

Visitor's Information

The home is privately owned and visiting is not permitted.

Lawnfield, The President Garfield National Historic Site
8095 Mentor Avenue
Mentor, Ohio

James A. Garfield purchased the Lawnfield estate in 1876 as a country home for his young and active family, which included five boys and a girl. Erected in 1832 by James Dickey, the farmhouse at Lawnfield was originally a small 1 1/2-story frame structure. Between 1877 and 1879 Garfield and his wife enlarged it to 2 1/2 stories, added a porch across the front and refurbished the interior.

After his nomination as president, he conducted much of his campaigning from his "front porch." He used one of the outbuildings as a campaign office. In March 1881, Garfield moved into the White House and he was never to see Lawnfield again. Four years later, Mrs. Garfield, who continued to live there, completed their plans by adding a library wing and several rooms to the rear. The structure has remained largely unchanged since that time.

Lawnfield is presently administered by the Lake County Historical Society which maintains a museum on the third floor and a library on the first. Other first floor rooms, as most rooms in the house, are furnished with original Garfield items and mementoes, as well as period pieces. The second floor contains the memorial library built by Mrs. Garfield. On top of a bookshelf is the large waxed funeral wreath sent by Queen Victoria to the family. The Wooten desk used by Garfield in his Washington office, with its 122 "filing" compartments, is in the far corner of the room. Display cases in the room contain the bible used when President Garfield took the oath of office and the manuscript of Garfield's inaugural address in his own handwriting.

At the northeast corner of the home is a small one-story building utilized in 1880 as the campaign office. A telegraph operator was installed here to send and receive messages; this is where Garfield received the news of his election. Mementoes and relics of the Garfield presidential campaign are on display.

Visitor's Information

Open Tuesday-Saturday, 10:00 a.m.-5:00 p.m.; Sunday, noon-5:00 p.m.
Closed January 1, Thanksgiving, December 25. Telephone: (216) 255-8722.

Admission: adults, $3.00, senior citizens, $2.00, children, $1.50.

Lawnfield is at 8095 Mentor Avenue, Mentor, Ohio. From the east take I-90 to the Mentor-Kirtland Route 306 exit. Turn right; take Rte. 306 for two miles north to Rte. 20 (Mentor Avenue). Turn right; take Rte. 20 for two miles east.

From the west follow above directions but turn left on the Rte. 306 exit from I-90.

Burial Site
Lake View Cemetery
12316 Euclid Avenue
Cleveland, Ohio

Two months after being shot by an assassin, Garfield died of his wounds on September 6, 1881, in Long Branch, New Jersey, where he had been taken at his own request. Cleveland was chosen as the burial site by his family and after lying in state in the nation's capitol, the president's body was taken by special train to Cleveland. There, the president's body lay in state in Public Square where thousands passed the casket to pay their respects. On September 26, the funeral procession of more than 5,000 people made its way down Euclid Avenue to Lake View Cemetery. After brief services the president's body was placed in a temporary vault.

The Garfield National Monument Association began collecting donations to build a memorial which was dedicated on Memorial Day, 1890. The monument is a tower constructed of Ohio sandstone, 180 feet high and 50 feet in diameter. The tower rests on a stone terrace surrounded by a porch.

Five panels depicting Garfield's life adorn the upper exterior of the porch. Using 100 life-size figures, Garfield is shown teaching, as a general during the Civil War, as an orator, taking the Presidential oath, and lying in state.

Inside the monument is the remarkable Memorial Hall which contains a marble statue of Garfield speaking before Congress. The sculpture is by Alexander Doyle, who obtained his marble from the famed quarries near Carrara, Italy, which were first used by Leonardo da Vinci. Surrounding the statue are columns of red polished granite. Above these is the interior dome of gold and stone mosaic complete with winged figures representing the grief felt by all portions of the nation when Garfield died. Circling these winged figures are wreaths representing each state and territory. Immediately below the dome are mosaic panels picturing a mourning procession. Stained glass windows light the hall and along with the decorative panels represent the 13 original states and Ohio.

In the crypt are the bronze caskets of Garfield and his wife, Lucretia. An American flag covers the President's casket.

Visitor's Information

Open daily 9:00 a.m.-4:00 p.m., April 1-November 19. Telephone: (216) 421-2665. Admission: Free.

Lake View Cemetery is located at 12316 Euclid Avenue at 123rd Street, Cleveland, Ohio. In Cleveland follow U.S. 20 (Euclid Avenue) east to 123rd Street.

Chester A. Arthur, 21st President, 1881-1885

Chester A. Arthur Birthplace (replica)

Chester A. Arthur Burial Site

Chester A. Arthur

Twenty-First President
1881 - 1885
Republican

The first president to come from Vermont, Chester Alan Arthur was born on October 5, 1830 in Fairfield. When he was fifteen he attended Union College, and graduated three years later a Phi Beta Kappa. He taught school in North Pownal, Vermont, (in the same school where James Garfield would teach penmanship three years later), while studying law. After admission to the bar in 1854 he spent the next twenty five years practicing law in New York City.

The woman Arthur married after he came to New York never lived to be First Lady. Ellen Lewis Herndon, the daughter of Commander William Lewis Herndon (who won fame as explorer of the Amazon River), had met Chester Arthur while in New York visiting relatives. They were married in 1859. A contralto-voiced singer, Ellen Arthur gave many concerts to raise money for charities. After a concert on a cold January night in 1880 she caught pneumonia, and died three days later.

During the Civil War Arthur was appointed quartermaster general of New York, gaining a reputation as an able administrator. In 1871 he was given the post of Collector of the Port of New York, a position which controlled the patronage of many other jobs. When President Hayes tried to place the office under Civil Service, Arthur fought the move but was removed from the job.

Chester Arthur had never held an elective office when he was nominated for the vice-presidency in 1880. His placement on the ticket was to placate the Stalwart faction of the Republican party, which was not pleased with the nomination of James Garfield. So when he assumed the presidency after the death of the Garfield in September of 1881, the Stalwarts believed they had a man who would return the country to the spoils system.

But the confidence the Stalwarts first had in Arthur soon turned to dismay; his sudden ascension to the presidency seemed to have brought on him a sense of duty. In his first annual message to Congress he advocated civil service reform and called for an investigation of the tariff. Arthur then pursued the prosecution of the "Star Route" mail route frauds, which proved embarrassing to the Republicans. He also vetoed large pork-barrel rivers and harbors appropriations.

After the Democrats won control of the House in 1882 they passed the Pendleton Act of 1883, which authorized the president to create a three member Civil Service Commission. It also required that certain lower federal jobs be open to competition through competitive examinations. Arthur implemented the Act, much to the dismay of the Stalwarts.

In other matters Arthur made himself popular with the electorate. Using surplus revenues, he lowered taxes and reduced the national debt. He also took some of the surplus and, over the objections of Congress, appropriated funds for the construction of four steel cruisers which would start America on the road to being a world naval power. In 1885 he dedicated the completed Washington Monument.

Though Chester Arthur had incurred the wrath of the Stalwarts, the Half-breeds did not forgive his past as a political hack and chose James Blaine to run in 1884. Arthur returned to New York City to practice law but lived less than two years after leaving office. He died on November 18, 1886 at the age of 56.

Historical Landmarks

Birthplace of Chester A. Arthur
Fairfield, Vermont

Chester Alan Arthur's Irish-born father, the Reverend William Arthur, moved to Fairfield in 1828 with his wife, Melvina Stone Arthur, and four daughters. In that year, William Arthur was ordained as a Baptist minister and Fairfield Center was his first church.

Although there has been controversy over the place and time of Arthur's birth, records and recollections lend strong credence to Chester Alan Arthur being born on October 5, 1830, in North Fairfield about three and one-half miles east of the Fairfield station.

In August 1903, dignitaries gathered at the birthsite to dedicate a polished Barre granite monument to Chester A. Arthur. At that time, all that remained of the small farmhouse and birthplace of Vermont's first native born president was a cellar hole.

In 1954,the Vermont Division for Historic Preservation reconstructed from an old photograph, the one-story clapboard house on its original foundation. The home is furnished with period furnishings and an exhibit tells the story of Arthur's life and rise to the presidency.

Visitor's Information

Open June 1-Columbus Day, Wednesday-Sunday, 9:00 a.m.-5:00 p.m. Telephone: (802) 933-8362.

Admission: adults, $1.00, children under 14, free.

Fairfield is in the northern part of Vermont near the Canadian border. From St. Albans, Vermont take Vermont Route 36 seven miles to Fairfield, turn left in the village. About one mile north bear right and follow this road four or five miles. The Historic Site is the first house on the right after the road becomes gravel.

Arthur House
123 Lexington Avenue
New York, New York

Chester A. Arthur lived in this house for most of his adult life. He moved to New York City in 1853 and at some unknown date he acquired this residence. It was here that Vice President Arthur took the oath of office at 2:00 a.m., September 20, 1881, after President James A. Garfield died as the result of an assassin's attack. He also returned here in 1885, after completing Garfield's term.

The residence, a five-story, brownstone rowhouse, has been considerably altered over the years as has the neighborhood. The house had a massive flight of stone steps leading to the front entrance at the second floor level but it has disappeared. A retail store occupies the front part of the first, or ground floor; another shop is on the second floor; and the remaining three floors have been divided into apartments. The entire neighborhood has completely changed. In Arthur's time it was a fashionable quarter of the city. Now fine, aristocratic looking residences have been turned into stores and offices.

Chester A. Arthur

On January 16, 1964, the 81st anniversary of the signing of the U.S. Civil Service Act by President Arthur, the Native New Yorkers Historical Association and the New York Life Insurance Company placed a bronze plaque on the building.

Visitor's Information

No Arthur furnishings remain in the building which is privately owned and closed to the public.

Burial Site
Albany Rural Cemetery
Cemetery Avenue
Menands, New York

Arthur suffered from Bright's disease, a potentially fatal inflammation of the kidneys, which was kept secret from the public, and was the reason he did not actively pursue nomination in 1884. With his chronic illness still a secret, Arthur returned to his New York City home and declined an offer to run for the U.S. Senate.

The day after boasting of improved health to his physician, Arthur died of a massive cerebral hemorrhage on November 18, 1886. He was buried beside his wife in Albany Rural Cemetery at Menands, New York.

Visitor's Information

Open daily 8:00 a.m.-4:30 p.m.

Albany Rural Cemetery is on Cemetery Avenue off Broadway in Menands, a suburb of Albany, New York. Take I-787 to NY 378W and follow to cemetery.

Grover Cleveland, 22nd and 24th President, 1885-1889, 1893-1897

Grover Cleveland Birthplace

Westland, Grover Cleveland's Home

Grover Cleveland Burial Site

Grover Cleveland

Twenty-Second & Twenty-Fourth President
1885 - 1889 & 1893 - 1897
Democrat

Stephen Grover Cleveland was born in Caldwell, New Jersey on March 18, 1837, the first President from that state. Four years later his family moved to western New York State. Because his father died when he was sixteen, Grover (he had dropped his first name) had to forgo college to work to support his family. An uncle helped him find work in Buffalo, where he studied law while clerking for a firm. He was admitted to the bar in 1859.

A Democrat, he was appointed assistant district attorney of Eire County when he was 26, but failed in his first attempt at elective office when he ran for district attorney. Several years later, when he was 33, he succeeded in being elected sheriff of Eire County. In 1881 he became Buffalo's mayor.

As mayor of Buffalo, Cleveland removed graft in municipal street cleaning and sewage projects. Running for governor in 1882 he beat the Republican candidate anointed by President Chester Arthur. As governor, Cleveland was an interesting mix of reformer and fiscal conservative, meeting with mixed success as the former he gained the respect of many Republicans for the latter.

The campaign of 1884 was filled with few issues and much personal attack. An appeal to anti-Catholic sentiment backfired when a protestant minister referred to the Democrats as the party of "Rum, Romanism, and Rebellion." Ammunition for the Republicans came from the fact that Cleveland, a bachelor until his presidency, had accepted responsibility for an illegitimate child, whom he later adopted. The Republicans chanted "Ma, Ma, where's my Pa?" Yet as it turned out, Cleveland's forthright response and honesty about the child gained him more votes than he lost. So when the results of the 1884 presidential election were tabulated, the Democrats could amend the chant "Ma, Ma, where's my Pa?" with "gone to the White House, Ha, Ha, Ha."

It had been almost thirty years since a Democrat had been elected to the Presidency, and they came to Washington in droves looking for jobs. Cleveland responded by dismissing tens of thousand Republicans from lower level federal jobs. But at the same time he also extended the number of jobs covered by the civil service provisions. Cleveland was the first president to see the threat from trusts, and he initiated investigations into the practices of the railroad, lumber, and cattle interests, the last of these which ultimately led to the return of eighty million acres of land to the public domain. During his first administration the Interstate Commerce act was passed, which helped begin the process of rail reform.

Cleveland angered the Civil War veterans with his appointment of two former Confederates to the cabinet, and infuriated them when he returned Confederate flags to the southern states as a symbolic gesture of good will. The veterans were further angered by the hundreds of vetoes he made of obviously fraudulent claims from dishonest veterans. Though he approved more of these claims than any other president, he was denounced by the veterans organization known as the Grand Army of the Republic (GAR) when he vetoed the Dependant Pension Bill passed by Congress, which he felt was too lavish.

The biggest problem Cleveland faced in his first administration was the tariff question. He was convinced that the high tariff was no longer necessary. He even devoted his entire annual message to Congress in 1887 to the issue. The Democrats responded with the Mills Bill which substantially reduced the tariff. The Republicans countered with their own high tariff. Neither bill passed.

During his first term Cleveland became the first and only president to be married while in office, when he wed 21 year old Francis Folsom, the daughter of his former law partner. Francis became the youngest of all the first ladies. Their daughter Esther, born in 1893, was the only child of a President born in the White House.

Cleveland's veto of the veteran's bill came back to haunt him in the election when, after renomination by his party, he faced Civil War veteran Benjamin Harrison of Indiana. Grover Cleveland lost the election even though he had won the popular majority by about 100,000 votes.

After leaving office Cleveland returned to his law practice in New York, becoming even more conservative in his attitudes towards business and developing an even stronger support for the gold standard. His personal popularity had increased so much by 1892 that the Democrats nominated him to run against Benjamin Harrison for a second time. Cleveland's running mate that year was Adlai E. Stevenson, whose grandson would himself be a Democratic candidate for the presidency in the 1950s. The Democratic ticket won again, and Grover Cleveland became our first and only president to serve two non-consecutive terms.

Only a few weeks after Cleveland's second inauguration, the nation entered one of its worst depressions. Banks failed and the nation's gold reserves fell. Cleveland engineered the repeal of the Sherman Silver Purchase Act and ordered the sale of three issues of gold bonds which, over a two year period, stabilized the gold supply. Times were hard for many Americans. When a large group of unemployed protesters, led by Jacob

S. Coxey of Ohio, tried to march on the Capital in favor of public-works programs, the police, under approval from Cleveland, were used to disperse the protesters.

One of Cleveland's campaign promises was to reduce the tariff, since he believed that high tariffs kept foreign goods out of the country which in turn caused customs collections to suffer. But an alliance of Democrats and Republicans from the Eastern states scuttled most of his plans in Congress, and the resulting tariff, known as the Wilson Gorman Tariff, left Cleveland and his allies unhappy. Further watering down Cleveland's plans was a decision by the Supreme Court which ruled the act's income tax provision unconstitutional.

In 1894, when the employees of the Pullman Palace Car Company went on strike after their wages were cut, some of the striking workers began cutting Pullman cars loose from trains and disrupting rail transportation. When a court order preventing the strikers from interfering with the mail was ignored, Cleveland sent in federal troops to Chicago to keep the trains moving.

Internationally, Cleveland used the Monroe Doctrine to settle a boundary dispute between Venezuela and British Guiana. But Cleveland was not an imperialist like most of the post-Civil War presidents. In fact, he opposed the annexation of Hawaii and was opposed to the American involvement in a tri-lateral protectorate (with Germany and Britain) over Samoa.

Though the depression was showing signs of abating in 1896, Grover Cleveland's actions during his second term had lost him the support of his party, and he was not nominated for a third term. He and Frances retired to Princeton, New Jersey, where Grover became a trustee of Princeton University, and a friend of its president, Woodrow Wilson. On June 24, 1908, he died in Princeton, NJ, at the age of 71.

Historical Landmark

Birthplace of Grover Cleveland
207 Bloomfield Avenue
Caldwell, New Jersey

On May 12, 1834, Reverend Richard F. Cleveland of Baltimore was chosen by the First Presbyterian Church of Caldwell, New Jersey, as pastor. He was a relative of Moses

Cleveland, the founder of Cleveland, Ohio. His wife, Ann Neal Cleveland, was the daughter of a publisher.

On March 18, 1837, in the rear room of the Presbyterian Manse, Stephen Grover Cleveland was born. He was named after the first minister of Caldwell in 1787, Stephen Grover, but the future 22nd and 24th U. S. president dropped his first name while still a boy.

The 2 1/2-story frame house built in 1832 has been restored and is administered by the New Jersey Department of Environmental Protection. The house contains a collection of objects associated with Cleveland including his old fashioned cradle.

Visitor's Information

Open Wednesday-Saturday, 9:00 a.m.-noon, 1:00 p.m.-5:00 p.m.; Sunday, 1:00 p.m.-5:00 p.m.; closed holidays. Telephone: (201) 226-1810.

Admission: Free.

The Grover Cleveland Birthplace is at 207 Bloomfield Avenue (State Route 506), Caldwell, New Jersey.

Westland
15 Hodge Road
Princeton, New Jersey

Westland was the home of Grover Cleveland from the time of his retirement from the presidency in 1897, until his death in 1908. During the last year of his second term in the White House, in 1896, he had decided to retire at Princeton, New Jersey. Mrs. Cleveland apparently selected the house, which had been built in the mid-19th century by Commodore Robert F. Stockton. Cleveland named it Westland in honor of a close friend and professor at Princeton University, Andrew F. West.

Westland was patterned after Morven, an elegant Georgian mansion built in Princeton in the 18th century by the prominent Stockton family. A 2 1/2-story, stone structure covered with stucco painted yellow, Westland had twin parlors on the first floor, spacious rooms, high ceilings, and handsome marble mantelpieces. Shortly after moving into the house, Cleveland added a two-story, flat-roofed wing containing a billiard room on the first floor and some bedrooms on the second. Through the years, other additions became so numerous that the rear of the structure was later detached and moved back on the lot to form a separate residence.

Visitor's Information

Westland is privately owned and visiting is not permitted.

Other Cleveland Residences

Grover Cleveland owned or stayed in other homes for varying periods of time. The homes which are still standing are privately owned and visiting is not permitted.

His boyhood home, from 1841 to 1850, is at 109 Academy Street, Fayetteville, New York.

When Cleveland married Frances Folsom in 1886, the couple honeymooned in a house now known as Grover Cleveland Cottage, on Deer Park Hotel Road off State Highway 135, Deer Park, Maryland.

After they were married, the couple's frequent escape from the White House was a 27-acre suburban farm Cleveland purchased. Called Oak View, it was located at 3536 Newark Street NW, Washington, D.C. A new house which retains some parts of the original property is on the site.

From 1891 until 1904, the Clevelands spent their summers on Buzzards Bay, Cape Cod, Massachusetts. Situated on Monument Point, it was a two-story clapboard cottage they called Gray Gables. Cleveland, an avid angler was drawn to the location by the fishing in the area. He recuperated here in 1893 from the secret operation on his cancerous left jaw. Fire destroyed the house in the 1970s.

Cleveland bought an old farmhouse near Tamworth, New Hampshire, which he used as a summer retreat from 1906 to 1908. Known as Cleveland House and enlarged by Cleveland, it is on Cleveland Hill Road, three miles west of Tamworth village.

Burial Site
Princeton Cemetery
29 Greenview Avenue
Princeton, New Jersey

Grover Cleveland lived in Princeton after leaving the presidency in 1987. In 1908, after a three month illness, Cleveland died on June 24. He is buried in Princeton Cemetery, in what is called President's Row, where almost all presidents of Princeton University are buried. The monument erected to the memory of Grover Cleveland is square and surmounted with an urn-shaped finial.

Visitor's Information

Open daily from sunrise to sunset. Telephone: (609) 924-1369.

Princeton Cemetery is located at 29 Greenview Avenue, Princeton, New Jersey. Take NJ Rt. 206 to Princeton, then east on Paul Robeson Avenue to Wiggins Street which is at the cemetery. Follow around to entrance on Greenview Avenue.

Benjamin Harrison, 23rd President, 1889-1893

Benjamin Harrison's Home

Tomb of Benjamin Harrison

Benjamin Harrison

Twenty-Third President
1887 - 1893
Republican

Benjamin Harrison, was born on August 20, 1833 in North Bend. Benjamin was the grandson of a president, great grandson and namesake of a signer of the Declaration of Independence, and the son of a member of the House of Representatives. He was the first president from Indiana.

He first attended Farmers College at Farmer's Hill, and after the death of his mother in 1850 transferred to Miami University in Ohio. There he met Caroline Scott, also a student, whom he fell in love with and married three years later. After graduation in 1852 he studied law in Cincinnati. He moved to Indianapolis after passing the bar, and became one of that city's leading lawyers. At 27 he was elected reporter of the Supreme Court of Indiana on the Republican ticket.

He helped organize the Indiana 70th Volunteer Infantry Regiment when the Civil War broke out, rising to the rank of breveted brigadier general after serving with Sherman in Georgia. When he returned from the war he continued his law practice while becoming active in Indiana politics, first losing a bid for the governor's office before winning a seat in the U.S. Senate in 1881. Defeated in a bid for a second term, Harrison returned to Indianapolis to resume his law practice.

Benjamin Harrison was the perfect candidate for the Republicans to run in 1888 to reclaim the White House. As a Union Army veteran he could, with relish, "wave the bloody shirt" and once more lay blame for the Civil War on the Democrats. Democrat Grover Cleveland's veto of the Dependent Pension Bill strengthened the emotional appeal of Harrison's campaign, as did the timely publication of a pro-Cleveland letter from the British minister to Washington that Cleveland failed to repudiate. Harrison was the last Union general to achieve the presidency.

Under Harrison and a Republican Congress many pieces of legislation were passed. His was the first billion dollar peace time budget. The Dependent Pension Act of 1890, which was a virtual duplicate of the bill vetoed by Cleveland, gave out about 160 million dollars a year to all disabled Civil War veterans, dependent widows, and minors. The navy got more money to build more steel ships, river and harbor improvements were also well funded, and free rural mail delivery was initiated. The Republicans managed to strengthen their majority in Congress by seeing to the admission of several Western states, (all highly Republican), and Oklahoma was purchased from the Native Americans.

In 1890 the Sherman Silver Purchase Act was passed. This bill required that the treasury to buy a certain amount of silver each month at market prices and pay for it with treasury certificates redeemable in gold. This was supposed to help increase money in circulation (which it didn't) and stifle the continued call by Westerners for the coinage of silver (it didn't do this, either). Strongly protectionist, Harrison signed into law the McKinley Tariff, which raised duties to their highest levels in peacetime. Public resentment against the tariff (and the Silver Purchase Act) was so strong that in the midterm election of 1892, the Democrats won a three-fourths majority in the House.

Harrison, like most of the late eighteenth century presidents, took the opportunity to flex American muscle abroad. He used troops from the USS Boston to assist a pro-American coup of Hawaii. A treaty of annexation was drawn up but was not passed during Harrison's administration. For Samoa, Harrison negotiated a three power protectorate with Britain and Germany.

America almost went to war with Chile during Harrison's term over the detaining of a steamer full of arms bound for forces revolting against the Chilean government. America's pro-government stance was not forgotten after the revolutionaries were successful. When Chilean rioters killed two American sailors and wounded twenty American citizens in Valparaiso, both countries prepared for war. Ultimately, Chile backed down and agreed to pay an indemnity to the United States.

Harrison failed to win re-election in 1892, losing to the man he had beaten in the previous presidential race, Grover Cleveland. Harrison's wife Caroline had passed away just a few weeks before the election, and he retired from politics and returned to Indianapolis, where he resumed his law practice. In 1895 he represented Venezuela at Paris in a boundary dispute with the British. He remarried in 1896, to his wife's niece, who was the White House secretary during his administration.

Benjamin Harrison died at the age of 67 on March 13, 1901 in Indianapolis.

Historical Landmarks

Birthplace of Benjamin Harrison
Loop Avenue
North Bend, Ohio

John Scott Harrison and Elizabeth Irwin Harrison, the parents of Benjamin Harrison lived on a portion of the big farm owned by John Scott's father, William Henry Harrison, in North Bend, Ohio. Benjamin was born here on August 20, 1833. When he was two, his grandfather built a two-story brick house for his son's family near his own home and Benjamin lived there until 1853. The house was called "The Point" because the 600-acre farm was between the Ohio and Big Miami Rivers. His grandfather became the ninth President of the United States when Benjamin was eight years old.

Visitor's Information

Neither Harrison's birthplace nor his boyhood home, The Point, are still standing. They were located in the vicinity of the Harrison Tomb State Memorial, a 14-acre memorial park which is named for the elder Harrison and contains his tomb. It overlooks the Ohio River just off U.S. 50, on Loop Avenue, in North Bend, Ohio.

Benjamin Harrison Home
1230 North Delaware Street
Indianapolis, Indiana

In February, 1874, Harrison contracted with architect H.T. Brandt to design and supervise building a home for the family with construction to begin in the Fall. Mr. and Mrs. Harrison and their teenage son and daughter moved in when the two-story house, which took twenty months to construct, was completed in 1875. Although located on what was then the outskirts of the town, it was still convenient to Harrison's Market Street law office and, at the same time, away from the hum of business.

Benjamin Harrison

The brick Italianate house had 16 rooms, an attic and basement standing on a double lot. A carriage house was constructed at the rear of the property. There was a side porch and along the front sidewalk ran a wooden picket fence. There was a grape arbor near the carriage house in the rear; the landscaping and planting of the oak and maple trees were done by James White.

At the completion of his presidency Harrison returned to Indianapolis alone, since his wife, Caroline Harrison, had died in Washington. In 1896, about the time of his second marriage, the ex-president made major changes and modernizations. Central heat, plumbing, electricity, and the Ionic-columned porch were added.

After his death in 1901, his second wife, Mary, and their daughter moved to New York and rented the home as a boarding house. In 1937, Mrs. Harrison donated the house to the Arthur Jordan Foundation to be used as a memorial to her late husband. The foundation worked with family members on a full scale restoration and family furniture and many keepsakes were returned to the home at that time. These included personal possessions such as books and mementoes of his career, his cradle which was also used by his grandfather's children, including his father, and the massive hand-carved bed in which Benjamin Harrison died.

Following another extensive renovation in 1974, the entire home was open to the public for the first time.

One of the most beautiful rooms, the front parlor appears as it did when decorated in 1896 for Harrison's new bride. Among its furnishings are cut-crystal chandeliers, an Aubusson rug and gold-lacquered mirrors. His law office furniture occupies a second-floor room and the former third-floor ballroom serves as a museum in which many artifacts of the Harrisons' professional and personal lives are exhibited.

Visitor's Information

Open Monday-Saturday, 10:00 a.m.-4:00 p.m.; Sunday, 12:30 p.m.-4:00 p.m. Closed January 1-31, Easter, Thanksgiving, December 25. Telephone: (317) 631-1898.

Admission: adults, $2.00, students, $1.00.

Benjamin Harrison

The Harrison Home at 1230 North Delaware Street is located near I-65. Southbound on I-65, take Meridan Street Exit, proceed east after exiting, cross Meridan to Delaware, turn left and proceed north on Delaware to the home. From northbound on I-65, use the Pennsylvania Street Exit, turn left and turn left again onto 11th Street, and turn left again onto Delaware. The house is on your left just beyond the viaduct.

Burial Site
Crown Hill Cemetery
700 West 38th Street
Indianapolis, Indiana

Benjamin Harrison died at his home, of pneumonia, on March 13, 1901. He is buried by the side of his first wife in the family plot in the Crown Hill Cemetery, Indianapolis.

A modest monument marks his last resting place. On the monument is inscribed his name, date of birth and his death, and there is listed a brief record of his public life. There is also carved on the stone a quotation taken from Alexander Pope's "An Epistle to Mr. Addison," beginning with the 67th line, which reads:

**Statesman, yet friend to truth; of soul sincere
In action faithful, and in honor clear.**

Visitor's Information

Open daily, April 1-September 30, 8:00 a.m.-6:00 p.m.; rest of year, 8:00 a.m.-5:00 p.m. Telephone: (317) 925-8231.

Crown Hill Cemetery is at 700 West 38th Street, Indianapolis, Indiana. From I-65 going south, exit at 38th Street and go east to cemetery. On I-65 north, exit at 29-30 Streets and go east on 29th Street to Illinois Street; turn left on Illinois to 34th Street, turn left onto 34th and follow to cemetery.

William McKinley, 25th President, 1897-1901

McKinley Memorial

The McKinley which includes Discover World - a Science Center, Museum of History, Science and Industry, Planetarium, and The National Memorial

McKinley National Memorial

William McKinley

Twenty-Fifth President
1897-1901
Republican

On January 29, 1843 William McKinley was born to a Niles, Ohio foundry-man and his wife. Young William McKinley's family soon moved to Poland, Ohio, the site of a local academy the father wished his children to attend. William eventually made it to Allegheny College, but when his father died he had to leave so that he could take a job teaching to help support his family.

William McKinley answered Abraham Lincoln's call for volunteers to fight in the Civil War when he was 18. He served with distinction, earning the praise of General Rutherford B. Hayes, another future president. (McKinley would later campaign for Hayes in his successful bid for Governor.) When McKinley returned after the war, he was a major.

After completing his law studies at Albany Law School and subsequently passing the bar, McKinley began practicing in Canton, Ohio. Two years later, at the age of 24, he became the county prosecuting attorney.

Around this time McKinley met and fell in love with Ida Saxton, the daughter of a prominent Canton banker. They were married in 1871. Ida's health was poor for most of her life, and for many years she was confined to a chair most of the time. She survived her husband by only six years, passing away in 1907.

In 1876 McKinley was elected to the United States House of Representatives, for the first of six terms. There, he was a consistent supporter of high tariffs and import duties. In 1889 he became chairman of the House Ways and Means Committee, and saw to the passage of the McKinley Tariff of 1890. In 1892 and 1894 the citizens of Ohio elected him governor.

The presidential campaign of 1896 was one of the more interesting, and was certainly one of the most important since the 1860 election. The Populist Party, finding itself in agreement with the Democrats on most issues, nominated their own William Jennings Bryan to lead their ticket. The parties essentially merged, both running Bryan against Republican William Mc Kinley. McKinley had been nominated thanks in great part to the behind-the-scenes manipulation of Ohio industrialist Mark Hanna.

William McKinley

During the campaign McKinley rarely strayed from the front porch of his Canton, Ohio home, where Hanna had him delivering what appeared to be spontaneous remarks, (but which were, in fact, pre-arranged speeches), down to audience members calling out questions. It was a tactic meant to avoid *the* subject of the campaign, the coinage of silver. Calling for a "Full Dinner Pail," McKinley won the election with the first popular vote majority since 1872.

Near the beginning of McKinley's first term large deposits of recently discovered gold were being introduced into the supply, inflating the currency and bringing easier credit. That, along with increased demands for American goods, helped propel America into prosperity, which in turn became a time of unparalleled growth of the trusts. In 1900 the Gold Standard Act was passed and established, once and for all, the gold standard, which would be the basis for the American monetary system.

McKinley's administration takes on great importance for what happened in foreign affairs, for by the end of his first term, America had emerged as a world power. The United States had long cast a jealous eye to Cuba, which was owned by the Spanish. In early 1898, a letter written by the Spanish minister in Washington, Dupoy de Lome, which severely criticized and mocked President McKinley was made public. McKinley, who had been against American intervention up to this point, had begun the effort to minimize the de Lome letter when, on February 15, the U.S.S. Maine, docked in Havana Harbor, blew up.

McKinley still attempted to avoid war, but while he negotiated with Spain for a peaceful solution, the country's attitude (most notably the business community, which moved quickly to a pro-war stance) shifted towards war. Though the Spanish agreed to every concession McKinley had asked for, he' went to Congress asking for a declaration of war. Congress passed the resolution.

The war did not last very long, nor was it confined to Cuba. Almost as soon as there was a declaration of war, Commodore Dewey sailed into Manila Harbor in the Philippines and sunk an aged fleet of Spanish ships. Several months later, when the necessary troops arrived, the Islands were taken. Meanwhile a blockade of Cuba was begun, and the army soon landed on the island. One of the regiments was led by the Assistant Secretary of the Navy, Theodore Roosevelt, who had resigned his post to recruit a regiment that he would lead into battle.

Santiago was taken in August and an armistice was signed on the twelfth. At a peace conference in Paris (to which McKinley had wisely sent three members of the Senate - they would end up voting on the treaty) it was agreed that Cuba would be granted independence, and that Puerto Rico, Guam, and the Philippines were to be ceded to the

United States. The war removed the last vestige of the Spanish empire from the Americas and strengthened America's ability to dig a trans-isthmus canal. It gave the United States several bases in the Pacific, as well as the burden of running the Philippines, a new and foreign land. America was a world power that, thanks to the unifying forces of the conflict, was more together than it had been since long before the Civil War.

There were other foreign matters, too. John Hay, McKinley's Secretary of State, acted against the slow absorption of China by foreign powers and their "spheres of influence," which included bases and ports in China. His 1899 letter to the major European powers proposing an "Open Door" Policy was met with approval, and Hay declared the policy to be in effect. The United States also took part in the First Hague Conference in 1899, which sought ways to promote world peace, establishing an international Court of Arbitration. The United States became the first country to submit a claim to the Court.

McKinley was easily renominated for another term of office by the Republicans in 1900. His running mate would now be the recent hero of San Juan Hill, Theodore Roosevelt. The inclusion of Roosevelt on the ticket was probably unnecessary, as most Americans favored the war (since it had been won so easily) and had grown tired of the free silver issue (now that the economy was going so well). McKinley beat William Bryan for the second time by the largest popular majority since Grant's second election in 1872.

McKinley and his wife returned to Canton for a brief respite from Washington in 1901. On September 6, 1901, William McKinley came to Buffalo, New York, the site of the Pan-American Exposition. Following a speech to the exposition, McKinley decided to engage in some hand shaking. A few minutes after four o'clock, while he was busy shaking hands with people filing through an exposition hall two shots rang out from the gun of anarchist Leon Czolgosz. The president fell, mortally wounded. Eight days later he died.

Perhaps the most touching epitaph came from the attending physician to William McKinley, Dr. Roswell Park, who said "Up to this time, I'd never really believed that a man could be a good Christian and a good politician."

Historical Landmarks

Birthplace of William McKinley
36 South Main Street
Niles, Ohio

McKinley's father, also named William, married Nancy Allison, a farmer's daughter, in 1827. William McKinley was born on January 29, 1843, in Niles, Ohio, a rural town with a population of about 300. The birthplace was a simple two-story frame building with a country store occupying part of the first floor. Near the birthplace was the little white school that McKinley attended as a boy. When he was nine years old, his parents decided that the school was not adequate and they moved to nearby Poland.

Visitor's Information

McKinley's birthplace is long gone from its Main Street location in Niles. In fact, McKinley is the only president whose personal residences have all been destroyed.

The Dollar Savings and Trust Bank building occupies the site where William McKinley was born. Its entranceway has a marker noting the McKinley site.

The Dollar Bank building is at 36 South Main Street, U.S. 422, Niles, Ohio. Telephone: (216) 544-9736.

National McKinley Birthplace Memorial
40 North Main Street
Niles, Ohio

Joseph G. Butler, Jr., a childhood companion and lifelong friend of William McKinley, was the first to conceive the idea to perpetuate the memory of the president by erecting a suitable memorial to mark his birthplace. Eventually, $500,000 was raised, mainly in small amounts from the American people. The largest single amount was from Pittsburgh industrialist, Henry Clay Frick, who donated $50,000. The only stipulation attached to his gift was that it be used to construct a library in the memorial.

The site occupies an entire square, which was contributed by the city of Niles, and is on the site of the school McKinley attended and within a stone's throw of the location of the frame house in which the president was born. It is an imposing structure 232 feet in length, 136 feet in width, and 38 feet high. In the central portion of the building is the Court of Honor flanked by two lateral wings, one designed for an assembly room, the other for the McKinley Memorial Library. Twenty-eight marble columns support the Court of Honor. Toward the rear is an impressive marble statue of McKinley. Flanking this statue are busts of members of McKinley's Cabinet and other prominent Americans. On the second floor, reached by a handsome marble stairway, is the collection of McKinley memorabilia and notable relics of all kinds associated with the life of William McKinley.

Visitor's Information

Open Monday-Thursday, 8:30 a.m.-8:00 p.m.; Friday and Saturday, 8:30 a.m.-5:30 p.m.; Sunday (during the school year), 1:00 p.m.-5:00 p.m. Closed holidays. Telephone (216) 652-1704.
Admission: Free.
The Memorial is at 40 North Main Street, in downtown Niles, Ohio.

The McKinley
800 McKinley Monument Drive N.W.
Canton, Ohio

The McKinley includes Discover World- a Science Center, Museum of History, Science and Industry, Planetarium, and The National Memorial. In the History Hall are tangible memories of the life of William McKinley: the clothing he wore, the furniture he used, political and personal mementoes representing his private life as well as his life as a public figure. This is the nation's largest collection of memorabilia from President McKinley's life.

The Ramsayer Research Library, located in the Museum, has a complete collection of McKinley books, newspapers, photographs and other memorabilia.

Visitor's Information

Open weekdays, 9:00 a.m.-5:00 p.m. (to 7:00 p.m. during summer); Sunday, noon-5:00 p.m. (to 7:00 p.m. during summer). Telephone: (216) 455-7043.
Ramsayer Research Library open Tuesday, Wednesday, Friday, noon-4:30 p.m.
Admission: adults, $5.00; age 60 and over, $4.00; ages 3-18, $3.00.

The Museum is located at 800 McKinley Monument Drive, Canton, Ohio. From north or south on I-77 use Exit 106 in Canton which leads to 13th Street N.W. Proceed east on 13th Street to bottom of hill, then take first right onto Monument Park Drive which leads directly to Museum.

Burial Site
McKinley National Memorial
800 McKinley Monument Drive
Canton, Ohio

On September 6, 1901, President William McKinley was shot by an assassin in Buffalo, New York. Eight days later McKinley lost his battle for life, his lips forming the words of his favorite hymn, "Nearer My God to Thee." His final words were, "Goodbye all. It is God's will. His will, not ours, be done."

His body was temporarily interred in Westlawn Cemetery while President Theodore Roosevelt appointed a commission to plan a memorial to McKinley. Thousands of men, women and children made voluntary contributions toward the fund for the memorial which was started in 1905 and was completed in 1907.

The tomb stands on a 75-foot high, grass covered hill overlooking the city of Canton. One hundred and eight steps lead to the entrance of the mausoleum. Over two million bricks were used in its construction. It is circular and domed, has a pink granite ashlar exterior, rises 96 feet above the ground, and measures 79 feet in diameter. The floor of the mausoleum is formed by different hued marble laid in a cross pattern. At the center, two polished dark-green, granite sarcophagi, resting atop a 10-foot square polished dark maroon granite base, contain the bodies of McKinley and his wife. The McKinley daughters, Katie and Ida, are entombed within the rear wall of the mausoleum. Both children died at early ages from childhood diseases. Midway up the steps, on a 13-foot-high pedestal, is a 9 1/2-foot high bronze statue of McKinley delivering his last speech in Buffalo.

William McKinley

Visitor's Information

The McKinley National Memorial is open the same hours as the McKinley Museum above and is handicapped accessible. Telephone: (216) 455-7043.
Admission: Free.

The Memorial is next to the McKinley Museum. See traveling directions above.

Theodore Roosevelt, 26th President, 1901-1909

Theodore Roosevelt's Birthplace

Sagamore Hill National Historic Site

Trophy Room, Sagamore Hill

Theodore Roosevelt Island

Theodore Roosevelt's Burial Site

Theodore Roosevelt

Twenty-Sixth President
1901 - 1909
Republican

The first President born in a city was Theodore Roosevelt, on October 27, 1858, in Manhattan. He was an asthmatic, sickly, myopic child, whose father sought to instill in the boy a drive not only for intellectual achievement but physical as well. Young Theodore worked out constantly on equipment installed in the Roosevelt home. The family's excursions to the country (for Teddy's asthma) fueled his ambition to be a naturalist.

Roosevelt graduated from Harvard University with a Phi Beta Kappa, the same year he married Alice Hathaway Lee, a Boston debutante. He went on to study law at Columbia University, and entered politics soon after graduation. His career in politics had barely begun (as a three time New York State Assemblyman) when both his wife Alice and his mother passed away on the same day. Brokenhearted, he left his only child, Alice, in the care of relatives, and moved to North Dakota to try ranching.

Theodore Roosevelt's attempt at cattle ranching failed and he returned to New York in 1886. At the request of Republican leaders he ran for the mayor's office, a race the party knew he had no chance of winning. Though Roosevelt lost the election, he did succeed in winning the hand of Edith Kermit Carow, whom he had known since childhood. They were married in late 1886, and after the honeymoon moved to Oyster Bay, Long Island, to a home Theodore had begun construction of in 1882.

Now back in the thick of politics, he travelled, making speeches on behalf of candidate Benjamin Harrison. When Harrison won the Presidency, Roosevelt was appointed to sit on the U.S. Civil Service Commission, a post he held until 1895. That year the mayor of New York appointed him president of the New York City Police Board. While serving in that office he exposed corruption on the force, raised salaries, and fought for safer working conditions.

Theodore Roosevelt was appointed Assistant Secretary of the Navy in William McKinley's first administration, but resigned after receiving permission to organize three regiments of cavalry for action in the Spanish American War. Anxious for action, his "Rough Riders" appropriated a troop transport, only to be unable to take their horses with them. The Rough Riders' charge up San Juan hill, although horse-less, made Roosevelt America's newest war hero.

Roosevelt returned to New York and easily won the governorship in 1898. During his term he sought for and received votes for higher taxes on the utilities and railroads, anti-trust legislation, bills to renovate tenements in New York City, conservation legislation, and got an eight hour day for state employees.

His reward for these progressive gains was to have the New York bosses secure his nomination for the Vice-Presidency, ostensibly to get him out of New York politics and into a job widely considered a dead end. The assassination of President McKinley changed those plans. On September 14, 1901, when Theodore Roosevelt took the oath of office as America's twenty-sixth president, Mark Hanna, the Ohio industrialist and party boss, (who never wanted Roosevelt on the ticket), spoke for most of the party regulars when he exclaimed "Now look, that damn cowboy is president!"

Roosevelt, in his first speech to Congress, attacked the trusts, and soon began the prosecution of the Northern Securities Company. Three years later, after a series of court battles, the company was ordered dissolved. The railroads were another favorite target of Roosevelt. The 1903 Elkins Act made rebates punishable, and the passage of the 1906 Hepburn Act (which increased the power of the Interstate Commerce Commission) allowed the government to fix maximum rates, nullify unreasonable rates, and inspect perishable goods being transported. Roosevelt's goal was never to eliminate big business, just its abuses, and during the rest of his term he secured indictments against twenty-five companies for anti-trust violations.

Roosevelt intervened on behalf of the American public in the Anthracite Coal Strike of 1902, when he threatened to use federal troops to re-open the mines. The owners submitted to arbitration, and the mine workers won a pay increase and a nine hour workday.

Theodore Roosevelt saw to the creation of a new cabinet level office in 1903, the Department of Commerce and Labor. He attempted on several occasions to secure legislation from Congress to give Federal protection to working women and children, and although he was unsuccessful, did get an employer's liability law passed which protected workers injured on any interstate railroad.

Roosevelt was a great lover of the outdoors and our first conservation president. Under his direction more land was set aside as public forest lands than his three predecessors combined. In 1902 he secured the passage of the Newlands Reclamation Act, which used the proceeds from the sale of federal lands in the West for the construction of irrigation projects. The establishment in 1907 of the Inland Waterways Commission helped protect waterways, forests, and other natural resources. During his administration Roosevelt created five national parks and fifty-five wildlife refuges.

The 1904 campaign was easily won by Roosevelt, who beat his Democratic opponent by the largest margin since Grant won his re-election in 1872. Roosevelt deftly played the political game, appointing men of character and ability to his administration who were also acceptable to the business oriented Republicans. TR even received over two million dollars in campaign contributions from business interests!

Aside from his continued attacks on the railroads and trusts, Roosevelt signed the 1906 Pure Food and Drug Act and the Meat Inspection Act. Inspired by a muckraker's exposure of those industries, the Acts established standards for processing, packing, and shipping of meat, forbade the use of harmful drugs, chemicals, and preservatives in food, and in 1911 were amended to forbid misleading labels on these goods.

Roosevelt's achievements in foreign affairs were no less impressive. His negotiation of the Russo-Japanese War (1904) resulted in the Treaty of Portsmouth (New Hampshire) in 1905. For his success, Theodore Roosevelt won the Nobel Peace Prize, the only American president to be so honored. He later signed the Root-Takahira Agreement with Japan, in which the two nations agreed to maintain the Open Door policy with China and respect each other's Pacific property.

The dream of an isthmus canal was finally begun during Roosevelt's second administration. Roosevelt aided a revolt in Panama (he had sent an American ship to support the rebels), to separate it from Columbia, then recognized Panama's independence one hour after the movement began. Fifteen days later he signed the Hay-Bunau-Varilla Treaty which gave the United States a perpetual lease of a ten mile wide zone across Panama for a canal. Canal construction began in 1906. When he inspected the early stages of construction, he became the first sitting president to leave U.S. soil.

Roosevelt's foreign policy, as described in Panama, was dubbed the "Big Stick." The Roosevelt Corollary to the Monroe Doctrine stated that the United States would intervene anywhere in the Caribbean or Central America if a weak nation were being threatened by an outside power. In 1920, he exerted pressure on Germany to stop its blockade of Venezuela.

Roosevelt opted not to run for the White House in 1908, but successfully passed the nomination to his Secretary of War, William Howard Taft. Returning from an African adventure two years later, Roosevelt found the Republican party split over support for President Taft, and many were calling themselves Roosevelt Republicans to distinguish themselves from the rest of the party. Roosevelt decided to pursue his party's nomination in 1912. When the Republicans renominated Taft, Roosevelt accepted the nomination of the Progressive Party, declaring that he was as "fit as a Bull Moose" to run for office.

It was fortuitous for the party that he was, for while sweeping through the country on a whistle-stop campaign, he was shot by a would-be assassin. The bullet was stopped by his glass case, and despite profuse bleeding from the wound, he delivered an hour and a half long speech. Despite this display of personal strength, the election of 1912 went to the third candidate in the race, New Jersey governor Woodrow Wilson. Roosevelt collected 88 electoral votes to Taft's 8, while Wilson got 434.

When war was declared against Germany in 1917, Roosevelt volunteered to fight, but his offer was turned down by President Wilson. He was proud, however, that all four of his sons (and one son-in-law) saw action. Two were wounded and one, Quentin, was killed.

Theodore Roosevelt was a prolific writer with forty books and over three thousand articles published on a range of subjects such as history, travel, and naturalism. During his term of office he became the first president to fly in an airplane, ride in a submarine, and the only one to see action in the Spanish-American War. Roosevelt was planning another run for the White House when he passed away on January 5, 1919 at Sagamore Hill.

Historical Landmarks

Birthplace of Theodore Roosevelt
28 East 20th Street
New York, New York

"Teedie," as he was called by his family, was born at 28 East 20th Street, New York City, on October 27, 1858. At his birth, the house, a four-story brownstone, stood in the midst of a prosperous residential neighborhood. Today it is surrounded by commercial lofts and rundown business buildings.

The house was one of Manhattan's first brownstone town houses with 15 rooms, a mansard roof, and a high front stoop leading to the entrance on the first floor above ground level. The first floor had a parlor and a library both opening to a hall with a dining room running across the full width of the house at the rear. On the second floor were three bedrooms, on the third floor three more, and servants quarters were on the fourth floor. Teedie was the second of four children of Theodore, Senior and Martha Bullock Roosevelt. The favorite place of the children was the wide porches across the back of the house and the one next door owned by Uncle Robert Roosevelt.

The house was furnished in what Roosevelt later characterized in his autobiography as "the canonical taste of the New York which George William Curtis described in the Potiphar papers," a period in which men of substance like to have their homes reflect the dignity and solidity of their traditions and lives. "The black haircloth furniture in the dining room scratched the bare legs of the children when they sat on it. The middle room was a library, with tables, chairs and bookcases of gloomy responsibility."

The family lived here until Roosevelt was fourteen. The house remained in the Roosevelt family until 1896. Gradually, as the surrounding neighborhood passed from a residential to a commercial area, the house underwent a series of changes that destroyed the original birthplace. In 1919, shortly after Roosevelt's death, the Women's Roosevelt Memorial Association (which later merged with the Theodore Roosevelt Association) raised funds to buy the site as well as the adjacent property, the house of Robert Roosevelt, uncle of Theodore. In 1921-23, the association reconstructed the birthplace home and converted the adjoining building into a museum and office. At the same time the two structures which had only been connected by a door leading from one porch to the other on the second floor, were made into a single unit.

In the reconstructed house, the living rooms and two bedrooms have been restored to the period of Teedie's boyhood. The parlor with its high ceiling, magnificent mirrors, crystal chandeliers and blue satin hangings, has the classic elegance of the period. To the children this was "... a room of much splendor open for general use only on Sunday evening or on rare occasions when there were parties." The front bedroom in which Roosevelt was born contains the original furniture and a portrait of his mother. Next to it is the nursery and beyond that his open porch used as a gymnasium. The restored building include many original Roosevelt items, and the museum preserves thousands of objects, pictures, and documents relating to his personal and private life.

Visitor's Information

The site is administered by the National Park Service in cooperation with the Theodore Roosevelt Association.

Open Wednesday-Sunday, 9:00 a.m.-5:00 p.m. Closed on Federal holidays. Telephone: (212) 26-1616.

Admission: adults, $1.00; under 17 and over 61, free.

Theodore Roosevelt Birthplace National Historic Site at 28 East 20th Street, New York City, can be reached via IRT and BMT subway stops at 23rd and 14th Streets or by bus.

Theodore Roosevelt National Park
Medora, North Dakota

This park, administered by the National Park Service, pays tribute to the contributions of the 26th President of the United States toward the conservation of the nation's natural resources. The 70,634-acre park comprises a South Unit near Medora and a North Unit near Watford City.

In the fall of 1883, Roosevelt came to the Badlands of North Dakota to hunt bison and other game. He became interested in ranching and acquired a partnership in the Maltese Cross Ranch, 7 miles south of Medora.

In 1884, he returned to North Dakota and established the Elkhorn Ranch. Roosevelt entered wholeheartedly into the life of the region and headed the Little Missouri River Stockmen's Association which he helped to organize. As his political career occupied more of his time, his visits to the Badlands became brief, and after a brutal winter in 1886-87 decimated his herd, he sold his ranches. Despite his failure as a rancher, Roosevelt once wrote, "I have always said I never would have been President if it had not been for my experience in North Dakota."

Visitor's Information

The Medora or South Unit is most relevant for Theodore Roosevelt. Stop at the Medora Visitor Center which has a museum with personal items of Roosevelt, ranching artifacts, natural history displays and an orientation film. Behind the Center is the Maltese Cross Cabin built in 1883-84, the only surviving building from either of Roosevelt's ranches.

The cabin is a three-room structure of hand-hewn pine logs. There are two doors, several glass-pane windows, mortar chinking, and a high-pitched shingled roof. All the furnishings are representative of the 1880's and a few of them are Roosevelt items.

Open daily 8:00 a.m.-8:00 p.m., June 8-September 4; 8:00 a.m.-5:00 p.m., September 5-September 30 and May 1-June 7; 8:00 a.m.-4:30 p.m., rest of year. Closed January 1, Thanksgiving, December 25. Telephone: (701) 623-4466.

Admission: $3.00 per vehicle per day, May-September; free, rest of year (most attractions closed Labor Day-Memorial Day).

The Medora or South Unit is 17 miles west of Belfield and 63 miles east of Glendive, off highway I-94.

Sagamore Hill National Historic Site
Cove Neck Road
Oyster Bay, New York

When Theodore Roosevelt was 15, his father established the family's summer residence at Oyster Bay, and the boy spent his vacations exploring the fields and woodlands on Cove Neck.

Six months after graduating from Harvard in 1880, Roosevelt bought the hill on Cove Neck where his house now stands. The cost was $30,000; and with two subsequent purchases, the area eventually comprised 155 acres of which he kept 95, selling the rest to an aunt and an older sister.

After his marriage to Alice Hathaway Lee of Boston, plans were drawn up for the house but before the final construction agreement was signed, Theodore's wife and mother died on the same day, February 14, 1884. All that was left of his marriage was his first born daughter, Alice, and to make sure he would have a suitable home for her he contracted to have built, at a cost of $16,975, the house that was to become known as Sagamore Hill. Roosevelt had originally planned to name the property "Leeholm" for his first wife. Within two years, however, he had begun seeing Edith Kermit Carow, a childhood friend, whom he married on December 2, 1886. Soon he called his estate Sagamore Hill for the Indian chief, Sagamore Mohannis who had signed away his rights to the lots over 200 years previously.

Thereafter, regardless of the position he held during a life of distinguished service, Sagamore Hill was the house to which he always returned. It was for more than 30 years, one of the most conspicuous homes in America and was the summer White House while Theodore Roosevelt was President.

Theodore Roosevelt

Sagamore Hill is a rambling, solidly built 22-room Victorian structure of frame and brick. The house reflected the hospitality, comfort and social stability of the owner. The foundations were almost two feet thick with rafters, joists and roof-boards in proportion. There were fireplaces all through the house, four on the first floor, four on the second, and a dumbwaiter for firewood came up from the cellar to feed them.

Today it has changed little from more than 90 years ago when it was the home of one of the most distinguished American families. On the first floor is a large center hall, the library that served as Roosevelt's private office, the dining room, Mrs. Roosevelt's drawing room, the kitchen and the spacious north room added in 1904. This room was designed by Roosevelt's friend, C. Grant LaFarge, son of John LaFarge, the artist. The 30 X 40 foot room is built of Phillipine and American woods and is crammed with trophies from hunting expeditions, books, paintings, flags, gifts from foreign leaders, and furniture. Appropriately called the Trophy Room, it dramatically reflects the spirit of Theodore Roosevelt.

The second floor contains the family bedrooms, nursery, and the guest rooms. The gun room housing Roosevelt's large collection of hunting arms is on the top floor. Other rooms include quarters for the maids and cook, a sewing room, a school room where some of the children were tutored, and T.R.'s bedroom as it was in his pre-college days. Around the south and west sides of the house is the spacious piazza from which Roosevelt looked out over Oyster Bay Harbor and Long Island Sound.

On the grounds are landscaped gardens, the pet cemetery where many of the Roosevelt family dogs are buried and, nearby, the Old Orchard Museum, formerly General Theodore Roosevelt Jr.'s home, containing audiovisual programs and exhibits on the career and family life of President Roosevelt.

Visitor's Information

Sagamore Hill is administered by the National Park Service.

Open daily, 9:30 a.m.-5:00 p.m.; closed January 1, Thanksgiving, December 25. Telephone: (516) 922-4447.

Admission: adults, $1.00; under 17 and over 61, free.

Sagamore Hill is at the end of Cove Neck Road, Oyster Bay, Long Island and can be reached by the Long Island Railroad. Taxis meet all trains. By car, Exit 41, NY 106 N, on the Long Island Expressway, I-95, leads directly to Oyster Bay where signs are posted along the way to Sagamore Hill.

Theodore Roosevelt Inaugural National Historic Site
641 Delaware Avenue
Buffalo, New York

This national historic site, operated by the National Park Service, features the Ansley Wilcox house. There, on September 14, 1901, Vice President Theodore Roosevelt recited the Presidential oath of office following the death of President McKinley, who had been shot by an assassin a few days earlier. The residence is among the few inaugural sites outside of Washington. Also, as one of the oldest houses in the city of Buffalo, it possesses local historical and architectural significance.

In 1883, Dexter P. Rumsey purchased the house as a wedding gift for his daughter Mary Grace and her husband, Ansley Wilcox, a prominent Buffalo lawyer. In the 1890's, Wilcox had the house remodeled which tripled the size of the entire structure. The result was a stately mansion.

One of Wilcox's close friends was Theodore Roosevelt, who called on him whenever he happened to be in Buffalo. When McKinley was shot, Roosevelt, who was then in Vermont on a speaking trip, rushed by train to Buffalo. He stayed at the Wilcox house, but on September 10, the condition of the president seemingly better after surgery, Roosevelt left to join his family for an outing in the Adirondacks. Three days later, he learned by messenger that McKinley was close to death. By the time he had reached Buffalo the next afternoon, the President had passed away.

After paying his respects to Mrs. McKinley, Roosevelt met with several Cabinet members and government officials in the library of the Wilcox House. There, at 3:15 p.m., on September 14, 1901, he took the Presidential oath of office. . That afternoon, in another room he drafted his first official document, a proclamation announcing McKinley's death and designating September 19 as a day of national mourning.

Theodore Roosevelt

The Wilcoxes continued to live in the house until their deaths in the 1930's. In 1963, when the structure faced demolition, a group of Buffalo citizens formed a committee to save it. Subsequently, Congress designated it as a national historic site, and in 1969 the Theodore Roosevelt Inaugural Site Committee and the National Park Service entered into a cooperative agreement for the administration and restoration of the site.

In addition to the exterior of the structure, many of the rooms, including the library where Roosevelt was sworn in, have been restored and furnished with period furniture. Items relating to President Roosevelt's inauguration and to the assassination of President McKinley are displayed and an audiovisual presentation is shown.

Visitor's Information

Open Monday-Friday, 10:00 a.m.-5:00 p.m., Saturday-Sunday, noon-5:00 p.m., April-December; Monday-Friday, 10:00 a.m.-5:00 p.m., Sunday, noon-5:00 p.m., rest of year. Closed January 1, Memorial Day, July 4, Labor Day, Thanksgiving, December 25. Telephone: (716) 884-0095.

Admission: adults, $1.00; under 17 and over 61, free.

The Theodore Roosevelt Inaugural House is on 641 Delaware Street near North Street, Buffalo, New York. Parking at the rear of the house is accessible from Franklin Street, a one-way street leading north from downtown Buffalo. Buses from downtown Buffalo stop in front of the site.

Theodore Roosevelt Island
Potomac River
Washington, District of Columbia

This island, an 88-acre natural area in the Potomac River, serves as an appropriate tribute to the conservation activities and interests of President Theodore Roosevelt. Although primarily a plant and wildlife preserve which provides a refuge for a variety of native plants and animals near the heart of metropolitan Washington, D.C., it is also the site of a monument honoring his Presidency and other accomplishments.

Theodore Island has borne a number of names. From "Anacostian" or "Analostan," the name given to it by the first white explorers, which they derived from a local Indian name, to "Mason's Island," named after the family that owned the island for 125 years after George Mason purchased it in 1717. Mason's son, also named George, is known for writing the Virginia Declaration of Rights and helping to draft the Federal Constitution.

In 1931, the Theodore Roosevelt Memorial Association bought the island and offered it as a gift to the American people. It was accepted by Congress the following year and is administered by the National Park Service.

The formal memorial designed by Eric Gugler is located in the northern center of the island, lending itself to the natural surroundings. A 17-foot bronze statue of the nation's 26th President, executed by Paul Manship, stands in front of a 30-foot high shaft of granite, overlooking an oval terrace. A step-down surrounding terrace is composed of a perimeter promenade encircled by a water-filled moat over which footbridges provide access to the memorial. From this terrace rise four 21-foot granite tablets, inscribed with the tenets of Roosevelt's philosophy on Nature, Manhood, Youth, and The State.

Visitor's Information

Open year-round during daylight hours. Telephone: (202) 426-6922 or (703) 285-2598.

Admission: Free.

Theodore Roosevelt Island is opposite the Kennedy Center of the Performing Arts on the Washington shore and the George Washington Memorial Parkway on the Virginia shore. It is accessible only by a pedestrian causeway from the Virginia shore or by boat. A parking area near the causeway is reached from the northbound lanes of George Washington Memorial Parkway on the Virginia side of the Potomac.

Theodore Roosevelt

Burial Site
Young's Memorial Cemetery
Cove Neck Road and East Main Street
Oyster Bay, New York

Theodore Roosevelt died unexpectedly of a blood clot in the heart on January 6, 1919. He is buried in Young's Memorial Cemetery, about 2 miles from Sagamore Hill. His first wife had been buried in New York City. His second wife died in 1948 and was buried beside him in Oyster Bay.

The funeral services were held in the Christ Episcopal Church in Oyster Bay where he had worshipped for 30 years. Family, friends, neighbors and relatives crowded the tiny church, and the bier was simply draped with the calvary flag of the Rough Riders.

The cemetery plot is on a ridge of an elevation which overlooks Oyster Bay and Long Island Sound.. The grave has a plain tombstone inscribed as follows:

Theodore Roosevelt
Born, October 27, 1858
Died, January 6, 1919
and his wife
Edith Kermit
Born, August 6, 1861
Died, September 30, 1948

Visitor's Information

The grave can be seen at all times during daylight hours.

Young's Memorial Cemetery is located at the intersection of Cove Neck Road and East Main Street, Oyster Bay, where you turn north to Sagamore Hill.

273

William Howard Taft, 27th President, 1909-1913

Birthplace of William Howard Taft

William Howard Taft's Burial Site

William Howard Taft

Twenty-Seventh President
1909-1913
Republican

William Howard Taft was born on September 15, 1857 in Cincinnati, Ohio. Law, it has been said, was bred into William Taft. His father, Alphonso (who had served as Grant's Secretary of War and Attorney General), and all of Alphonso's sons were lawyers. So it was no surprise when William graduated from Yale in 1878 he pursued a law degree, at the Cincinnati Law School.

Taft's first job was as a law reporter for the Cincinnati Times. At 24 he became the assistant prosecuting attorney for Hamilton County. A year later he was the collector of internal revenue. Taft then practiced law until 1887, when he was appointed a superior court judge.

Just a year before his judicial appointment Taft married his childhood sweetheart, Helen Herron, an accomplished pianist whose father was Rutherford B. Hayes' law partner. Mrs. Taft would later leave Washington with one of its most enduring yearly traditions when she arranged for the gift, from the Mayor of Tokyo, of 3,000 Japanese Cherry Trees to be planted near the Potomac.

Taft began a steady climb through the judiciary which he hoped would ultimately land him in the Supreme Court. In 1890, at the age of 33, he became the Solicitor General, at 35 a United States Circuit Court Judge and the Dean of the Cincinnati Law School.

In 1900 President McKinley appointed him the first Governor of the newly acquired Philippines. He organized a democratic government, built roads, post offices and banks, organized a school system, and improved sanitation. Because of these projects and his promotion of Phillipino self determination, he was positively revered among those people. His commitment to the Philippino people was so strong that he twice turned down President Roosevelt's offer of a seat on the United States Supreme Court, a lifelong dream.

Taft and his family returned to America so that he could assume the post of Secretary of War in Roosevelt's Cabinet. While in that post he also served as the provisional governor of Cuba and helped to end internal strife there. In 1908, after Roosevelt decided not to run for another term, he chose Taft to carry on his policies. Roosevelt's popularity and influence assured Taft the nomination of the party and victory in the general election.

Taft was criticized for his work in the arena of foreign affairs. His reciprocity treaty with Canada (which provided for mutual reductions in tariff duties), was opposed by American farmers because of the competition from Canadian food products. Many Canadians suspected the treaty was part of a plan by the United States to annex them, and their parliament rejected it. In China, Taft's administration followed what was called "Dollar Diplomacy," where American bankers were induced to finance railroads in that country. Similar actions in the Caribbean ultimately led to military intervention in Nicaragua.

Despite these problems, William Taft's administration did produce some splendid pieces of progressive legislation. By extending its jurisdiction, the Interstate Commerce Commission became one of the most powerful federal agencies in Washington. The Publicity Act (1910) forced congressional candidates to reveal their campaign contributions. Taft also pushed through two amendments to the Constitution favored by the progressives. The sixteenth amendment instituted the income tax, and the seventeenth amendment (actually becoming law a few weeks into Wilson's administration) provided for the direct election of Senators by the people.

Taft brought twice as many anti-trust suits against monopolies as did Roosevelt. The postal savings system was established, which among other things meant there was now a place for rural Americans to safely put their money for short periods of time. Also helping rural America (and stimulating the mail order houses such as Sears and Roebuck) was the liberalization of parcel post to allow for the delivery of large packages. The eight hour day was instituted for people on government contracts. It is also noteworthy that during Taft's administration the last of the 48 contiguous states, Arizona and New Mexico, were admitted to the Union.

Taft's signing of the Payne-Aldrich Tariff, which continued a high tariff policy the progressives were against, began a rift between himself and the Progressive wing of the Republican party. This rift widened when Taft failed to involve himself in the House of Representative's successful moves to limit the power of the dictatorial Speaker, Joseph Cannon.

Taft lost even more progressive support when he dismissed a Department of Interior employee, Gifford Pinchot, for making public accusations that his boss, Secretary of the Interior Richard Ballinger, was derelict in his duty for allowing private individuals to gain control of public lands. Though a Congressional Committee found Ballinger innocent, Taft's firing of Pinchot was met with more anger from the Progressives, notably Theodore Roosevelt, who had just returned from his trip abroad.

When Taft won the Republican Party nomination for the presidency in 1912, Roosevelt bolted to Bob LaFollette's Progressive Party and won their nomination, much to the anger of LaFollette. Meanwhile, the Democrats nominated New Jersey Governor Woodrow Wilson as their standard bearer. Taft and Roosevelt ended up splitting the Republican vote, and Wilson won.

William H. Taft left the presidency (he once called it "the loneliest place in the world") but did not retire from public life. He became Kent Professor of Law at Yale University, the President of the American Bar Association, and chairman of the American Red Cross. In 1921, Taft achieved his lifelong goal of becoming Chief Justice of the United States Supreme Court, when nominated by President Harding and approved by the Senate. Taft's feelings were best expressed by his statement that "Next to my wife and children, the Court is the nearest thing to my heart." He thus became the only President to also serve in our nation's highest court.

Taft resigned from the Supreme Court in 1930, and passed away a month later, on March 8. He then became the first President to be buried at Arlington National Cemetery.

Historic Landmarks

Birthplace of William Howard Taft
2038 Auburn Avenue
Cincinnati, Ohio

After receiving a law degree in Connecticut, in 1838, William Howard Taft's father, Alphonso Taft, settled in Cincinnati, Ohio. Alphonso, whose father was a Vermont judge, became a successful lawyer, a nationally prominent figure in the Republican Party, and served in President Ulysses S. Grant's Cabinet. In 1851, he purchased a house in Mount Auburn, at 2038 Auburn Avenue, then a country suburb of Cincinnati, He had been married in 1841 and had five children but his wife died in 1852. At the end of 1853, he married again, to Louise Maria Torrey of Millbury, Massachusetts.

William Howard Taft was born on September 15, 1857, in a first floor bedroom of the family home. William lived in the house until 1874, the year he entered Yale University.

In 1876-77, while the elder Taft was serving as Secretary of War and then Attorney General under President Grant, the family moved to Washington.

The Tafts reoccupied the house in 1885, and William Howard lived with them until after his marriage the next year, when he acquired his own residence in the city. Subsequently, his career necessitated his relocation to Washington.

After his father died in 1891, his mother went to Massachusetts to live with a sister. In 1899, she sold the house.

When Alphonso acquired the house, it was a square brick structure in the Greek Revival style and had two stories over a basement. He renovated the entire structure, including the erection of a small captain's walk, or observatory, on top of the almost flat roof. He also constructed at the rear a three-story brick ell. A fire in 1878 required rebuilding and additional changes were made. A succession of owners over the years substantially altered the interior and exterior. In 1961, the William Howard Taft Memorial Association leased the building to preserve it as a shrine to the Taft family. It acquired full title to the structure seven years later and the following year transferred it to the National Park Service which has restored the house and grounds. Four restored rooms reflect the family life of the Tafts during the years 1857 to 1877. Museum exhibits emphasize the long and dedicated career of William Howard Taft and the Taft family.

Visitor's Information

The Taft birthplace is a national historic site operated by the National Park Service.

Open daily, 10:00 a.m.-4:00 p.m.; Closed Thanksgiving, December 25, and January 1. Telephone: (513) 684-3262.

Admission: Free.

The house at 2038 Auburn Avenue is one block north of the intersection of Auburn and Dorchester Avenues in Cincinnati, Ohio.

Taft's Washington Home
2215 Wyoming Avenue NW
Washington, District of Columbia

When William Howard Taft returned to Washington as Chief Justice of the Supreme Court he bought a white brick house at Wyoming Avenue for $75,000. He lived there from 1922 to 1930; his last home. This brick house had white pillars, nine bedrooms and several fireplaces. The third floor was completely filled by the Chief Justice's library, which was reached by an elevator installed by Taft. The structure is one of the few former presidential homes in Washington identified by an historical marker.

Visitor's Information

The house is currently the Embassy of the United Arab Emirates.

Burial Site
Arlington National Cemetery
Arlington, Virginia

Taft was a hard-working Chief Justice, arising at 5:15 in the morning and working until 10 p.m. He watched his health carefully and to keep his weight down (it was about 300 pounds) he walked the three miles between his home and the Court almost every morning and evening. But finally the strain of overwork became too great. Bad health, chiefly due to heart trouble, forced his retirement on February 3, 1930. Taft died on March 8, 1930, and was buried in Arlington National Cemetery.

Visitor's Information

Open daily, 8:00 a.m.-7:00 p.m., April-September; 8:00 a.m.-5:00 p.m., rest of year. Telephone: (703) 697-2131.

Arlington National Cemetery in Arlington, Virginia, is adjacent to Washington and accessible from there via the Memorial Bridge.

Woodrow Wilson, 28th President, 1913-1921

Birthplace of Woodrow Wilson

Woodrow Wilson Boyhood Home

Woodrow Wilson House Museum

Woodrow Wilson House Museum-Interior

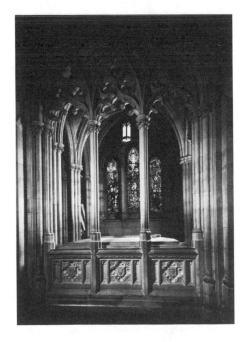

Woodrow Wilson Crypt

Woodrow Wilson

Twenty-Seventh President
1913 - 1921
Democrat

Thomas Woodrow Wilson was born on December 28, 1856. His father was a Presbyterian minister, and moved quite often as he found new parishes to lead. When Thomas was a year old, his family moved to Atlanta, where they lived during the Civil War. (Two of Wilson's uncles were Union Generals.) When he was fourteen his family moved again, this time to Columbia, South Carolina, only to move again three years later, to Wilmington, North Carolina.

After graduating from Princeton in 1879 (where he was known as a serious student and an able debater), he attended the University of Virginia for law, and after passing the bar set up a practice in Atlanta. But the law did not satisfy him, and he returned to school, studying history and political science at Johns Hopkins. At this time, in 1885 Wilson married Ellen Louise Axton, whom he had been courting for a few years.

Wilson became Bryn Mawr's first professor of History while continuing his studies at Johns Hopkins. In 1886 he earned his Ph.D. in political science, our only President to have that distinction. He left Bryn Mawr to teach at Wesleyan, where he also coached the football team. In 1890 he returned to Princeton as a lecturer, and became its president in 1902. Some much publicized squabbles with the college over various issues caught the attention of the New Jersey Democratic Party, which convinced him to run for governor. His victory in 1911 was a landslide, and as governor he made progressive gains in that state's election, corporation, labor, and public utility laws.

The next year, at the Democratic National Convention, Wilson's name was placed in nomination by William Jennings Bryan, the three time Democratic candidate. He won, and in the general election, thanks to party divisiveness between the Roosevelt Progressives and the Taft Regulars (which split the Republican vote), Woodrow Wilson won decisively. He became the first Southerner to be elected to the presidency since before the Civil War. The Democrats also won control of both Houses of Congress.

Wilson became the first President since John Adams to address Congress in person when he pressed for large reductions in the tariff. He was also the first President to hold regularly scheduled news conferences, and the first to appoint a woman to a subCabinet level post.

Before the First World War demanded most of his attention, Wilson pursued the passage of reform legislation. Despite the work begun by Roosevelt and Taft, trusts were still finding ways to operate around the law, and in 1914 two bills were passed which made Wilson a hero to the small businessman attempting to compete against large corporations. The Federal Trade Commission was formed to enforce fair trade practices and was given the power to serve injunctions and "cease and desist" orders against firms which did not follow the Commission's orders.

After a politically bloody fight, Wilson won passage of lower import rates with the Underwood Tariff (1913). The Federal Reserve Act (1913) created a central banking system. A new form of currency, the Federal Reserve Note, soon became the nation's primary form of exchange.

Wilson then saw to the passage of the Clayton Antitrust Act, which was labeled by unions as "Labor's Magna Carta." Other laws which improved labor's lot were the La Follete Seaman's Act of 1915, which mandated better conditions and wages for merchant seamen. The Adamson Act (1916) gave railroad workers an eight hour day. Wilson's administration also began taking a larger role in the nation's farms by making aid available to build and staff rural schools and for the building of rural roads.

During Wilson's second term the Eighteenth Amendment, the terms of which were later spelled out in the Volstead Act, prohibited the manufacture and sale of any alcoholic beverage. The Nineteenth Amendment, which extended the right to vote to women, was passed by Congress in 1919 and became law in 1920.

Though the war in Europe would come to dominate American foreign policy, the Caribbean demanded a great deal of attention during Wilson's first term. Wilson fought for and won the repeal of the Panama Canal Tolls Act which exempted United States ships in coastwise trade from paying for transit through the canal. In 1916 he sent the Marines to Santa Domingo to prevent a revolution and protect American business interests. European intervention was prevented by United States military action in Haiti in 1915. Wilson signed a treaty with Nicaragua in 1914 which gave the United States the right to keep naval bases, and in 1917 purchased the Virgin Islands from Denmark for $25 million.

In 1914 Wilson ordered the capture of Vera Cruz in retaliation for the capture of American sailors by Mexico. After a contingent of Mexican soldiers, led by Francisco "Pancho" Villa, attacked and killed Americans in Columbus, New Mexico, Wilson had General John J. Pershing pursue Villa into Mexico.

Wilson won election to a second term with promises of continued American neutrality in the European war. "He kept us out of war," was the campaign slogan. Wilson had tenaciously kept the country away from the conflict, despite Britain's attempts at limiting American shipping (to enforce its blockade of Germany) and Germany's sinking of several ships at the cost of some American lives (in their effort to enforce their own blockade of the British Isles). Despite his desire for neutrality, however, Wilson asked Congress to pass several defense measures in 1916 which authorized construction of battleships, increased the size of the army, and created an agency which would see to the proper use of the nation's resources during war.

After his 1916 election, Wilson attempted to get the belligerents to agree on his own peace plan which was based on "peace without victory." It was turned down by them all, and Germany continued to sink American merchant vessels, forcing Wilson to break diplomatic ties with Germany. He then sought the Senate's approval to arm merchant ships. After a Senate filibuster prevented the vote from passing, Wilson used a War of 1812 law to arm them anyway. But despite the weapons, four American vessels were sunk by the Germans in March of 1917.

On April 2, 1917, Wilson spoke before Congress declaring that "the world must be made safe for democracy." On April 6, the declaration for war was passed by the Senate. In May, the draft began with the passage of the Selective Service Act. A number of agencies were created to control various industries needed for the war effort, such as railroads, fuel, certain manufacturing, and food.

The war effort also produced a national hysteria against the German people, thanks to the Committee on Public Opinion, which was run by newspaperman George Creel. The Espionage Act, the Trading with the Enemy Act, and the Sedition Act, passed between June of 1917 and May of 1918, compromised some civil liberties in order to insure order and support of the war in America. Wilson accepted the laws as means to achieve his goal of a new world order, one based on peace.

Wilson began his peace offensive with his January 1918 announcement of his Fourteen Points to Congress. They called for, among other things, free trade between nations, freedom of the seas, the abolition of secret diplomacy, and most importantly, the establishment of a League of Nations. As Allied victories continued, forcing the German Kaiser to flee to Holland, many Germans saw the Fourteen Points as a peace they could live with, and the Armistice was signed on November 11, 1918.

Unfortunately for Democrat Wilson's plans, the American people had voted in a Republican Congress in the election of 1918, the first such repudiation of a President during war. Wilson made a tactical error, too. He went to the Peace Conference without taking any important Republicans with him, a fact, combined with the American public's desire for revenge against the Germans, made the outlook for ratification poor.

Despite warnings from his doctors that the rigors of six years in office had left him weak, Woodrow Wilson embarked on a country wide speaking tour in favor of the Peace

Treaty and the League of Nations. After traveling more than 8,000 miles in less than a month, making speeches in favor of his plans, Wilson suffered a stroke in September of 1919. He was left paralyzed, and although his mind was still sharp, he was too weak to perform most of his duties. His last year in the White House was spent in seclusion, tended to by his second wife who carried out many of his day to day business. (His first wife, Ellen, had passed away in early 1914 and in late 1915 Wilson married a young widow named Edith Bolling.) In his condition he was unable to fight for the Peace Treaty, which was defeated by the Senate. This defeat shattered Wilson's dream for the League of Nations, which was rendered useless without American participation.

Wilson was rewarded for his work on the League of Nations with the Nobel Peace Prize in 1920, the second time the honor had been bestowed on an American president. He lived for three years after leaving the presidency, spending his time writing and practicing law. He passed away on February 3, 1924. Edith, it is interesting to note, lived long enough to attend the inauguration of John F. Kennedy in 1961.

Historical Landmarks

Woodrow Wilson Birthplace and Museum
24 North Coalter Street
Staunton, Virginia

In 1846, the First Presbyterian Church of Staunton built a residence for use as a manse. Nine years later, the Reverend Joseph R. Wilson, who had come to Virginia in the early 1850s to teach at Hampden-Sydney College, accepted an appointment with the Staunton Church and moved in. On December 28, 1856, his wife, Jessie, gave birth to their first son and third child, Woodrow.

The rectangular, 12 room, brick structure , painted white, represents the Greek Revival style. It sits on the slope of a steep hill. Because the ground floor is below street level on the street side, the house presents two stories on that side and three at the rear. Architectural features of interest include a wide and impressive rear three-story portico with huge Doric columns and double balcony overlooking a terraced Victorian garden.

Woodrow Wilson

The handsome house is restored to its appearance when the Wilson family lived there. Trained interpreters guide visitors through the twelve rooms which contain many original furnishings including Wilson's crib and the chair in which his mother rocked him, and many items that belonged to his parents.

Augmenting the guided tours of the Birthplace is a newly opened Museum of seven exhibit galleries telling in depth the many accomplishments of Wilson as an author, scholar, university president, governor, and statesman. Rare artifacts, photographs, family and personal possessions help to narrate the fascinating life and career of Wilson. President Wilson's 1919 Pierce-Arrow sedan, immaculately restored, that he bought from the White House fleet and used until his death, is exhibited in the garage gallery of the new museum.

Visitor's Information

Open daily, 9:00 a.m.-5:00 p.m. except January 1, Thanksgiving, December 25, and the Sundays of December, January and February. (Closing time is extended to 6:00 p.m. during the summer months.) Telephone: (703) 885-0897.

Admission: adults., $5.00; over 62, $4.00; ages 6-12, $1.00.

The birthplace is at 24 North Coalter Street, Staunton, Virginia. From I-81 take Exit 57 west to Coalter Street and turn right.

Woodrow Wilson Early Boyhood Home
419 Seventh Street
Augusta, Georgia

In 1857, the Reverend Joseph R. Wilson, left Staunton, Virginia, to become the pastor of the First Presbyterian Church in Augusta, Georgia. This house served as the church manse and Woodrow lived here until 1870. The three-story brick house is adjacent to the church at 642 Telfair Street.

Visitor's Information

The house is privately owned and visiting is not permitted.

Woodrow Wilson Boyhood Home
1705 Hampton Street
Columbia, South Carolina

Woodrow Wilson lived in Columbia for four years. Three of those years, 1872-1874, were spent in this house. Wilson's father was a Presbyterian minister and the family had moved often. This Tuscan Villa style house was built by Wilson's parents and was the only home the family ever owned.

The teenage Wilson witnessed in Columbia a town, still occupied by Federal troops, rebuilding itself in the aftermath of Sherman's wartime march which burned out its business district. The time the Wilsons spent in Columbia seemed to have meant a great deal to the family as Wilson's parents are buried in Columbia's First Presbyterian Church Yard.

The house is a good example of a minister's Victorian home. Its furnishings are of this period and include the bed in which the future President was born, his mother's bureau, bedside table and a four volume set of the Bible, a gift to her from her husband. Remnants of gas lighting fixtures remain and the marbleized mantels are original to the house. In the front gardens a large tea olive plant and several magnolia trees remain from Mrs. Wilson's plantings.

Visitor's Information

Open Tuesday-Saturday, 10:15 a.m.-3:15 p.m.; Sunday, 1:15 p.m.-4:15 p.m. Closed mid-December-January 2 and major holidays. Telephone: (803) 252-1770.

Admission: adults, $3.00; ages 6-21, $1.50.

The Wilson Boyhood Home is at 1705 Hampton Street, Columbia, South Carolina. Take I-26 to I-126 to Bull Street, turn right for about six blocks and turn left onto Hampton Street and the house is two blocks ahead.

Woodrow Wilson House Museum
2340 S Street NW
Washington, District of Columbia

This is the only former President's house open to the public in the nation's capital. The house, in the Embassy Row section of Washington, was purchased by Wilson in 1920 as a surprise for his second wife, Edith Bolling Wilson. On finishing his term of office in 1921, Wilson retired directly to this residence. He lived here for nearly three years until his death in 1924. Mrs. Wilson continued to live in the house for nearly forty more years. Upon her death in 1961, the property became a historic house museum that is maintained by the National Trust for Historic Preservation.

Visitor's Information

Visitors watch an introductory film on the efforts of Woodrow Wilson to secure a just and lasting conclusion to World War I, after which they are personally guided through the house and its varied collection of family furnishings, presidential gifts, and other memorabilia representing Wilson's career as a scholar, educator and statesman. Among the highlights of the collection are the President's inaugural Bible, his White House Cabinet chair, his typewriter, the pen used to sign the Declaration of War against Germany, a casing of first shell fired by American forces in World War I, portrait photographs of British and Belgian Royal Families, a framed mosaic from the Vatican, and numerous table-top statues.

Open Tuesday-Sunday, 10:00 a.m.-4:00 p.m. Closed Mondays and major holidays. Telephone: (202) 387-4062.

Admission: adults, $4.00; senior citizens and students, $2.50; under 7, free.

The Woodrow Wilson House Museum, 2340 S Street NW, is in the Upper Dupont Circle/Kalorama area. It is a 15 minute walk from Metro (Red Line); at Dupont Circle exit, take Q Street exit; travel northwest on Massachusetts Avenue NW to S Street and turn right.

Burial Site
Washington National Cathedral
Massachusetts and Wisconsin Avenues NW
Washington, District of Columbia

For almost three years after his term ended in March 1921, Wilson lived in quiet retirement but he remained an invalid from his stroke in 1919 and never regained his health. On February 3, 1924, he died in his sleep.

Various places were offered to Mrs. Wilson as a place of burial for her husband. His birthplace, Staunton, Virginia was mentioned; the President offered Arlington National Cemetery; and Princeton offered President's Row in Princeton Cemetery where all presidents of the university, but two, are buried. Mrs. Wilson declined all and chose a crypt in the Washington National Cathedral (Cathedral Church of St. Peter and St. Paul).

The sarcophagus of President Wilson was made in Boston of cream color limestone. It has a single decoration, the Cross of the Crusader, chosen by his wife because she believed it best illustrated his outstanding characteristics.

Visitor's Information

Open for tours Monday-Saturday, 10:00 a.m.-noon, 12:30 p.m.-3: 15 p.m.; Sunday, 12:30 p.m.-2:45 p.m. Telephone: (202) 537-6200.

Admission: donations.

The Washington National Cathedral is on Mount St. Alban at Massachusetts and Wisconsin Avenues NW.

Warren Gamaliel Harding, 29th President, 1921-1923

Warren G. Harding's Home

Tomb of Warren G. Harding

Warren G. Harding

Twenty-Ninth President
1921 - 1923
Republican

The first President born after the Civil War was Warren Gamaliel Harding, on November 2, 1865 in Corsica, Ohio. He was the oldest of eight children born to a homeopathic physician and his wife. Warren Harding attended Ohio Central College and after graduation worked on a farm, made brooms, and was a construction laborer. He began to attend law school, but at nineteen quit to take a job as a reporter on the Marion (Ohio) *Democratic Mirror*.

Harding's father had been part owner of a newspaper, and much of Harding's youth was spent in the paper's print shop, which explains his lifelong ambition to own a newspaper. In 1884, he started on the road to fulfilling that dream when he and two friends bought the Marion *Star* for $300. He became its editor and later the sole owner in 1891. It was at this time that young Warren met, fell in love with, and married the divorced daughter of a prominent Marion banker. Florence Kling was a music teacher and five years Harding's senior when she began working at the paper. As business manager she was soon an integral part of its success.

Warren Harding took an interest in local politics and began supporting Republican candidates. He had a natural flair for politics, and in 1900 was himself elected to the Ohio Senate. Four years later he became the state's lieutenant governor. Though he lost his bid for the governorship in 1910, he was elected to the United States Senate in 1914. Harding began gaining national attention in 1916, after being made Chairman of the Republican Party.

The Republican Convention of 1920 was a deadlock between General Leonard Wood and Illinois Governor Frank Lowden until, in the classic "smoke filled room" in a Chicago hotel, Harding's name was broached. The next day the convention gave its affirmation to Warren Harding to lead them back into the White House. President Woodrow Wilson, declaring the election a "solemn referendum" on the Treaty of Versailles, could only watch as the Democrats' choices for President, James Cox, Governor of Ohio, and Vice-President, Franklin Roosevelt, Assistant Secretary of the Navy, lost decisively. The country, tired of war and of Wilson's idealism, were drawn to Harding's promises of a "return to normalcy." The election returns were the first broadcast over radio, and Harding would later become the first President to give a speech over the radio.

Some of Harding's choices for his Cabinet reflected the very best in ability and integrity. Henry Wallace, a farmer's advocate, became Secretary of Agriculture, former Supreme Court Justice Charles Evans Hughes, Secretary of State, and Herbert Hoover, who had run the food management program during the war, Secretary of Commerce. But two of his other choices for the Cabinet would turn out to disgrace the administration, as would men selected for other government positions.

The head of the Veterans Bureau, Charles Forbes, was convicted of skimming a large portion of the Bureau's $250 million budget. Jesse Smith, an old friend of the President was involved in another scam with Thomas Miller, the Alien Property Custodian, who had accepted bribes in exchange for allowing the resale of an American metal company to the Germans. The Attorney General, another Ohioan named Harry Daugherty, was dismissed from office for selling liquor permits and pardons, among other illegal acts.

Perhaps the most explosive and damaging affair surrounded the actions of Secretary of the Interior Albert Fall, who had Harding transfer the rights to two oil reserves (Elks Hill in California and Teapot Dome in Wyoming) to his control, after which he sold the rights to an oilman who had "loaned" him a large sum of money. Fall was convicted of bribery and became the first Cabinet officer to go to prison.

Andrew Mellon, one of America's most successful businessmen, was named Harding's Secretary of Treasury. This reflected Harding's belief that there should be "more business in government." Under Mellon, taxes for the wealthy went down dramatically. Government budgeting methods were streamlined with the passage of the Budget and Accounting Act. Businessmen were appointed to head many of the regulatory agencies (such as the ICC, FTC, and Tariff Commission) that had been their combatants during the Progressive era, changing their thrust from regulatory to advisory. In 1922 the Fordney-McCumber Act, aside from continuing high tariffs, created a Tariff Commission, and gave the President the power to raise and lower tariffs by fifty percent.

Harding's Secretary of State, Charles Hughes, was given the power to convene an international conference to settle issues that were not being addressed by the Treaty of Versailles. The Washington Conference, held from 1921 to 1922, resulted in three major treaties dealing with territorial rights, naval strength, and a moratorium on shipbuilding. The countries attending the conference also agreed on an open door policy towards China. One of Harding's last efforts in the foreign arena was to propose United States membership in the World Court, which was not acted upon until 1926.

In 1923 Warren Harding, reeling from the scandals plaguing his administration, took off on a speaking tour of the West. On July 2, while in Seattle after a visit to the Alaska territory, Harding suffered an attack of what was first believed to be indigestion. A month later, at the Palace Hotel in San Francisco, Harding died from a cerebral thrombosis. He was 57.

Historical Landmarks

Birthplace of Warren Gamaliel Harding
State Highway 97, east of County Road 20
Corsica, Ohio

The Harding birthplace, which was built in 1856, was a saltbox cottage on the outskirts of Blooming Grove, now Corsica, a rural town in north-central Ohio, about twenty-five miles northeast of Marion, Ohio. This was the house to which Dr. George Tyron Harding, a farmer and later a homeopathic physician, brought his bride, Phoebe Elizabeth Dickerson, in the fall of 1864. They had been married on May 6, 1864, three days before he left to fight in the Civil War.

Warren G. Harding, the first of eight children, was born in this house on November 2, 1865. In 1872, the family moved to Caledonia, Ohio, where Warren spent most of his boyhood until 1880.

Visitor's Information

Harding's birthplace was torn down in 1896. A historical marker identifies the site, now a field, and a small stone marker lies on a corner of the actual location of the cottage on State Highway 97 just east of its junction with County Road 20

The family home in Caledonia was a white frame house which is identified by a marker on the northwest corner of South and Main Streets. The house is privately owned and visiting is not permitted.

Warren G. Harding

The Harding Home and Museum
380 Mount Vernon Avenue
Marion, Ohio

Warren G. Harding married Florence Kling DeWolf, whose father was one of Marion's wealthiest and most prominent Republicans, July 8, 1891. In the year before their marriage they planned and built the house now known as the Harding Home, where they were married. They occupied the house until they left for the White House in March 1921.

A 2 1/2-story frame structure in the Queen Anne style, the residence has a gabled roof, green clapboard siding, and cream-colored trim. The large Colonial Revival porch, of which one end is rounded, dominates the front of the house. The base of the balustraded porch is fieldstone, as are the pedestals, which support paired Ionic columns.

On the first floor is a large front hallway, parlor, library, and dining room. The second floor contains the master bedroom, whose bay windows overlook the roof of the porch and the front lawn; two other bedrooms; a maid's room, and a bathroom. Almost all the interior woodwork is oak.

When Mrs. Harding died in 1924, the year following President Harding's death, her will left the home, with its original furnishings, and more than 2,000 mementoes, gifts, etc. received by President and Mrs. Harding during his administration as President, to the Harding Memorial Association with the request that the home be preserved for the public. In 1926, the Harding Memorial Association opened a museum in the rooms on the ground floor. During the winter of 1964-65, the house was restored in detail to its condition at the turn of the century. The original gas lights, wired for electricity were put back in place and decorations, especially wallpaper, duplicated in authentic detail. The original furniture and furnishings were returned to their positions in accordance with a chart made at the time they were put in storage.

The Harding Museum is housed in a building at the rear of the Harding Home. It was built after the Harding nomination of 1920 and served as the working press headquarters for the presidential campaign. It was transformed into a museum during the restoration of the Harding home and displays pertinent items from the thousands of mementoes and other materials commemorating Harding's career.

Warren G. Harding

Visitor's Information

Open May 25-September 2, Wednesday-Saturday, 9:30 a.m.-4:30 p.m.; Sunday, noon-4:30 p.m.

Admission: adults, $2.50; senior citizens, $2.00; children 6-12, $1.00. Telephone: (614) 387-9630.

The Harding Home and Museum, 380 Mount Vernon Avenue, Marion, Ohio, can be reached via U.S. Route 23. Take Route 23 to Vernon Heights Boulevard and follow to Mount Vernon Avenue.

The Harding Memorial
Vernon Heights Boulevard
Marion, Ohio

In June 1923, President and Mrs. Harding began a trip across the continent and to Alaska, which ended with his death in San Francisco, on August 2. Following services in Washington, D.C., a funeral train carried the President's body to Marion, where it was placed in a temporary tomb at Marion Cemetery. On December 21, 1927, the bodies of the President and Mrs. Harding, who died in Marion in 1924, were moved from the temporary tomb to the newly constructed Harding Memorial.

The Harding Memorial is a circular monument of white Georgia marble which contains the sarcophagi of President Harding and his wife, Florence Kling Harding. Its appearance suggests in general a round Greek Temple. The diameter of the base of the monument is 103 feet and its height is 52 feet.

The monument is situated in the midst of 10 acres of landscaped grounds. Rows of maples form the shape of a Latin cross, the tomb being placed at the intersection of the arms of the cross. The total cost of the monument, landscaping and grounds was $783,108.56. It was paid for with voluntary gifts from the public with many thousands of dime contributions from school children throughout the country.

The graves are covered by two slabs of Emerald Pearl Labrador Granite. As one enters the Memorial, President Harding occupies the tomb to the left, which is marked by a bronze palm wreath. Mrs, Harding occupies the tomb to the right, which is marked by a bronze wreath of roses.

Visitor's Information

Open daily dawn to dusk.

The Harding Memorial on Vernon Heights Boulevard can be reached via U.S. Route 23 which intersects Vernon Heights Boulevard.

Calvin Coolidge, 30th President, 1923-1929

Calvin Coolidge's Birthplace

Coolidge Homestead

Calvin Coolidge's Burial Site

Calvin Coolidge

Thirtieth President
1923 - 1929
Republican

America's only President to be born on the 4th of July was John Calvin Coolidge, in Plymouth Notch, Vermont in 1872. "Classic New England" is the best way to describe growing up in this small Vermont town, and Calvin Coolidge came to embody that spirit. He worked and studied hard, graduating from Amherst College in 1894, where he was awarded a prize in a national competition for the best essay on the causes of the Revolutionary War. He studied law in Northampton, Massachusetts, and was admitted to the bar in 1897.

In Northampton Calvin Coolidge met Grace Goodhue, a graduate of the University of Vermont who taught the deaf. Grace's personality was said to be quite different from Calvin's, but he took an immediate fancy to her, and after a short courtship, married her in 1905. Later, as first lady, Grace would play matchmaker, bringing aviator-hero Charles Lindbergh and Anne Morrow together. She was also an avid baseball fan, and while living in the White House spent a good deal of time in front of a radio listening for the latest scores.

In 1897 Calvin Coolidge was elected to the City Council in Northampton, Massachusetts. This turned out to be the beginning of a steady climb up the political ladder. The following year he became city solicitor, then in 1905, when he was 32, Clerk of the Courts. At the age of 35 he was a state legislator and at 38, mayor of Northhampton. Two years later he returned to the Massachusetts State House as a Senator, and at 44 became the Lieutenant Governor. He became Governor in 1919.

In September of that year the Boston Police Department went on strike to protest the firing of men who had attempted to unionize the force. Coolidge's strong stand against the department (to break the strike he called out troops to patrol the streets) made him a national figure when he proclaimed "There is no right to strike against the public safety by anybody, anywhere, anytime." The following year, when the Republicans sought someone to balance the ticket with dark-horse Warren Harding of Ohio, Coolidge's name was placed in nomination and accepted by the convention.

Calvin Coolidge

On August 3, 1923, Calvin Coolidge was visiting his boyhood home in Plymouth Notch when the news came by telegram that President Harding had died. The family gathered in the Coolidge sitting room where Calvin's father, a notary public, gave his son the oath of office over the family Bible.

Coolidge spent the remainder of Harding's term cleaning out much of the corruption that had been left by his predecessor and appointing special prosecutors to remove corrupt office-holders. This won him further respect among the voters, who were also enjoying the economic boom of the twenties. In 1924 Coolidge was nominated by the Republicans for another term of office, and then went on to win big in the general election against Democrat Robert La Follette.

"The business of America is business," Coolidge declared, and during his administration many of the regulatory agencies strengthened by Roosevelt, Wilson, and Taft were weakened by his appointment of businessmen in leadership positions. Coolidge kept most of Harding's Cabinet, and Secretary of the Treasury Andrew Mellon was able to secure large tax cuts for the very wealthy...money saved that went into the booming stock market. Under Coolidge the federal government canceled its involvement in regional projects such as the Muscle Shoals project in Tennessee. His refusal to support various agricultural projects meant that farmers were unable to share in the prosperity of the twenties as crop prices tumbled. By the end of his five and one half years in office Coolidge had vetoed more Congressional legislation than any other President.

Relations with Mexico, which were strained after that country nationalized foreign owned properties, improved during Coolidge's second term. American troops were removed from Nicaragua in 1927, helping to ease relations with that country, too. In 1924 the Dawes plan reduced the debt owed to America by its former World War allies. Other treaties were signed which reduced interest rates and extended the time for repayment. The Kellog-Briand Pact, signed in 1927, was a well-meaning treaty signed by many nations of the world which renounced war in favor of peaceful methods for settling disputes. Lacking any way to enforce the pact, it was largely ignored. The Geneva Conference in 1927 also failed to keep countries from building up their navies.

Though there was a tradition of eschewing a third term, the Republicans were keen on Coolidge to run in 1928. His declaration "I do not chose to run" was typically succinct and the decision characteristically irreversible. It was later learned that Coolidge had suffered a heart attack in early 1927 and was advised for health reasons against another term in office.

Calvin and Grace Coolidge retired to Northampton. Apparently the throngs of people who came by their home for a glimpse of the former first family caused them to move to a larger, more secluded estate on the Connecticut River. There, Coolidge wrote several articles and finished his autobiography. He died on January 5, 1933 at the age of 60, and is buried with Grace in Plymouth Notch, Vermont, beside their son Calvin, Jr.

Historical Landmarks

Birthplace of Calvin Coolidge
Off State Route 100A
Plymouth Notch, Vermont

Calvin Coolidge was born on Independence Day, July 4, 1872, in the downstairs bedroom of his parents' small five room, 1 1/2-story house in Plymouth Notch, Vermont, next to the general store owned by his father. He was the first child of John Calvin and Victoria Josephine Moor Coolidge. Five generations of Coolidges, dating back to Captain John Coolidge, a Revolutionary soldier and one of the town's first three selectmen elected in 1789, had lived in Plymouth Notch.

When Calvin was four years old, the family moved across the road to what is now called the Coolidge Homestead.

Coolidge Homestead
Off State Route 100A
Plymouth Notch, Vermont

This simple, 1 1/2-story frame and clapboard farmhouse was the boyhood home of Coolidge. When he bought the house in 1876, for $375, John Coolidge added the front piazza and bay windows in the sitting room. Calvin lived in the house until 1887, the year he entered Black River Academy, in nearby Ludlow. In 1895, upon graduating from Amherst College, he took up the practice of law and settled in Northampton, Massachusetts.

Calvin Coolidge

Through the years, while pursuing a successful political carer, Coolidge returned to Plymouth Notch to see his family. On one of these occasions, during the night of August 2, 1923, when he was serving as Vice President of the United States, he was awakened with news of President Harding's sudden death in San Francisco. In a dramatic ceremony, held about 2:47 a.m. on the morning of August 3, 1923, in the sitting room of the homestead, Coolidge's father, a notary public and justice of the peace, swore him into office as President.

When his father died a few years later, Coolidge inherited his boyhood home but continued to spend most of his time in Northampton.

Visitor's Information

By purchase or gift, the State of Vermont acquired the Coolidge Birthplace and Homestead and many surrounding buildings including several associated with Calvin Coolidge, and they are preserved and maintained by the Vermont Division for Historic Preservation as the Plymouth Notch Historic District. This rural village, population around 400, is almost unchanged since the turn of the century.

The Birthplace has been restored to its appearance in 1872, when the President was born, and is furnished with original family furnishings, possessions and artifacts. The Homestead is virtually the same as it was the night Coolidge's father gave him the oath of office. The sitting room, known now as the Oath of Office Room, displays the table, Bible, and kerosene lamp used in that ceremony. Other rooms also contain original furnishings. Above the General Store, which was owned by his father, is Coolidge Hall, which was opened to the public for the first time in 1991. This hall, used by the local grange and for weekly dances , was Coolidge's summer White House office in 1924.

The Calvin Coolidge Visitor's Center, which should be the starting point for a visit to Plymouth Notch, contains a museum with a pictorial review of President Coolidge's life and an exhibit of presidential portraits and gifts.

Open daily, Memorial Day through mid-October, 9:30 a.m.-5:00 p.m. Telephone: (802) 672-3773.

Admission: adults, $3.50; under 14, free.

Plymouth Notch is 6 miles south of U.S. 4 on Vt. 100A. Entrance to the Visitor's Center is on Vt. 100A.

Coolidge's Northampton Home
21 Massasoit Street
Northampton, Massachusetts

Calvin Coolidge married Grace Goodhue, who had moved to Northampton from Vermont, on October 4, 1905. In 1906, when Grace was six months pregnant, they moved into half of a two family home; later they occupied all of it. It was a simple frame house with a dining room, kitchen, parlor, and front porch. There were three bedrooms upstairs plus a bath and the attic. They kept this house for twenty-four years. They lived here until they left for the White House and returned in March 1929, after Coolidge's Presidency was over.

Coolidge had been in the White House for six years and was known to everyone. An endless stream of tourists and sightseers from everywhere in the country walked or drove by his house hoping to catch a view of him on the porch. For the sake of privacy, the Coolidges moved to a new house, "The Beeches."

Visitor's Information

The house is privately owned and visiting is not permitted.

The Beeches
16 Hampton Terrace
Northampton, Massachusetts

The three-story, 16 room house, built in 1914-15 for Dr. Henry MacCracken, a professor of English at Smith College, is on a five-acre parcel of land. The house has a deeply gabled L at the southerly corner and windows are grouped and divided into small panes. The home derives its name from eighty beeches planted on the large property. It provided ample privacy for the Coolidges and the Coolidge family lived here from 1930 to 1937. The former President died in the house in 1933.

The current owners, who bought the house in 1990, informed the authors that previous owners had remodeled the kitchen and bathroom making it no longer acceptable as an historic site.

Visitor's Information

The home is privately owned and visiting is not permitted.

Calvin Coolidge Memorial Room
Forbes Library
20 West Street
Northampton, Massachusetts

There was much debate in Northampton about what kind of "Coolidge Memorial" would be best but Mrs. Coolidge made her views clear. She thought a special room for the President's books and memorabilia would be most appropriate. When she moved from The Beeches, she had given the Forbes Library 900 books, chiefly presentation copies, furniture and other memorabilia from Calvin's private library. This was added to the stock of material, including Coolidge's gubernatorial correspondence and an extensive photo collection already gathered by the Forbes' librarians. Mrs. Coolidge's last public appearance, before she died in 1957, was at the dedication ceremonies when the Calvin Coolidge Memorial Room was first opened in 1956.

The Forbes Library began its Coolidge collection in 1920 when he was nominated as Vice President on the Republican ticket. Coolidge took an active interest in this work and deposited family pictures and many souvenirs and gifts received during his Presidential years. As recently as 1985, John Coolidge, son of the president, donated some 150 files of his father's personal correspondence.

Visitor's Information

Open daily, 9:00 a.m.-5:00 p.m.., Sunday, 2:00 p.m.-6:00 p.m. Telephone: (413) 584-6037.

Admission: Free.

State Route 9, which becomes Main Street in Northampton, intersects with West Street, the location of the Forbes Library.

Burial Site
Plymouth Notch Cemetery
Plymouth Notch, Vermont

When the Coolidges left Washington at the end of his presidency in 1929, they returned to Northampton, Massachusetts. He kept busy by serving on various boards and writing. But he was distraught by the Depression which had started with the stock market crash eight months after he left office, and deepened in the winter of 1932. His health was not good; he felt weak and complained that he was too old for his years, that the responsibilities he had carried had burnt him out. On January 5, 1933, Mrs. Coolidge found him lying on the floor of his bedroom, where he had died of a heart attack.

Former President Herbert Hoover, Eleanor Roosevelt, and thousands of mourners came to Northampton. The funeral services were held at Edwards Church and Coolidge was buried in the Plymouth Notch Cemetery next to his son, Calvin, Jr., who had died while he was President. When his wife, Grace Goodhue Coolidge died on July 8, 1957, she was buried alongside him. Six generations of Coolidges, along with neighbors and friends are buried in this town cemetery which was established before 1800.

A simple granite headstone marks the President's grave.

Visitor's Information

Open sunrise to sunset.

The Plymouth Notch Cemetery is about a mile southwest of the Coolidge Homestead on the south side of Vt. 100A.

Herbert Hoover, 31st President, 1929-1933

Herbert Hoover Birthplace

Hoover-Minthorn House

Herbert Hoover Presidential Library and Museum

Burial Site of Herbert Hoover and wife

Herbert Hoover

Thirty-First President
1929 - 1933
Republican

Our first President of the Quaker persuasion and only one to hail from Iowa is Herbert Clark Hoover, who was born on August 10, 1874 in West Branch. By the time Herbert was ten both his parents had passed away, so he and his two siblings went to live with an uncle. The family was poor, but Herbert worked hard on the farm while forging ahead with his education.

When he was fifteen he went to work in Oregon for another uncle, and while there managed to gain entrance to the first class of Stanford University. Hoover worked at various jobs to pay the tuition, and earned his degree in engineering in 1895. Though his first job was shoveling ore in a mine near Nevada City, his engineering skills soon propelled him upwards. He worked in Australia mining for gold, and, thanks to his "nose for gold," was responsible for his company's tremendous profits.

After being offered a chance to run the company's business in China, Hoover decided that he finally had the position of stability he wanted to marry his Stanford sweetheart and former Iowa native, Lou Henry. After their marriage in 1899 they sailed to China, where aside from mining, the Hoover's found themselves caught up in the Boxer Rebellion. Herbert gained international prestige for his role in saving the European community besieged by the rebels. Lou participated in the distribution of food and the nursing of the sick and wounded.

Hoover next became the company's mining consultant, and he and Lou travelled extensively around the world, almost never seeing the home they had purchased in 1902 in Monterey. When the First World War broke out, Hoover was asked to assist in the operations to rescue Americans caught in belligerent countries. He then accepted the post as head of the Belgian Relief Committee, an assignment he performed so well that he is credited with saving countless lives in Europe.

Upon the United States' entry into the World War, Hoover was made the U.S. Food Administrator, where he was responsible for increasing U.S. food production and cutting consumption through a program of volunteerism. After the war he headed the American Relief Organization which fed thousands of starving people from both sides of the conflict.

Among the many accolades he received from grateful Europeans was the naming of an asteroid, Hooveria, by an Austrian astronomer, the first such honor bestowed on a President. After completing that assignment, he was appointed to Harding's Cabinet as Commerce Secretary, a post he held through the Coolidge Administration.

Herbert Hoover's success as a businessman and public servant had made him a symbol of the Republican philosophy of limited federal government and more private initiative. As such he was nominated for the presidency on the first ballot at the Republican convention, and ran extolling the virtues of an American system that had brought the country to new heights of prosperity. "A chicken in every pot" was the Republican slogan that year (even though Democratic opponent Al Smith of New York said it first). For the first time since the Civil War, Texas, Florida, Virginia, and North Carolina, all formerly part of the Democratic "Solid South," went Republican as Hoover steamrolled to victory in 1928.

Hoover immediately set to work on the farm surplus problem by calling a special session of Congress, which passed the Agricultural Marketing Act of 1929. This law created the Federal Farm Board which, among other things, worked to help farmers create marketing cooperatives which were meant to help improve the farmer's plight. Hoover also signed, against the advice of many economists, the Hawley-Smoot Tariff, which would raise protective rates to their highest levels.

Though a few economists worried about the effects of large amounts of stock market speculation as well as a slowdown in building, industry, and agriculture, most people felt secure that prosperity would continue. But a selling spree at the New York Stock exchange in October of 1929 ballooned into a full blown panic. The stock market crash that followed led to the falling of a series of economic dominoes, and the country slid inexorably into a depression.

Hoover, believing that while American policies were partially to blame, felt it was the economic hardships suffered by the Europeans which were keeping the Depression from being short-lived. Since his own experience had shown the success of volunteerism, Hoover extolled the country to take measures into their own hands, and he asked businesses to maintain wages and keep plants open, while asking labor to voluntarily spread the work that was available by taking part-time shifts.

Herbert Hoover pursued, on a much smaller scale, many of the ideas that Franklin Roosevelt would succeed with in his administration, including taking to the radio with speeches explaining his plans for recovery. In 1930 he asked Congress to appropriate money for public works projects and for the establishment of the Reconstruction Finance Corporation, which would lend federal money to local governments for works projects. The Home Loan Bank Act of 1932 helped people in danger of losing their homes to refinance their mortgages. In 1931 Hoover declared a one year moratorium on the payment of international debt.

Hoover's administration was beset by people seeking relief from what was quickly becoming the nation's worst depression. Though he was not responsible for the depression, his name became synonymous with it. Millions were unemployed and homeless, many camping outside major cities in collections of shacks known derisively as "Hoovervilles." They paraded around in pants with the pockets pulled out (to show their empty state), and called them "Hoover flags."

In 1932, 12,000 veterans descended on Washington to demand early payment of their benefits, in what became known as the Bonus March. When the Patman Bill, which advocated the early disbursement of veterans benefits, failed to pass, more than half the veterans accepted Congress' offer for fare money home. But about five thousand refused to leave, setting up their own "Hooverville" on the mall near the Capital. The army, commanded by Douglas MacArthur, was called in to disperse the veterans. After a skirmish which cost the lives of two of the Bonus Marchers, MacArthur's troops used tear gas and tanks to remove the men.

The Republicans renominated Hoover in 1932, but he was unable to run against the Depression, let alone New York Governor Franklin Roosevelt, who promised Americans a "New Deal." Hoover lost all but six states that November. He returned to his Palo Alto, California home where he worked on administrating the Hoover Library of War, Revolution, and Peace. He also completed several volumes of his memoirs. After Lou's death in 1944 Herbert moved to New York City.

As a sign of the stature that Hoover had maintained (despite the setbacks the country suffered during his term as President), in 1946 President Truman asked him to coordinate post-World War Two relief planning, and during the Truman and Eisenhower administrations he chaired a commission which studied ways to improve the efficiency of the executive branch of government. He died on October 20, 1964, at the age of 90.

Historical Landmarks

Birthplace of Herbert Clark Hoover
Herbert Hoover National Historic Site
Downey and Penn Streets
West Branch, Iowa

Herbert Hoover was born on August 10, 1874, in a small simple, 14-by-20 foot, cottage built by his father, Jesse in West Branch, Iowa, a predominantly Quaker community of about 350 persons. "Bertie," as he was then affectionately called, was the second of three children born to Jesse and Hulda Minthorn Hoover. Jesse, a blacksmith, erected a shop across the street. In 1879, after the arrival of his third child, he moved the family to a larger residence about a block to the south, which is no longer extant. Jesse's premature death the following year and that of his wife in 1884, orphaned their three children. Herbert at first went to live with an uncle, Allen Hoover, on his farm just northeast of West Branch. In 1885, however, he was sent to Newberg, Oregon, to reside with another uncle, Dr. Henry J. Minthorn.

The Hoover birthplace was a three-room frame cottage with small front and rear porches. The two main rooms were the bedroom, the birthplace of Hoover; and a combined living room, kitchen, and dining room. The third room, formed by an enclosed portion of the rear porch, served as a summer kitchen or spare sleeping room.

Herbert Hoover's birthplace was designated a National Historic Site in 1965 and is administered by the National Park Service. At the site are the restored birthplace cottage at its original location with as much of the original Hoover furniture as could be acquired, a replica of Jesse Hoover's blacksmith shop, the one-room West Branch elementary school Hoover may have attended which was moved here, and the Friends Meetinghouse where Herbert Hoover worshipped with his family. Also on the site are the Presidential Library-Museum, and the gravesite where Hoover and his wife are buried, which are described below.

Visitor's Information

A walking tour of the Hoover site begins at the National Park Service Visitor Center where interpretive displays capsulize the Hoover career and orient visitors to the late 19th century farm community into which Hoover was born in 1874, which they will be seeing.

Open daily, 8:00 a.m.-5:00 p.m.; closed January 1, Thanksgiving, December 25. Telephone (319) 643-2541.

Admission: adults, $1.00, under 17 and over 62, free.

The Visitor Center for the Herbert Hoover National Historic Site is on Parkside Drive and Main Street, 1/2-mile north from Exit 254 off I-80.

Herbert Hoover

Hoover-Minthorn House Museum
115 South River Street
Newberg, Oregon

The house was built in 1881 by Jesse Edwards, the Quaker founder of Newberg. Dr. Henry Minthorn (uncle and later foster-father of Herbert Hoover) bought it in 1884, the year he was appointed superintendent of Friends Pacific Academy (forerunner of today's George Fox College).

Shortly after Dr. and Mrs. Minthorn and their three children moved into their comfortable new home, the tragic death of their young son occurred. The grief and sense of loss Dr. Minthorn felt at losing his only boy prompted him to write to Iowa to his young nephew, Herbert Hoover, inviting him to come west and to become part of their family. Hoover was ten years old, and since the death of his parents had been living with other relatives.

Hoover accepted his uncle's invitation and joined the Minthorn family in Newberg. He was raised in the Quaker faith of his late parents, and attended Friends Pacific Academy. In 1889, Dr. Minthorn resigned his position and moved his family to Salem, including Hoover.

The Hoover-Minthorn House was purchased and restored with funds donated by friends of Hoover. The restored structure, the oldest house still standing in Newberg, contains original furnishings, photographs and mementoes of Hoover's boyhood years in the house.

Visitor's Information

Open March-November, Wednesday-Sunday, 1:00 p.m.-4:00 p.m.; December and February, Saturday-Sunday, 1:00 p.m.-4:00 p.m.; closed January and holidays. Telephone: (503) 538-6629.

Admission: adults, $1.50; over 65, $1.00; students, $.50.

Herbert Hoover

The Museum is located in Newberg, 23 miles southwest of Portland. Take I-5 south from Portland to State Route 99W; follow it into Newberg and at River Street turn left and proceed to house.

Hoover Home
623 Mirada Avenue
Palo Alto, California

After World War I, Hoover returned to California and he and his wife, Lou Henry Hoover, who he had met when they both were students at Stanford University, decided to build a house. Mrs. Hoover had long dreamed of having a home on a hill on the Stanford campus. Plans for the house started in 1918 but it was not until 1920 that they could move in. Mrs. Hoover had selected the site and worked with the architect to help design the two-story mission style house. Because they loved fireplaces with fires in them, almost every main room in the house had a fireplace including the living room terrace and the front entrance hall. However, Hoover's involvement with war relief work, his subsequent service as Secretary of Commerce, and his later becoming president gave him little time to enjoy his new home. At the end of his presidency he and his wife spent some time in Palo Alto but in 1934 moved to a suite in the Waldorf Towers in New York City where they remained for the rest of their lives. When Mrs. Hoover died in 1944, the Palo Alto house was given to Stanford University for use as the official residence of its president.

Visitor's Information

The house is a private residence and visiting is not permitted.

Herbert Hoover Presidential Library and Museum
Parkside Drive
West Branch, Iowa

The Library serves as a research center, preserving and making available to researchers the historical materials of Herbert Hoover and his times. The collection contains 5 million documents and nearly 20,000 books plus photographs, film, microfilm and sound recordings.

The Museum illustrates the life and times of Herbert Hoover from 1874 to 1964. Included are Hoover's accomplishments as a mining engineer followed by fifty years of public service as administrator of food relief programs during both World Wars, Secretary of Commerce and President of the United States. New exhibits will enable visitors to walk through recreations of Mr. Hoover's Waldorf Towers hotel suite, his Camp Rapidan fishing retreat, and a World War I era Belgian relief warehouse. Many other interactive exhibits convey the life story of America's 31st president.

Visitor's Information

Open daily, 9:00 a.m.-5:00 p.m.; closed January 1, Thanksgiving, December 25. Telephone: (319) 643-5301

Admission: Adults, $1.00; under 15, free.

The Library-Museum is located on the grounds of the Herbert Hoover National Historic Site. It is 1/2 mile north from Exit 254 off I-80.

George Fox College
Newberg, Oregon

Herbert Hoover, the only president to have lived in Oregon, attended Pacific Academy, the forerunner of George Fox College.

The Herbert Hoover Academic Building, named after Hoover, contains a variety of Hoover memorabilia in display cases on both levels. A brass sculpture is the form of a profile of the former president is on the west wall of the Hoover Building. It is designed to be best viewed from a distance and is clearly visible as Hoover's portrait a block away. A large bronze plaque in Hoover's honor, dedicated in 1930, is located in Wood-Mar Hall, main floor.

Herbert Hoover

Visitor's Information

Open weekdays, 8:00 a.m.-5:00 p.m.; closed holidays.   Telephone: (503) 538-8383

Admission: free.

Newberg is 23 miles southwest of Portland. Take I-5 south from Portland to State Route 99W which goes into Newberg.

Hoover Institution on War, Revolution, and Peace
Hoover Tower
Stanford University
Palo Alto, California

The Hoover Institution, an independent institution within the frame of Stanford University, was founded in 1919 by Herbert Hoover, who searched Europe during World War I for documents that today form the basis for the research center's library.

The 280-foot Hoover Tower, the first building erected for the Institution's exclusive use, was dedicated in 1941.

Within the Hoover Tower complex, which contains the Herbert Hoover Memorial Building, the Lou Henry Hoover Building and an Exhibit Pavilion, are exhibits devoted to each of the Hoovers. They highlight Hoover's fifty years of international and national public service and include displays of memorabilia which range from Hoover's fishing gear to a Peruvian funeral plaque from the pre-Inca period (600-1000 A.D.) that was given to President-elect Hoover in 1928 while he was on a "good neighbor" tour of Latin America.

The Lou Henry Hoover exhibits are designed to explain the lifelong interests she shared with her husband; a commitment to scholarship, voluntarianism, and humanitarian work. They also feature her special collections of Chinese porcelain, Belgian lace, and silver from many countries.

Herbert Hoover

Visitor's Information

Open Monday-Friday, 11:00 a.m.-4:00 p.m. Telephone (415) 723-2053.

Admission: free. (There is a charge for the observation deck at the top of the Hoover Tower: Adults, $1.00; senior citizens and under 13, $.50; families, $2.50.)

Palo Alto is 32 miles south of San Francisco.

Burial Site
Herbert Hoover National Historic Site
Parkside Drive and Main Street
West Branch, Iowa

Herbert Hoover died at age 90 in his suite at the Waldorf Towers on October 20, 1964. His flag-draped coffin was carried with full military honors to Washington, D.C., to lie in state in the Capitol rotunda. On October 25, 80,000 people assembled in West Branch to observe the burial ceremony in the Herbert Hoover National Historic Site on a hillside overlooking his birthplace. A few days later the body of Mrs. Lou Hoover, who died in New York in 1944, was reinterred here. Landscaping provides a circular setting for the flat white marble gravestones with a view down the valley to the birthplace.

Visitor's Information

The gravesite is about 1/4 mile southwest of the birthplace cabin.

Open daily 8:00 a.m.-5:00 p.m.; closed January 1, Thanksgiving, December 25. Telephone: (319) 643-2541.

Admission: free.

The visitor center for the Hoover National Historic Site is on Parkside Drive and Main Street, 1/2 mile north from Exit 254 off I-80.

Franklin Delano Roosevelt, 32nd President, 1933-1945

Home of Franklin D. Roosevelt

Franklin D. Roosevelt's Campobello Island Cottage

Little White House

Burial Site of Franklin D. Roosevelt and wife

Franklin Delano Roosevelt

Thirty-Second President
1933 - 1945
Democrat

Franklin Delano Roosevelt was born to a wealthy family on January 30, 1882 in Hyde Park, New York. As befits a young man of his class, Franklin traveled and studied in Europe and then attended Groton. He earned his B.A. in History at Harvard in only three years, graduating with the class of 1904.

While attending Harvard, Franklin met a distant cousin named Anna Eleanor Roosevelt, and a year after graduation they were married. Eleanor had a genuine desire for social reform, and took to public service with the same intensity as Franklin. She pursued the cause of international peace, becoming one of the most admired women of the twentieth century.

After Harvard Franklin Roosevelt attended Columbia University Law School. He was admitted to the bar in 1907, and soon entered politics, winning a seat in the New York State Senate as a Democrat from a highly Republican district. He was re-elected in 1912. After leading the fight for Woodrow Wilson's nomination in 1912, Roosevelt was rewarded with the post of Assistant Secretary of the Navy. In 1920 he was nominated by the Democratic Party as James Cox's running mate, but was beaten by the Republican team of Harding and Coolidge. Given the sentiment towards Wilson at the time, the defeat was not considered politically serious. He returned to Hyde Park and practiced law.

Although not as rugged as his cousin Theodore, Franklin loved the outdoors, especially swimming. While vacationing at the family's home at Campobello Island in 1921, he was stricken with infantile paralysis, which left his legs crippled. He fought back to win his mobility, winning a partial victory. From that point on he could walk only with heavy metal braces. However, this handicap did not prevent him from winning the Governorship of New York in 1928 and 1930. From there, he launched himself into the fight for the presidency in 1932.

Nominated by the Democrats on the first ballot, Franklin Roosevelt's air of assurance and his promises to the nation for a "New Deal" swept him into office. Once there, he surrounded himself with Cabinet members of the highest caliber to help him bring the country out of what had become its worst depression. Among them was the first woman,

Francis Perkins, who assumed control of the Labor Department. For other advisors, Roosevelt eschewed, for the most part, the business leaders that Harding, Coolidge, and Hoover had relied on, choosing instead many academicians, who were dubbed the "Brain Trust."

The day after his inauguration on March 4th Roosevelt, in order to prevent runs on banks, declared a bank holiday which closed them all until confidence could be restored. Four days later Congress was called into special session, at which time they passed the Emergency Banking Act which set out to stabilize the banking system. This was the first act passed during what came to be known as the "Hundred Days," a whirlwind of legislation designed to start the country on the road to recovery. Roosevelt, like his predecessor, took to the radio (in what he called his "fireside chats") to explain his policies to the nation.

Government salaries, budgets of government agencies, and veterans benefits were reduced. The powers of the Federal Reserve Board were increased and the Federal Insurance Deposit Corporation, which guaranteed individual bank accounts, was established. Roosevelt carried out his campaign promise to repeal Prohibition, and in December of 1933 the Twenty-first Amendment was ratified, making the production and sale of alcohol legal again.

The threat of violence in the farm belt was averted with the passage of the Agricultural Adjustment Act in May of 1933. Its aim was to restore the buying power of the farmer to higher levels. The Farm Credit Administration was also created around this time to help farmers refinance at lower interest rates. Other bills helped the farmer's plight, but it was not until the drought of 1934-1935 created such horrific "dust bowl" conditions, forcing a great number of farmers to quit, that a measure of parity was achieved.

Meanwhile, agencies were being created which provided federally funded jobs so the unemployed could survive, maintain their dignity, and help to improve America's infrastructure. The Civilian Conservation Corps (CCC) employed young men in the forests and parks. The Federal Emergency Relief Administration (FERA) gave money for food, clothing, and shelter to those families unable to provide for themselves. The Civilian Works Administration (CWA) would provide work relief to over four million Americans. The Public Works Administration (PWA) built large public structures such as buildings and waterworks, using private firms.

Two of Roosevelt's agencies created controversy. The National Recovery Act (NRA), passed in June of 1933, prepared and enforced codes of fair competition for businesses and industries. Businesses that cooperated with the Act and agreed to abide by their industries standards were awarded a blue eagle, which was the NRA's symbol. Although

95% of American businesses were awarded the blue eagle, many corporations found loopholes around collective bargaining and wage agreements, leaving labor leaders wary of the New Deal. One of the NRA's accomplishments was that it ended child labor and helped industry increase production.

The Tennessee Valley Authority (TVA) built hydro-electric plants which produced electricity for a seven state region, managed flood control and inland navigation of its rivers, and a host of other health and recreational projects. The Hoover and Grand Coulee Dam projects were also begun.

A second round of programs created by Roosevelt in 1935 was dubbed the Second New Deal. It consisted of more far-reaching programs intended to bring the country out of the still devastating depression, such as the Social Security Act of 1935 which provided, among other things, a federal pension for people over the age of 65. Still in effect today, the Social Security system is one of the most far reaching and lasting programs from the Roosevelt years. Others were the National Labor Relations Board (NLRB) which provided stronger guarantees for collective bargaining by labor, and the Public Utility Holding Company Act, which gave the government the power to put the financial practices of utilities under federal control. The Rural Electrification Administration (REA) furnished electricity to rural areas not served by private utilities.

The election of 1936, in which Franklin Roosevelt beat Kansan Alfred Landon, was notable for several reasons. The 523 to 8 electoral vote count was the most lopsided since 1820. And 1936 was the first time a scientific sampling of voters by the Gallup organization correctly predicted the outcome of the election. (A weekly magazine was less fortunate. They had predicted a Landon victory, and after the election went out of business because of their miscalculation.)

The Supreme Court had declared many parts of the New Deal unconstitutional, prompting Roosevelt to brand them "nine old men." Unable to nominate judges until one of the current members died or quit, in 1937 the President used his influence in Congress to have a law sponsored which would permit him to appoint up to six additional justices if any over seventy chose not to retire. The outrage against Roosevelt's attempt to "pack" the court came from all parts of the political spectrum, resulting in the only serious defeat of his administration, when the bill died in committee a year later.

The last piece of New Deal legislation passed in 1938. The Fair Labor Standards Act provided a minimum wage of 40 cents per hour and a forty hour week, no child labor under 16, and time and a half for overtime.

Franklin Roosevelt's administration was faced with immense domestic challenges during his first two terms. But there were several international situations that would ultimately become his greatest tests, and lead him to the decision to run for an unprecedented third term.

In the Western Hemisphere Roosevelt pursued what he called a "Good Neighbor" policy. To allow him to concentrate on domestic problems, he withdrew the United States from Haiti and Nicaragua, and terminated the customs receivership in the Dominican Republic. He also abrogated the Platt Agreement when trouble broke out in Cuba. In other regions, Roosevelt signed the Tydings-McDuffie Act which granted the Philippines independence over a ten year period. He also recognized Russia in 1933.

Roosevelt sought solidarity among the nations of North and South America. At the Buenos Aires Conference in 1936 and the Lima Conference in 1938 the nations of the hemisphere agreed to the principle of collective security. The 1940 Act of Havana declared that an act of aggression against one country would be an act against them all.

The reason for these calls for solidarity was the danger posed by militaristic Japan, Italy, and Germany during the thirties. Congress, intent on keeping America out of its second war in as many generations, passed a series of neutrality laws. Here Roosevelt ran headlong against Congress, and as far back as 1934 sought an increase in the size of the U.S. Navy. Congress did not approve such a measure until 1938. In 1937 Roosevelt delivered his "Quarantine Speech," in which he condemned the aggressor nations and called for an international quarantine against them.

When war finally broke out in September of 1939 Roosevelt sided with the British and their allies. He favored delivering all possible American aid short of war, and after calling Congress into session, secured a loosening of the neutrality laws. The arms embargo was replaced with a cash and carry policy which permitted sales to all the belligerents. (In reality it helped the allies). Nazi victories in Europe began to swing the tide in favor of preparedness, and in 1940 a Selective Service Act was passed which called for the registration of all men 21 to 35 years of age. The Office of Production Management was created to mobilize industry for war.

As FDR mulled over the field of possible candidates for President in 1940, he was concerned that none of them had a strong enough commitment to the allies, or that any would be able to prepare the country for war. He therefore sought and was granted nomination for a third term in 1940, breaking the tradition held by every two term president since Washington. To increase bi-partisan support he even placed two Republicans in his Cabinet. He was opposed by Republican Wendell Wilkie, who was supported by anti-New Dealers and Isolationists, as well as those citizens who felt that two terms was enough for any man.

Roosevelt prevailed, and soon after the election requested 7 billion dollars from Congress for the production of war materials. Opposition to American involvement in the war was still strong, even as late as 1940, forcing Roosevelt to be more clever in his attempts to help the British. One such ploy was the Lend-Lease plan, in which Britain was "lent" eight naval bases and fifty destroyers left over from World War One. After the June 1941 invasion of Russia, Roosevelt had lend-lease extended to the Soviet Union, even though the Soviets had been a German ally when the war began. An August meeting with British Prime Minister Winston Churchill solidified American cooperation in the Allied effort when they made a joint statement called the Atlantic Charter. By late 1941 Roosevelt knew he had taken America as far as it would willingly go into the conflict.

On December 7, 1941, the Japanese attacked the American naval base at Pearl Harbor, Hawaii. The next day, Franklin Roosevelt, in a speech to a joint session of Congress, declared the 7th of December as a "date that will live in infamy," and asked Congress for a declaration of war, which he got with only one dissenting vote.

Roosevelt's next task was to mobilize the country for the war. Taxes were increased and, under the auspices of the War Powers Act, Roosevelt was given the power to reorganize the federal government as well as regulate business and travel in the country. The War Production Board directed industry, the War Labor Board regulated wages and saw to labor relations, the War Manpower Commission sent workers to areas they were needed most, and the Office of Defense Transportation directed the movement of troops and supplies, and the Office of Price Administration set prices and rationed certain goods.

Running the country, directing the war effort, and traveling abroad to meet with the Allies during the war took its toll on the President, but despite his exhaustion he accepted the Democrat's call to run for a fourth term. Roosevelt would change Vice-Presidents, however, replacing Henry Wallace with Harry S. Truman of Missouri. Their opposition, led by Thomas Dewey of New York, failed to wrest back the White House, as the country heeded the campaign calls "Don't change horses in mid-stream," and "Let Roosevelt finish the job!"

In February of 1945, with the war near an end and Allied victory assured, Roosevelt met with Joseph Stalin and Winston Churchill to make preparations for the world after the war. These included the partitioning of Germany and the disposition of territory in Eastern Europe. During this time he had also led the fight for a strong United Nations after the war.

Only three months after his fourth term began, Franklin Roosevelt passed away at his Warm Springs, Georgia home. The outpouring of grief for the President was tremendous. April 12, 1945, remains one of those days that, like the attack on Pearl Harbor, John Kennedy's assassination, and the Challenger accident, remain indelibly fixed in the mind of every American alive at the time. He was buried, according to his wishes, on the grounds of his Hyde Park home.

Historical Landmarks

Birthplace of Franklin D. Roosevelt
U.S. Route 9
Hyde Park, New York

The 32nd President of the United States was born in this home overlooking the Hudson River on January 30, 1882. He was the only child of James and Sara Roosevelt. James Roosevelt was a wealthy Vice-President of the Delaware and Hudson Railway. His wife was a member of the wealthy Delano family. When Franklin was born his mother was 28 years old and his father was 54.

Franklin Roosevelt spent much of his time here. This is where he lived as a toddler, as a youngster and as a sheltered child who was also taught perseverance and responsibility. This is where he brought his bride, Eleanor, in 1905, and where they raised their five children.

The central part of the building, the oldest section, dates to the early 1800's. It was a clapboard framehouse when purchased in 1867 by James Roosevelt.

The main house has undergone many renovations and additions with the passage of years. In 1915-16, it assumed its present form. The central part, its clapboards removed, was covered with stucco and fronted by a porch with a sweeping balustrade and a small colonnaded portico. On each end, a two-story wing was added, giving the whole structure an H-shape. As finished in 1916, the residence consisted of 35 rooms and 9 baths.

During Roosevelt's presidential years the house served as a "summer White House" and was the scene of several conferences and events of national and international significance.

The house was given to the Federal government by Roosevelt and his mother and it was designated a National Historic Site in 1944 and is administered by the National Park Service. It was opened to the public after Roosevelt's death, and little in the house has been changed since that time. Most of the furnishings date from the 1850's through the 1920's and only a few items postdate 1930. Portraits include those of various family members, and many of the paintings reflect Roosevelt's nautical interest.

Franklin Delano Roosevelt

Visitor's Information

Open daily, 9:00 a.m.-5:00 p.m.; closed Tuesdays and Wednesdays, November-March; and January 1, Thanksgiving, and December 25. Telephone: (914) 229-9115.

Admission: $4.00 (includes admission to Roosevelt Museum); under 16 and over 62, free.

The Franklin D. Roosevelt National Historic Site is on the New York-Albany Post Road (U.S. 9), 2 miles south of Hyde Park and 4 miles north of Poughkeepsie. From New York City, you can reach the site over the Henry Hudson Parkway. the Saw Mill River Parkway, and the Taconic State Parkway. Approaches from the west side of the Hudson River are by the Mid-Hudson Bridge at Poughkeepsie, the Rip Van Winkle Bridge at Catskill, or the Kingston-Rhinecliff Bridge at Kingston.

Roosevelt Campobello International Park
Campobello Island
New Brunswick, Canada

This 2,800-acre park is a joint memorial by Canada and the United States, and a symbol of the close relationship between the two countries.

In Franklin Roosevelt's affections, Campobello Island ranked second only to Hyde Park. From 1883, when he was one year old, until he was stricken by polio in 1921, he spent most of his summers on this rugged and beautiful island on Passamaquoddy Bay where a group of New York and Boston entrepreneurs had purchased a large section of land and promoted it as a summer resort for wealthy Americans.

James Roosevelt, Franklin's father, purchased four acres and a partially completed house in 1883. By the summer of 1885 this house was completed and the Roosevelt's, James, Sara Delano and young Franklin became summer residents. The site of that house, known in later years as "Granny's Cottage," was just north of the present Roosevelt Cottage, which Sara purchased in 1910, and later gave to Franklin and Eleanor.

Franklin Delano Roosevelt

It was at Campobello, in 1921, when he was 39 years old, that Roosevelt was crippled by an attack of polio and he did not return to the island until 1933, while serving his first term as President.

In the Roosevelt Cottage, visitors can view the room used by President Roosevelt during his 1933 visit, his bedroom, Mrs. Roosevelt's writing room, the living room, dining room, kitchen, laundry, nursery and family bedrooms, including the room where Franklin D. Roosevelt, Jr. was born. Most of the furnishings were used by the Roosevelt family and Roosevelt's den contains memorabilia from his childhood and the years of his presidency.

Visitor's Information

The Park's Reception Centre provides an introduction to the Park. Two films are shown in the Centre. "Beloved Island" is a portrait of the island and its impact on Franklin Roosevelt. "Campobello-The Outer Island" is an interpretation of the natural areas of the island and its shores.

Open daily, late May to mid-October, 9:00 a.m.-5:00 p.m., Eastern Daylight Time. Telephone: (506) 752-2922.

Admission: Free.

The principal access to Campobello is The Franklin D. Roosevelt Memorial Bridge at Lubec, Maine. Follow Maine Route 1 to Route 189 to Lubec and cross Roosevelt Memorial Bridge to New Brunswick Route 774. The Park is about 1 1/2 miles from Canadian Customs.

Little White House State Historic Site
State Route 85W
Warm Springs, Georgia

Roosevelt first came to Warm Springs in 1924 to test its pools as an aid in recovery from the infantile paralysis which struck him in 1921. Finding exercise in the warm buoyant water beneficial, he built a modest home on a site he selected on the slopes of Pine

Mountain. It has six rooms, three bedrooms, a combination living and dining room, the entry and kitchen.

The Little White House is substantially as it was when Roosevelt died there in 1945. Many items on display reflect his interests: these include his collection of ship models denoting his great love of the sea; Fala, his dog is remembered by a chain still hanging in a closet, and a riding quirt marks his enthusiasm for horseback riding. The famous unfinished portrait which was being painted of the President by Elizabeth Schoumatoff when he was fatally stricken is in the house. In the garage is Roosevelt's 1938 Ford convertible, fitted with hand controls which enabled him to drive it alone.

The Walk of the States, featuring stones and flags from each of the states, flank the ornamental walkway to the Franklin D. Roosevelt Museum. Here visitors learn about his life and career. A film of Roosevelt in Georgia, "A Warm Springs Memoir of Franklin D. Roosevelt" depicts scenes of his activities in and around Warm Springs.

Visitor's Information

Open daily, 9:00 a.m.-5:00 p.m.; until 6:00 p.m. June-August; closed Thanksgiving and December 25. Telephone: (404) 655-3511.

Admission: adults, $3.00, ages 6-12. $1.50.

The Little White House is located 70 miles south of Atlanta, on State Route 85W one-quarter mile south of the Warm Springs traffic light.in Warm Springs, Georgia.

The Franklin D. Roosevelt Library and Museum
U.S. Route 9
Hyde Park, New York

The Franklin D. Roosevelt Library, the first of the Presidential Libraries, represented a departure in American archival history. From the earliest days of the Republic the papers of American Presidents were considered their personal property and were taken with them upon retirement. As a result, valuable records were lost or destroyed. Roosevelt made known his intent to break with this precedent. A joint resolution of Congress followed in 1939 which established Presidential Libraries as part of the National Archives.

The research collections in the Roosevelt Library are made up of manuscripts and other documents (more than 16,000,000 pages), the most important of which are the papers bequeathed by FDR. They reflect his entire life, as well as an important part of the history of our time. Eleanor Roosevelt's papers are also housed in the Library together with those of many of the contemporaries and associates of both the President and Mrs. Roosevelt. In addition, there are nearly 40,000 books, including the President's personal library of 15,000 volumes; a large collection of photographs and other audiovisual material; and the President's private collections on the U.S. Navy and on the history of Dutchess County and the Hudson Valley.

The museum contains extensive displays on the life and career of FDR, including photographs; an extensive array of objects that he used personally or received as gifts; selected items from his collection on the U.S. Navy; and many of his family letters, speeches, state documents, and official correspondence. Among these are the President's statement on the significance and purposes of the Social Security Bill when he signed it into law on August 14, 1935; his message to Congress of December 8, 1941, calling for a Declaration of War on Japan; and the letter from Einstein that led to the development of the atomic bomb.

Visitor's Information

Open daily 9:00 a.m.-5:00 p.m.; closed January 1, Thanksgiving, December 25. Telephone: (914) 229-8114.

Admission: Roosevelt Museum and Home, $4.00; under 16 and over 62, free.

The Franklin D. Roosevelt Library and Museum is located on the grounds of the FDR National Historic Site (Birthplace/Home). See above for travel directions.

Burial Site
Franklin D. Roosevelt National Historic Site
U.S. Route 9
Hyde Park, New York

On March 29, 1945, President Roosevelt left for a rest at Warm Springs. On April 12, he was working at his desk while an artist, Elizabeth Schoumatoff, painted his portrait. Suddenly he fell over in his chair and he whispered, "I have a terrific headache." These were Roosevelt's last words and he died a few hours later of a cerebral hemorrhage

The grounds of his birthplace house, in the family rose garden northeast of his home, was chosen by Roosevelt as his burial place. Here, on April 15,1945, he was laid to rest. Seventeen years later, Mrs. Roosevelt was buried beside him on November 10, 1962. A rose garden was traditional with the family, for the surname Roosevelt was adopted from the Dutch "field of roses" in the ancestral land, and perpetuated in the family coat of arms: Three roses on a shield, surmounted by a casque and three feathers.

A white marble tombstone, with a slight touch of color highlighting its natural beauty, stands immediately north of the grave. Known as "Imperial Danby," it is from the quarry in Vermont that produced the marble for the Thomas Jefferson Memorial in Washington. President Roosevelt drew up the plans for the tombstone, which is 8 feet long, 4 feet wide, and 3 feet high.

Visitor's Information

The grave is located on the grounds of the Franklin D. Roosevelt National Historic Site (Birthplace/Home). There is no charge to view the burial site. See above for visiting days and travel directions.

Harry S. Truman, 33rd President, 1945-1953

Birthplace of Harry S. Truman

Harry S. Truman's Home and Summer White House during his presidency

Harry S. Truman Library

Burial Site of Harry S. Truman and wife

Harry S. Truman

Thirty-Third President
1945 - 1953
Democrat

Harry S. Truman was born on May 8, 1884 in Lamar, Missouri. His middle name is simply S, due to a family squabble over which Truman ancestor, Solomon or Shippe, would be honored. The Truman family moved several times when Harry was a boy, finally settling in Independence when he was five. When his father was financially ruined while trading in grain futures, Harry was forced to give up his plans for college, and he went to work as a bank clerk, an usher at a movie house, and a piano player, before settling in for twelve years as a hired hand on his grandfather's farm.

When the first World War broke out, Harry helped recruit a regiment, and he was given the rank of first lieutenant. When he arrived in France he was placed in command of a battery, leading his men into several battles with distinction. He returned to Independence a major, and finally married Elizabeth (Bess) Wallace, a childhood friend to whom he had been engaged before the war.

The Trumans opened a haberdashery in Kansas City, but it failed after two years. Harry returned to school, studied law, and entered politics. Although associated with "Boss" Prendergast of Kansas City, Harry was honest in the pursuit of his duties as overseer of county highways, and was elected county Judge in 1922 while still studying the law. Four years later he was elected presiding judge. In 1934 Truman won election to the United States Senate for the first of two terms. While in the Senate he gained fame for his work on the "Truman Committee," which was created to check waste in the Defense Department. (By some estimates he helped save the government almost three billion dollars.) The now nationally respected Truman was placed on the 1944 Democratic Ticket with Franklin Roosevelt, which won in November.

On April 12, 1945 President Roosevelt, who had been in declining health, passed away while on a trip to Warm Springs, Georgia. "Last night," Truman said the next day, "the moon, the stars, and all the planets fell on me."

On May 7, 1945, after the German army surrendered, the Allies began concentrating on the defeat of Japan. Informed of the plans for the atom bomb only after Roosevelt died, Truman made the decision to use the Atomic bomb on Japan to shorten the war. It was a decision that he would have to defend for the rest of his life, but one from which he never wavered. As had been hoped, the bomb brought a quick end to the Pacific war when Japan surrendered unconditionally on August 15, 1945.

Truman was faced with several problems now that the war was over. The Russians systematically began installing pro-Communist governments in the Eastern European countries where they still had troops. Short of war, which Truman rejected, there was nothing the Allies could do to stop them. He was able to make his stand, however, when the Soviet Union attempted a take-over of Berlin. A year-long coordinated Allied effort to supply the city, known as the Berlin Airlift, kept the Allied sections of the city out of Russian hands.

Truman found there were other ways he could fight what he perceived as a worldwide Communist threat, such as his appropriation of $400 million worth of economic aid for Greece and Turkey, both of which were fighting Communism from within. He declared that it was the United States' obligation to support countries in such a struggle. This became known as the Truman Doctrine.

It was after the announcement of the Truman Doctrine that Secretary of State George Marshall announced his plan for recovery in Europe. The Marshall Plan funds, which totalled in the billions, not only provided desperately needed relief to millions of people, but also headed off Communist advances for the loyalties of some countries. Truman's Four Point Program, also begun in 1949, sent money to underdeveloped countries for scientific and technical aid.

One of the main points of Roosevelt's plan for the world after the war was the establishment of a strong United Nations. United States involvement under Truman helped make the U.N. a viable means for settling world problems. In 1949 America entered into its first military alliance during peacetime since the Revolution when it joined the North Atlantic Treaty Organization (NATO), which was made up of countries committed to opposing Russian advances on the European continent.

In late June of 1950 the North Koreans, supported heavily by the Russians, invaded South Korea. The United Nations Security Council met and declared that the North Koreans were the aggressors. Truman decided to commit U.S. troops in support of the U.N. Resolution, and World War Two hero General Douglas MacArthur was called upon to lead the effort. As the war dragged on a feud developed between MacArthur and Truman over the goals of the war (MacArthur wanted permission to take the war into China and to use the atomic bomb if he felt it necessary). Citing the general's public insubordination, Truman relieved him of his command.

Domestically, Truman's years in office were equally difficult. After the war, prices that had been kept low by the Office of Price Administration rose after the agency's demise, causing a period of inflation in 1946. Labor began striking to secure higher wages and better benefits, which caused a further spiraling of prices. When the United Coal Miners struck and created a coal shortage, Truman seized the mines. The President also took over the railroads when its workers went off the job. Both strikes were settled after Truman threatened to draft all the workers for striking against the government. Truman later regained some of his lost support from labor when he vetoed the Taft-Hartley Act in 1947, although the Republican Congress (elected in 1946) was able to override his veto.

Harry Truman began the slow establishment of civil rights in America when he appointed a commission to study the issue in 1946. Their report, "To Secure These Rights," was a blueprint for solving many of the problems encountered by black Americans. Though Trumans's attempts at enacting these suggestions were voted down by Congress, he was successful in desegregating the armed forces and strengthening the Civil Rights section of the Justice Department.

In 1947, the Republican Congress passed the 22nd Amendment (which was ratified in 1951) which limited the President to two elected terms. Truman's comment was that the Republicans had secured Franklin Delano Roosevelt's place in history as the only President to serve more than two terms.

With the liberals angry over Truman's hard line against the Russians and the conservative Southerners angry over his Civil Rights stance, Truman faced a 1948 re-election battle not only from the Republicans but also from two candidates who had bolted from his own party. Despite polls and political pundits who declared that "Truman is a gone goose", Truman embarked on a nationwide whistle-stop campaign to take his message to the people. The "experts" who predicted a Truman defeat had clearly forgotten the people who had been helped by Truman's programs such as laborers, farmers, and minorities. He beat his major opponent, Republican Thomas Dewey, by a wide margin. The photograph of him holding up a newspaper declaring Dewey the winner is a classic.

Truman's second term was marked by a series of domestic programs that came to be known as the Fair Deal. But although he was able to secure a housing bill in 1949 and raise the minimum wage, most of his other programs, including civil rights legislation, were killed by the coalition of Southern Democrats and Northern Republicans.

Under Truman, the atomic bomb became not just a weapon but a way of life. After creating the Atomic Energy Commission in 1947 to regulate the new industry, he made an attempt to stop the spread of nuclear weapons in the world. When the Russians rejected the plan, it was dropped by the rest of the members of the U.N.

The fear of Communism in the United States began to grow during Truman's terms in office. He established new procedures for weeding out Communists from the government which subjected applicants to loyalty investigations. But Truman also believed there were limits to what the government could do. In September 1950, after the Hiss Investigation, the Rosenberg Spy Case, and other Cold War incidents, Congress passed strict legislation (called the McCarren Internal Security Act) to monitor and control Communists in the United States. Truman vetoed the bill, although it was overridden.

Truman's last years in office were fraught with many problems. The war in Korea had dragged on for two years with no results, and the country was suffering from another bout with inflation. During 1951 some of Truman's advisors and appointees were involved in scandals which grabbed headlines. A freezer given to military aide Harry Vaughn by a grateful friend created a stir, and was followed by a tax-fixing scandal in the Revenue Department, and another in the Reconstruction Finance Corporation. By 1952, Truman, who was personally untouched by the scandals, had had enough of Washington and decided not to run for another term.

Harry Truman retired to his home in Independence, Missouri, where the former President was a familiar sight around the small town. He wrote his autobiography, which was titled *Mr. Citizen*, and helped establish, fund, and run the Harry S. Truman Library in Independence. Outspoken to the end, Harry Truman died on December 26, 1972 at the age of 88 in Kansas City, Missouri.

Historical Landmarks

Birthplace of Harry S. Truman
1009 Truman Avenue
Lamar, Missouri

The corner lot, 80 by 150 feet, where the birthplace is located, was purchased by a Simon Blethrode in October, 1880 for $78.20. When a house was built on the property, he sold it to John Anderson Truman, Harry Truman's father, for $685.00 on November 14, 1882. After John Truman had married Martha Ellen Young in 1881, they set off on their own and moved to Lamar where John continued farming and dealing in livestock. He conducted his livestock business from a lot located diagonally across the street from his house which he purchased in March, 1883 for $200.

Harry S. Truman

The small white frame house, 20 by 28 feet, has 6 rooms, 4 downstairs and two rooms upstairs. The house had no electricity, basement, running water, storage attic, clothes closets or bathroom. Beside the house is a woodshed, or smoke house, and the hand-dug 36 foot deep cistern. An outdoor toilet is at the rear.

Harry Truman was born in the downstairs southwest bedroom, May 8, 1884. That bedroom measures only 6 feet 6 inches by 10 feet 9 inches. On the day Harry was born, his father proudly planted an Austrian pine tree at the corner of the house and nailed a mule shoe over the front door to celebrate his first child's birth.

Harry was named for his uncle, Harrison Young. He was given the middle initial "S" but no middle name so that both grandfathers, Solomon Young and Anderson Shippe Truman, could claim that he was named for them.

When Harry was 10 months old the Truman family sold the home and stock lot across the street, March 3, 1885, for $1600 and moved to Harrisonville, Missouri.

The United Auto Workers of America bought the house for $6,000 in 1957 and donated it to the state. The house has been restored and redecorated with furnishings from the period of the Trumans' occupancy. It is now a State Historic Site operated and maintained by the Division of Parks and Recreation, State of Missouri.

Visitor's Information

When Truman was born, the population of Lamar was 800 and the house had no number on a street without a name. The street was later named Truman Avenue.

Open Monday-Saturday, 10:00 a.m.-4:00 p.m.; Sunday, noon-4:00 p.m.; closed January 1, Easter, Thanksgiving, December 25. Telephone: (417) 334-2279.

Admission: Free.

Harry S. Truman Birthplace State Historic Site is located two miles east of U.S. 71, one block off Highway 160 in Lamar, Benton County, Missouri.

Harry S. Truman

Truman's Boyhood Home
909 West Waldo Street
Independence, Missouri

This house, built about 1886, was bought by John and Martha Truman in 1895, when Harry was eleven years old. They lived there for seven years until financial difficulties forced them to sell the house in 1902. They eventually moved in with Martha's father, Solomon Young, on his 600-acre farm at Grandview, a suburb of Kansas City.

Visitor's Information

Later additions to the house have greatly altered the appearance of the house. It is now a private residence and visiting is not permitted.

Truman Farm Home
12301 Blue Ridge Boulevard
Grandview, Missouri

The home, built in 1894, is in the northwest part of Grandview. Harry left his job at a bank in Independence, to help his parents run the family's farm in Grandview, from 1906 to 1917. During the ten years before his World War I duty, Truman farmed the six hundred acres and tended to livestock while serving as a soldier, Mason, postmaster and school board member in the Grandview area.

The two-story white frame house has been authentically restored using both original furnishings and appropriate period pieces from the early 1900's. The chicken coop, smokehouse, outhouse and garage are also open to visitors.

Visitor's Information

Open, Friday-Sunday, April 15-November 15, 9:00 a.m.-5:00 p.m. Telephone: (816) 881-4431.

Admission: adults, $2.00, ages 5-13 and over 62, $1.00.

Grandview is nineteen miles south of Independence. The Truman Farm Home can be reached by taking I-435 south to 71 Highway south, and exit at Blue Ridge Boulevard in Grandview.

Harry S. Truman National Historic Site
219 North Delaware Street
Independence, Missouri

This is the house in which President and Mrs. Truman lived from their marriage in 1919 until their deaths, and where their daughter, Mary Margaret, was born. When Truman married Elizabeth (Bess) Virginia Wallace, they moved into a second floor bedroom of her maternal grandparents' home, which they shared with Bess' mother, Madge Gates Wallace, and Grandmother Gates. In 1924, Madge Gates acquired title to the house and after her death in 1952, it became the property of the Trumans. After President Truman's death in 1972, his widow kept the house as it was during his lifetime. Ten years later when she died, her will bequeathed the house to the nation.

The neighborhood surrounding the house is the Harry S. Truman National Historic Landmark District. It is largely unchanged from the time when the ex-President strolled its sidewalks each day. The Truman house is one of the earliest and architecturally most interesting buildings in the historic district.

The frame house, asymmetrical in design and combining several mid-19th century architecturally styles, is 2 1/2-stories high and contains 14 rooms. A hip-and-gable roof, pierced by tall arched dormers, tops the structure. Dominant features of the west, or front, facade include the balastraded porch, which is bracketed and has elaborate wooden jigsaw trim; scroll gables; and the massive and highly ornamented bay that juts out from one side of the central doorway. The main porch extends from this bay around the north side of the house; a similar but smaller one is on the south side. Narrow sashes filled with colored glass flank the windows on the first two stories of the bay. Extending from the rear, or east, facade of the dwelling is a two-story ell housing the kitchen. A one-story porch resting on high brick piers and partially screened for summer use, surrounds the ell's eastern and southern sides.

Harry S. Truman

The house is crowded with the Trumans' furnishings and other possessions including Harry Truman's library, portraits of family members, the baby grand piano 8-year-old Margaret received for Christmas in 1932, which accompanied the family to the White House, and other family heirlooms and more recent Truman purchases.

Visitor's Information

The Ticket Information Center (223 North Main Street at Truman Road) issues tickets for Truman home tours on a first-come, first-served basis. Visitors should arrive early in the day to avoid long waits for tours. The center also has an audiovisual program about the home. This National Historic Site is administered by the National Park Service.

Open daily 8:30 a.m.-5:00 p.m.; no tours on Mondays between Labor Day and Memorial Day. Closed January 1, Thanksgiving, December 25. Telephone: (816) 254-7199.

Admission: $1.00; under 16 and over 62, free.

From I-435, east on Truman Road; or from I-70, north on Noland Road to Truman Road and turn west.

Harry S. Truman Courtroom and Office
Independence Square Courthouse
Independence, Missouri

The old courthouse sits in the center of historic Independence Square, where the Civil War's Battle of Independence was fought. Truman's political career took root in the small office in the 1930's, shortly after builders remodeled the Independence Courthouse and added on his new quarters.

Truman's image as an honest, hard worker won him his second term as administrative judge. From the same courtroom and office, Truman launched a statewide campaign that took him to the United States Senate and ultimately to the Presidency.

In 1972, the courthouse attained Registered National Historic Landmark status, and due to the growing interest in Truman's life and times, the Jackson County Parks and Recreation Department restored his office and courtroom in 1973.

Coupled with "The Man From Independence," a 30-minute audiovisual look at Truman's career, guided tours reveal how Truman became one of the most successful and beloved public servants of the twentieth century.

Visitor's Information

Open Wednesday-Saturday, 9:00 a.m.-5:00 p.m., Sunday, 1:00 p.m.-5:00 p.m., April 15-November 15; by appointment, rest of year. Closed January 1, Thanksgiving, December 25. Telephone: (816) 881-4467.

Admission: adults, $2.00; over 65 and under 14, $1,00.

From I-70, exit at Truman Road and travel east to Liberty Street, turn right one block to the Independence Square Courthouse.

Harry S. Truman Library and Museum
U.S. Highway 24 and Delaware Street
Independence, Missouri

The Truman Library's primary purpose is to preserve the papers, books, and other historical materials relating to President Truman and to make them available for research and public display.

The Library consists of a public museum and research archives containing more than 14 million pages of manuscript material, including approximately 5 million pages from the Truman Administration White House files, more than 40,00 books, 71,000 serials, and more than 1,400 microfilm copies of printed materials. Its audiovisual collection consists of approximately 87,000 still pictures, 500 hours of disc and tape recordings, more than 400 motion pictures and 75 hours of video tape recordings.

Harry S. Truman

There are more than 24,000 objects in the museum exhibit collection, only a small portion of which are on display at any one time. Most of the items were received by Mr. Truman while he was President. The exhibits in the Library's museum emphasize the career of Harry S. Truman, the history of the Truman Administration, and the nature and history of the American Presidency. Among the permanent exhibits are the large mural painting in the entrance lobby, "Independence and the Opening of the West" by Thomas Hart Benton, the table on which the United Nations Charter was signed, a reproduction of the Oval Office as it appeared during the Truman Administration, and the office used by Mr. Truman in his retirement years, which can be viewed from the Library's Courtyard.

Visitor's Information

Open daily, 9:00 a.m.-5:00 p.m.; closed January 1, Thanksgiving, December 25. Telephone: (816) 833-1225.

Admission: $2.00; over 62 and under 16, free.

The Library is on U.S. 24 (Independence Avenue) and Delaware Street. From I-435, east on U.S. 24; or from I-70, north on Noland Road to U.S. 24 and turn west.

Key West Little White House Museum
111 Front Street
Key West, Florida

President Truman first came to Key West in 1946 when his physician, Brigadier General Wallace H. Graham, ordered him to take a vacation. Truman fell in love with Key West and returned 20 more times during his presidency and another five times after he left office. He spent 175 days of his presidency in Key West where he first occupied the commandant's quarters at the Key West Navy Base because the house was vacant and he didn't want to put anyone out.

Called the "Little White House" since Truman's first visit, the building was officially known as Quarters A and B and dates back to 1890 when a New York contractor received

347

$7,489 to build two frame buildings, two stories high. In the early 1900's, the two homes were converted into one and became the home of the base commandant.

The house has been restored to its 1948 appearance and contains Truman possessions and memorabilia. It was opened to the public in 1991. Items on display include the piano where the sheet music is open to Chopin, the desk where he sat, and the south porch of the house, or "poker porch" features Truman's original poker table, made by the Navy out of mahogany. Many of the home's furnishings are original, left there after the Navy abandoned the Truman Annex in 1974 after Truman died.

Visitor's Information

Open everyday, 9:00 a.m.-5:00 p.m.

Admission: adults, $6.00; under 12, $3.00. Telephone: (305) 294-9911.

The Little White House Museum is in the Truman Annex at the southwest corner of Front and Caroline Streets.

Burial Site
Harry S. Truman Library and Museum
U.S. Highway 24 and Delaware Street
Independence, Missouri

On December 5, 1972, Truman was hospitalized for pulmonary congestion. The former President then developed kidney failure which led to his death on December 26, 1972.

Both President Harry S. Truman and Mrs. Truman, who died nearly ten years later, are buried side by side in the courtyard of the Harry S. Truman Library in Independence.

Visitor's Information

Please see above information on Harry S. Truman Library and Museum.

Dwight David Eisenhower, 34th President, 1953-1961

Dwight D. Eisenhower's Birthplace

Lt. & Mrs. Eisenhower lived in Fort Sam Houston, Officer Quarters, 1916-1917 (right stairwell, second floor, left side)

Dwight D. Eisenhower Library

Eisenhower Family Home

Eisenhower Farm House, Eisenhower National Historic Site

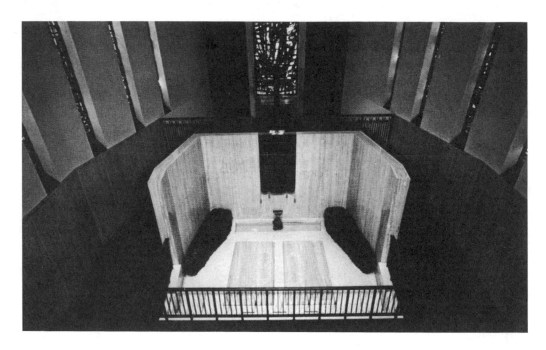

Tomb of Dwight D. Eisenhower and wife

Dwight D. Eisenhower

Thirty-Fourth President
1953 - 1961
Republican

Our first President from Texas was David Dwight Eisenhower who was born in Denison on October 14, 1890. The family moved shortly to Abilene, Kansas where Dwight's father found work in a creamery. Young Dwight (who had reversed the order of his given names) worked in that creamery following his high school graduation, but left after receiving an appointment to the West Point Military Academy in 1911. Although he previously passed the midshipman's exam, the Navy had rejected him because at 21 he was overage.

He was an excellent student at West Point, and played football until he broke his knee. In 1915, after graduating in the top third of his class, he was posted as a second lieutenant at Fort Sam Houston in San Antonio, Texas. There he met and fell in love with Iowa native Mary (Mamie) Doud. They were married in 1916.

Eisenhower remained in the United States during World War One, establishing and commanding the tank training center at Camp Colt in Gettysburg, Pennsylvania. Among other assignments in the years between the two World Wars was a stint as the assistant to General Douglas MacArthur in the Philippines. After U.S. entry into the Second World War, Ike was assigned to the War Department, where he worked on plans for allied operations in Europe. In 1942 he became the Assistant Chief of Staff for General George Marshall, earning recognition for his strategic and organizational talents. Later that year he was placed in command of the European Theater of Operations, directing the allied invasion of North Africa, Sicily, and Italy. These victories swiftly made Eisenhower a household name on both sides of the war.

In late 1943 Eisenhower was appointed the Supreme Allied Commander in Europe. From that position he planned the hugely successful Allied invasion of France on June 6, 1944. Later that year he was awarded the rank of General of the Army and given something that not even General George Washington could lay claim to, a fifth star. In 1945 he achieved his most important goal, the unconditional surrender of Germany.

Eisenhower returned to the United States after the war to become Army Chief of Staff, at which time he supervised the demobilization and integration of the army into the newly formed Department of Defense. In 1948 he published his memoirs of the war, *Crusade in Europe*. He left the army that year to become President of Columbia University, but in 1950, at the request of President Truman, Eisenhower returned to the military to become Supreme Commander of NATO.

Courted by both Republicans and Democrats again in 1952, Eisenhower took stock of his political feelings and accepted Republican party members' request to run for the presidency. He faced a tough challenge within that party from conservative Robert Taft, but ultimately won the nomination. He was opposed in the general election by Illinois Governor Adlai Stevenson, whose intellectual skills, while great, were no match for the General's charisma. Ike and his running mate, Senator Richard Nixon of California, won by a landslide.

Eisenhower had a great deal of respect for businessmen, and his Cabinet was almost completely staffed with them. (When the president of the Plumbers and Steamfitters Union was appointed Secretary of Labor, one critic labeled the Cabinet "nine millionaires and a plumber.") Eisenhower ran the cabinet in a manner not unlike the way he ran his field command, handing out objectives his staff members were expected to complete, without bothering him with the details.

His administration created a new Cabinet level office, Health, Education, and Welfare. He also created a new cabinet level office, called Chief of Staff, in which he placed former New Hampshire Governor Sherman Adams. Adams' job was to attend to the President's schedule, filtering appointments and information as he saw fit.

The Eisenhower years (he easily won re-election over Stevenson again in 1956) are generally considered prosperous ones for America, although the actual economic boom occurred between 1954 and 1956. The rest of the time Ike and his Cabinet battled with an unbalanced budget (which was brought under control by 1956) and recessions in 1953 and 1958.

Down on the farm, the Agricultural Act of 1954 (also known as the Eisenhower-Benson plan) introduced a sliding scale for price supports in an effort to reduce farm surpluses. Two years later another Agricultural Act created a "soil bank" plan which paid farmers to either leave certain portions of their land idle or turned into forests or pastures.

In 1959 Ike signed the Landrum Griffin Act, which was aimed at curbing organized labor abuses. That same year, when the United Steel Workers went on strike (crippling several industries), Eisenhower asked the courts for an 80 day injunction under the Taft-Hartley Act, to provide for a cooling off period.

Personally committed to the improved personal welfare of Americans, in 1954 and 1956, Eisenhower extended Social Security benefits to four million more workers, including farmers, clergy, and local government workers. About a billion dollars was spent on education during his first term alone on school lunches, student aid, construction, and research facilities. The Interstate Highway Act of 1956 began the greatest road building program in America's history.

Though Eisenhower favored private funding of utilities, he entered into an agreement with Canada for the building of the St. Lawrence Seaway. It was Eisenhower's belief that private companies could do a better and cheaper job of developing natural resources, and in 1953 he signed the Submerged Lands Act, which granted offshore oil and gas rights to states that bordered those areas.

Civil rights became a dominant issue during the Eisenhower years. The separate but equal doctrine was struck down by the Supreme Court in 1954 (in Brown vs. Board of Education), and several times the President called on federal troops to enforce desegregation laws. He signed the Civil Rights Act of 1957, which was the country's first civil rights bill since 1875. This Act created a Commission on Civil Rights to investigate discrimination in voting rights, and gave the Department of Justice the power to enforce the voting laws. Three years later the Civil Rights Act of 1960, which mandated federal penalties for those who used violence to obstruct the Civil Rights Act, was passed by Congress and signed by Eisenhower.

When Ike ran for president in 1952 he vowed to go to Korea if elected. After assuming office, Ike did go, and in July of 1953 an armistice was signed which ended the war. Elsewhere in Asia, the United States signed a mutual security treaty with Nationalist China for the defense of Formosa. In 1955 the U.S. joined SEATO, the South East Asian Treaty Organization whose members agreed to mutual defense.

Eisenhower backed the U.N.'s condemnation of the Israeli, British, and French attack on Egypt in 1956. The next year the "Eisenhower Doctrine" committed the United States to help Middle Eastern countries resist communism. In 1958, at the request of the Lebanese president, American troops were sent to Lebanon to help fight internal subversion.

The death of Soviet Russia's leader Joseph Stalin in 1953 led to a temporary thaw between the East and West. A treaty was signed by France, Great Britain, America, and Russia which created an independent Austria. In 1955 Eisenhower called a summit in Geneva between the major western powers and the Soviet Union. But tensions returned to their previously heightened states after Russia put down a revolt in Hungary in 1956.

The 1957 launch of the first artificial satellite into earth orbit by the Soviet Union shocked America. The following year Eisenhower created the National Aeronautics and Space Administration and the National Defense Education Act, which provided funds for the study of mathematics, science, and foreign languages.

In an attempt at detente, Eisenhower invited the Soviet leader, Nikita Khrushchev, to tour the United States in 1959. The short period of friendliness that developed was called the "Spirit of Camp David," named for the President's Maryland retreat where some of his talks with the Soviet leader were held. But tensions returned after an American U-2 spy plane was shot down over Russian territory in 1960. The downing took place while the two leaders were holding a summit in Paris. Khrushchev immediately terminated conference and rescinded an invitation for a visit by Eisenhower to Russia.

In 1959 Fidel Castro overthrew the government of Cuba and aligned himself with Russia and Communist China. To respond to the Cuban threat to export Communism in the region, Eisenhower had Congress appropriate money for a "Marshall Plan" for Latin America.

After his two terms were up Ike retired to the Gettysburg home he and Marie had purchased in 1950. He spent his days writing his memoirs, painting, fishing, and living to see the completion of the Dwight D. Eisenhower Center and Library at Abilene, Kansas. Dwight Eisenhower died on March 28, 1969 at Walter Reed Hospital in Washington, D.C., and was buried at Meditation Chapel, at the Eisenhower Center in Abilene, Kansas.

Historical Landmarks

Birthplace of Dwight David Eisenhower
Eisenhower Birthplace State Historical Park
208 East Day Street
Denison, Texas

Eisenhower's ancestors were German and Swiss immigrants who came to America in the 1730's to seek religious freedom. His parents, David Jacob Eisenhower and Ida Elizabeth Stover Eisenhower belonged to the River Brethren, or the Church of the Brethren in Christ. They opposed war or any kind of violence.

Dwight David Eisenhower was born on October 14, 1890 in a modest two-story frame house in Denison, Texas. His parents named him David Dwight but called him Dwight. By the time he reached high school, he had reversed his names. About two years after his birth, the family moved to Abilene, Kansas. He was the only one of seven boys born to the Eisenhowers who was born in Texas. Recognition of his birthplace was late in coming. Even Eisenhower was unaware of the house since he listed Tyler, Texas as his birthplace upon entering West Point. During World War II, the principal of Lamar Elementary School in Denison initiated the research which identified his birthplace. Subsequently, the house was restored and with the surrounding city block, it was turned into a park.

Although a quilt in the bedroom where the future president was born is the only authentic Eisenhower possession in the house, the furnishings were chosen to be representative of the 1890's. The exterior has been restored and a railed upstairs porch which had been part of the house when built circa 1880 was reconstructed.

Visitor's Information

Open daily, 8:00 a.m.-5:00 p.m., June-August; 10:00 a.m.-noon, 1:00 p.m.-5:00 p.m., September-May; closed January 1 and December 25. Telephone (903) 465-8908.

Admission: adults, $1.00; ages 6-11, $.50.

Denison is north of Dallas on U.S. Route 75 and the Birthplace Park is on East Day Street at the corner of Lamar Avenue.

Fort Sam Houston Museum
Building 123
Fort Sam Houston, Texas

Dwight D. Eisenhower lived at Fort Sam Houston twice, 1915-1917, and 1941. The earlier of his two principal residences is designated as the Eisenhower BOQ (building 688), and in June 1941 when he was transferred to Fort Sam Houston as 3d Army Chief of Staff, Colonel and Mrs. Eisenhower moved into Quarters 179 on Artillery Post Road. Both are marked on historic tour literature distributed to visitors by the Fort Sam Houston Museum. While visitors are welcome on the post, none of these buildings are open to the public. Visitors may drive by and take pictures, however.

Dwight D. Eisenhower

The Museum tells the history of Fort Sam Houston and the US Army in the San Antonio area from 1845 to the present. The Museum usually has a display about the Eisenhowers' time at Fort Sam Houston.

Visitor's Information

Open Wednesday-Sunday, 10:00 a.m.-4:00 p.m. Telephone: (512) 221-6117.

Admission: Free.

Fort Sam Houston is within the city limits of San Antonio between I-35 and Harry Wurzbach Highway, about 2 1/2 miles from the Alamo.

Eisenhower Center
200 Southeast 4th Street
Abilene, Kansas

The Eisenhower Center is the popular name given to the five building complex which makes up the Dwight D. Eisenhower Library. The Center includes a Visitors Center, the Dwight D. Eisenhower Library, the Museum of the Presidential Library, the Family Home, and "A Place of Meditation," the final resting place of Dwight D. Eisenhower.

Visitors Center

An orientation motion picture shown in the auditorium of the Visitors Center reviews the life and work of Dwight D. Eisenhower. It also explains the functions of the Library in those areas not open to the general public.

Dwight D. Eisenhower Library

The Library building was designed as a research institution and contains almost 19 million Eisenhower-era documents. The exterior is native limestone and provides a contrast to the extensive use of imported marble in the interior of the building. The walls of the lobby and corridors are of bookmatched Loredo Chiaro marble from Italy. Floors in the public areas are Roman Travertine trimmed with Breche d'Alep and Rouge Fleuri marble from France. The ornamental bronze work reflects the Great Plains environment by the use of a motif of buffalo heads and native bluestem grass.

Eisenhower Museum

The Museum is constructed of Kansas limestone, and was dedicated on Veteran's Day, 1954. Exhibits in four major galleries contain items associated with President Eisenhower, his wife, Mamie Doud Eisenhower, and other members of the Eisenhower family. The materials are arranged in both a chronological order as well as thematically. The Introductory Gallery provides a synopsis of Eisenhower's life and career from his early childhood through his service as President of the United States. His major careers, military leader and 34th President of the United States, are developed in depth in separate galleries.

The exhibits in the Military Hall gallery include his early military career from West Point to the beginnings of World War II. In the World War II section, Eisenhower's role is illustrated by the use of photographs, objects and documents including his 1942 Cadillac staff car from Europe and the model of the artificial harbor, Mulberry Harbor, and the D-Day invasion. The White House years focus on the campaign "Whistle Stop Tour" of 1952 and various highlights of his eight years in the White House. The Presidential Gallery includes gifts to the Eisenhowers from foreign governments and Mamie Eisenhower's clothes, china, and jewelry.

Eisenhower Family Home

A simple frame structure, typical of family homes in Kansas in the late nineteenth century, the Eisenhower Home was occupied by members of the family from 1898 until 1946. All the furnishings of the Home are original and reflect the simple and practical environment in which President Eisenhower and his brothers grew to manhood. The interior of the house, with the family furniture and mementoes arranged as they were at the time of Mrs. Ida Elizabeth Eisenhower's death, is shown to visitors by trained guides.

Visitor's Information

Open daily, 9:00 a.m.-4:45 p.m. Closed January 1, Thanksgiving, December 25. Telephone: (913) 263-4751.

Admission: ages 16 and over, $1.00. This is for admission to the exhibit areas of the Museum. No fee at the other buildings.

The Eisenhower Center is located in Abilene, Kansas, two miles south of the Abilene exit, off I-70, on Kansas Highway 15 (also called Buckeye Avenue).

Eisenhower National Historic Site
Gettysburg, Pennsylvania

The Eisenhower farm house was the only home ever owned by the Eisenhowers. The house, grounds, and buildings are carefully preserved. The house, 2 1/2-stories high and painted white, consists of two sections. The northern part, in which the entrance way is centered, is of frame. It contains the living room; dining room; and at the rear, a glass-covered porch overlooking the lawn. In the brick south section are the kitchen; the "Old Dutch Room," which preserves the original Dutch oven and fireplace; a study; two bedrooms; two baths; and a laundry room. Six bedrooms, five baths, and a studio occupy the second floor. Northwest of the farmhouse is a two-room guest cottage that was originally a garage. Also on the immediate grounds are the large stock barn, a skeet-shooting range, and a putting green. Original furniture, photographs and many of the President's paintings and other items are displayed.

Visitor's Information

Access to the Eisenhower National Historic Site, which is administered by the National Park Service, is only by a shuttle bus that leaves from the Eisenhower Tour Information Center on Pa 134 (Taneytown Road).

Open daily, April-October; Wednesday-Sunday, rest of year; shuttle buses run 9:00 a.m.-4:00 p.m. (717) 334-1124.

Admission: adults, $2.25; ages 6-12, $.70. (Includes transportation and entrance fee.)

The Eisenhower Tour Information Center is in the lower end of the Gettysburg National Military Park Visitor Center, on Pa 134 (Taneytown Road) near its intersection with Business U.S. 15 (Emmitsburg Road).

Dwight D. Eisenhower

Burial Site
Place of Meditation
Eisenhower Center
200 Southeast 4th Street
Abilene, Kansas

Dwight D. Eisenhower had a history of heart trouble and had suffered a heart attack near the end of his first term as President on September 24, 1955. As the years passed, his heart trouble became more serious. In May, 1968, he entered Walter Reed General Hospital in Washington, D.C. His condition became worse, however, and he died on March 28, 1969. After services in Washington his body was interred in the Place of Meditation, in the Eisenhower Center, across from the Eisenhower Home. Mamie Doud Eisenhower was interred there in November 1977. The Eisenhowers' first born son was interred in 1966.

Built of native limestone, the building harmonizes with the other modern structures of the Center. Outstanding elements of the interior design of the building are the richly colored windows, the Travertine marble wall panels, the walnut woodwork, and the large embroidered hanging, which carries the words of the prayer that President Eisenhower wrote for his first Inaugural Address, on January 20, 1953. There is a meditation portion of the building where, according to General Eisenhower's wishes, it was hoped that visitors would reflect upon the ideals that have made this a great nation and pledge themselves again to continued loyalty to those ideals.

Visitor's Information

See above information for Eisenhower Center.

John F. Kennedy, 35th President, 1961-1963

Birthplace of John F. Kennedy

Hammersmith Farm

John F. Kennedy Library and Museum

John F. Kennedy's Burial Site

John F. Kennedy Memorial

The Sixth Floor exhibition

John F. Kennedy

Thirty-Fifth President
1961 - 1963
Democrat

John Kennedy was the second of four sons born into a wealthy Boston family on May 29, 1917. His grandfather was mayor of Boston, and his father, Joseph P. Kennedy, was a successful businessman, chairman of the SEC during the 1930s, and later Ambassador to England.

Kennedy attended Canterbury and Choate, then attended Princeton for a semester before jaundice forced him to leave. He was then accepted to Harvard, graduating "cum laude" with the class of 1940. His thesis was later published under the title *While England Slept* and became a bestseller. Appointed an ensign in the Navy in the fall of the 1941, he was given command of a P.T. boat after the Japanese attack on Pearl Harbor. His boat was later sunk by the Japanese near the Solomon Islands and his actions during that incident, in which he saved the lives of his crew, became legendary, and were the subject of a book and film called *PT 109*.

After the war he tried newspaper work, but was drawn inexorably into politics by a family that looked to him to take up the task originally assigned to his older brother Joe, who had been killed in the war. In 1946 he ran for and won a seat in the House of Representatives from the Eighth Congressional district in Massachusetts. This seat, which was occupied at one time by the legendary James Michael Curley, would later be occupied by Kennedy's nephew Joseph.

In 1952 Kennedy ran for Senator against a strong Republican candidate, Henry Cabot Lodge, and won. Interestingly, it was Lodge's father who had beaten Kennedy's grandfather in a 1916 race for the same seat.

While serving in the House, John Kennedy met Jacqueline Bouvier, a graduate of George Washington University who was working for a newspaper. In 1953, after he entered the Senate, they were married.

In 1954, while convalescing from several operations for his back, (which he had injured as a youngster playing football and further aggravated during the war), John Kennedy wrote his Pulitzer Prize winning book, *Profiles in Courage*, which dealt with Congressmen who had displayed political courage.

John F. Kennedy

In 1956 he narrowly lost the Democratic party's nomination for the Vice-Presidency, but in 1960, after winning re-election to the Senate in 1958 by an overwhelming majority, he was able to secure the Democratic nomination for the presidency. John Kennedy's Catholicism was just one of the side issues during the 1960 Presidential Campaign. Only 42 years of age, many felt he was too young and too inexperienced for the job. But a series of wins in some crucial primaries convinced the delegates to the Democratic Convention that he was the man to take on Richard Nixon in the general election.

The campaign of 1960 is best remembered for the four televised debates to which Kennedy had challenged Nixon. Kennedy's debating skills, along with the youthful visage (which many had once feared would hamper the candidate), helped him win those debates, and a close election that November. John F. Kennedy became the youngest man ever elected President, and the first Roman Catholic.

His administration began with an energizing inaugural address in which he said "Ask not what your country can do for you, ask what you can do for your country." In March of 1961 an embodiment of that spirit, the Peace Corps, was begun. Thousands of volunteers (among them future President Jimmy Carter's mother, Lillian) would accept assignments as teachers and technicians in underdeveloped countries around the world. The Peace Corps not only helped the people of these poorer nations, but helped offset the influence of Communist nations attempting to sway sentiment in the Third World. It was this struggle with the Communist Bloc that devoured most of Kennedy's attention.

Some of his responses were economic, such as the Alliance for Progress in Latin America, a program which sent billions of dollars to that region. This plan failed to achieve most of its goals early on, and was subject to much debate in Congress.

A political settlement in Laos, where Communists were gaining ground in their attempt to lead the country, was achieved after the Seventh Fleet and large numbers of ground troops were sent to countries surrounding Laos.

Other responses were military and clandestine, as with Kennedy's increased support of South Vietnam's conflict with Communist North Vietnam. Aside from sending troops to the region, he assured the fall of a corrupt South Vietnamese government when he withheld aid. His hope that an honest non-Communist government would solidify South Vietnam's ability to fight the North Vietnamese was never met, and more United States troops were being committed to helping the South Vietnamese as 1963 wound down.

Soon after taking office, Kennedy was told of a plan, formulated in the last year of the Eisenhower administration, to incite a revolution in Cuba. The President, looking to score an early victory against Communism, allowed the plan to proceed. But Castro's forces were well prepared for the April, 1961 invasion, and Kennedy's refusal to commit military support doomed the plan. The Bay of Pigs was Kennedy's first defeat as President and his most embarrassing.

In June of 1961, Kennedy met face to face with Soviet leader Nikita Khrushchev in Vienna. During that meeting Khrushchev demanded that the West recognize East Germany as an independent power by the end of the year. Tensions between the two superpowers escalated over the issue, and as fears of war rose, Kennedy asked Americans to build bomb shelters. In August, the Soviets defiantly erected a wall between East and West Berlin, but later dropped their demands for East German recognition.

Kennedy's greatest crisis came in late 1962, when reports of Soviet Union short and medium range ballistic missiles in Cuba were corroborated by high altitude reconnaissance photographs. Kennedy responded with a naval blockade of the island and demanded that the Russians remove the missiles. The world teetered closer than it ever had to nuclear war, but within two weeks Kennedy's "brinkmanship" forced the Soviets to agree to American demands, and the missiles were removed. Kennedy used his new prestige at home and abroad to get the nations of the world to sign a nuclear test ban treaty, which was ratified by the Senate in September of 1963.

The theme of Kennedy's administration was "The New Frontier." Though the phrase was meant to embody social and economic reforms, it was John Kennedy's embrace of the space program which perhaps had its greatest and most far reaching effect. Following the successful return of America's first astronaut, Alan Shepard, (whose 15 minute sub-orbital flight came after the Russians had orbited the first man in space) the President spoke before Congress to issue a challenge. He declared that America should make it a national goal to land a man on the moon and bring him safely back. John Kennedy never lived to see it, but only eight years later two Americans became the first humans to walk on the surface of the moon.

Kennedy entered the White House seeking the passage of liberal domestic social legislation. The Housing Act of 1961 appropriated almost 6 billion dollars for public housing, the Area Redevelopment Act created an agency to stimulate growth in depressed areas, Congress increased the number of people covered by a minimum wage as well as the minimum wage, and a more liberal Social Security Law was also passed.

When the steel industry raised its prices in 1962 (after Kennedy had gotten the big steel makers to agree to absorb their rising costs), the President threatened anti-trust suits and federal investigations of the industry. Steel prices were brought down in the face of these moves, but a year later the industry was able to increase prices without Kennedy's involvement. Kennedy's struggles with the economy were made harder when a stock market panic in mid-1962 led to the worst economic decline since 1937.

Kennedy's administration also faced a declining gold supply. During 1963 the country began issuing $1 Federal Reserve notes, backed in silver instead of gold. Perhaps the most significant economically related act of his administration was the Trade Expansion Act of 1962, which gave the President the power to reduce tariff duties in return for concessions by other countries, and provided for federal aid for businesses hurt by foreign competition.

Kennedy, although personally committed to the Civil Rights movement, was unable to get legislation past Southern conservatives. However, efforts by his brother Robert, who was the country's Attorney General, helped the cause of desegregation in several instances by using the powers of the federal government. In 1962, for example, under Robert Kennedy's orders, federal troops were used to protect James Meredith, the first black man to enroll at the University of Mississippi. Near the end of his administration, John Kennedy submitted a far reaching civil rights bill, but it was not passed until after his death.

On November 22, 1963, while making a nationwide political trip in preparation for the upcoming national election, John F. Kennedy was shot while riding in a motorcade making its way through Dallas, Texas. He died en route to the hospital. Though his administration was experiencing a great deal of criticism from many parts of the nation, his death was greeted with tremendous sorrow and grief across the country and by people all over the world who had been touched by his vision. He was buried four days later at Arlington National Cemetery.

Historical Landmarks

Birthplace of John F. Kennedy
83 Beals Street
Brookline, Massachusetts

John Fitzgerald Kennedy was born on May 29, 1917, in the Boston suburb of Brookline. The house at 83 Beals Street had been purchased by Joseph P. Kennedy in 1914, in anticipation of his marriage to Rose Fitzgerald. They moved into it on returning from their wedding trip. Both parents were well-educated members of prominent, prosperous, and politically active Irish-American families.

John F. Kennedy spent his babyhood in this house. In 1921, when he was 4 years old, the family moved a few blocks away to the northeast corner of Abbottsford and Naples Roads.

They lived here until 1927, when they moved to 5040 Independence Avenue in the Riverdale section of The Bronx, New York. Both of these homes are privately owned and visiting is not permitted.

The Beals Street house passed through six owners before the family bought it back in 1966 and deeded it to the federal government. It is operated by the National Park Service. It is a nine-room, clapboarded structure dating from 1907, has a gabled and dormered roof and a small front porch. The first floor contains a hall, living room, dining room, and kitchen; the second floor, a hall, study, guest room, nursery, master bedroom (where John was born), and bath. It has been restored to its 1917 appearance and the furnishings are either original or other Kennedy family items, period pieces, or reproductions. The recorded voice of the President's mother describes the significance of each room.

Visitor's Information

Open daily, 10:00 a.m.-4:30 p.m.; closed January 1, Thanksgiving, December 25. Telephone: (617) 566-7937.

Admission: adults, $1.00; over 62 and under 16, free.

To reach the site, take Allston, Brighton, Cambridge Exit from Massachusetts Turnpike Extension. Proceed towards Allston along Cambridge Street and turn left onto Harvard Street. Turn left from Harvard Street onto Beals Street. The house is easily reached by public transportation.

Kennedy Compound
Irving and Marchant Avenues
Hyannis Port, Massachusetts

The Kennedy Compound consists of about 6 acres of waterfront property along Nantucket Sound. It contains the homes of Joseph P. Kennedy and two of his sons, Robert F. and John F. Kennedy. During the late 1950's and early 1960's, the latter utilized the compound as a base for his Presidential campaign and as a summer White House and Presidential retreat until his assassination in 1963.

John F. Kennedy

To the right on Marchant Avenue, stand the triple-gabled eighteen-room Big House, the residence of former Ambassador Joseph P. Kennedy; to the left is Attorney General Bobby Kennedy's twelve-room cottage, to the rear and farthest back from the sea is the eleven-room, two-story, white shingled summer White House. All three buildings are white frame clapboarded structures typical of vacation residences on Cape Cod.

Visitor's Information

The compound is still privately owned by the Kennedy family and visiting is not permitted.

Hammersmith Farm
Ocean Drive
Newport, Rhode Island

Hammersmith Farm was the childhood summer home of Jacqueline Bouvier, daughter of Mrs. Hugh D. Auchincloss, the farm's last private owner; it was sold in 1977. The property's original owner, William Brenton, a Colonial surveyor, was one of the original founders of the town of Newport. He owned well over 1,000 acres of land at the end of Aquidneck Island and named it Hammersmith Farm for his birthplace in England. In 1887, John Winthrop Auchincloss purchased the 97 acre farm and commissioned a New York architect to design a 28 room shingle "cottage" which was to be the summer residence to the Auchincloss family for four generations. Hugh D. Auchincloss, Sr. bought the property from his brother, John, in 1894. He commissioned Frederick Law Olmsted, designer of New York's Central Park, as the landscape architect. The grounds and gardens were then sufficiently elaborate to require a maintenance corps of about 30 gardeners.

When Hugh D. Auchincloss, Jr. married Janet Lee Bouvier in 1942, they continued to maintain Hammersmith as a working farm. Two prominent events in Newport's social history were the debut of Jacqueline Bouvier in 1947 and six years later, the wedding reception of Jacqueline and Senator John F. Kennedy, with over 1,200 guests in attendance.

During the Presidency of John F. Kennedy, he and his family frequently visited at Hammersmith. A Presidential Flag in the foyer is reminiscent of the summers of 1961-1963, when Hammersmith was the Newport "Summer White House." The house is furnished as it was during the Auchincloss ownership. Of particular interest is an upstairs study where a handsome desk is marked with an engraved plaque commemorating bills signed by the President when he was in residence.

Visitor's Information

Open daily for guided tours, April 1 to mid-November; weekends mid-March and Mid-November. Spring and fall hours, 10:00 a.m.-5:00 p.m.; Memorial Day weekend through Labor Day, 10:00 a.m.-7:00 p.m. Open early December for special Christmas tours. Telephone: (401) 846-0420.

Admission: adults, $6.00; children ages 6-12, $3.00.

From Boston follow Rt. 128 to Rt. 24 S to Rt. 114 S.
From New York follow Rt. I-95 N to Rhode Island exit 3 (Rt. 138) and signs for the Newport Bridge.
Once in Newport, follow signs for Ocean Drive and Fort Adams State Park. Hammersmith is adjacent to Fort Adams.

John F. Kennedy Library and Museum
Columbia Point
Boston, Massachusetts

The John F. Kennedy Library, on a site overlooking Boston Harbor, opened in 1979. With its geometric design, made up of a circle, a triangle and a square, the Library has won high praise for architect I.M. Pei. Archive rooms offer more than 30 million pages of documents, of which the papers of John F. Kennedy comprise one third of the total. There are transcripts of 1,200 interviews with leading figures of the times and a collection of printed material of more than 35,000 catalogued volumes. An additional audiovisual department holds nearly 150,000 still photographs, more than 6.5 million feet of motion picture film, and over 7,000 sound recordings.

The Library's museum portrays the life of John F. Kennedy, traces the career of his brother, Robert F. Kennedy, and illustrates the nature of the office of the President of the United States. The exhibits incorporate film, tape recordings, photographs, slides, letters, speeches, and hundreds of objects from the Library's extensive collection.

John F. Kennedy

Visitors to the museum watch a half-hour biographical film, "John F, Kennedy 1917-1963," produced exclusively for the Library. The exhibits seen after the film are organized in sequential sections around a central area containing the President's desk. The sections include, 1. Formative Years, 2. A Career in Congress, 3. The Kennedy Administration, 4. The President and the Press, 5. Personal Interests, Cultural Affairs, and Family Life, 6. Day in the Life of the President, 7. Office of the President, 8. Robert F. Kennedy, and 9. RFK Remembered. The presidential desk in the center of the exhibits looks as it did on November 21, 1963, when he left for Texas. His treasures are still there: the coconut shell with the message which led to the 1943 rescue of the PT 109 crew in the Solomon Islands, the gold Inaugural Medal, and the alligator desk set from General Charles De Gaulle of France.

Visitor's Information

Open daily, 9:00 a.m.-5:00 p.m.; closed January 1, Thanksgiving, December 25. Telephone: (617) 929-4523.

Admission: age 16 and over, $4.50; senior citizens, $2.50; under 16, free.

To reach the Library by car, take I-93/Rte. 3 to Exit 14 north or Exit 15 south and follow signs to University of Massachusetts and JFK Library. Public transportation via MBTA Red Line to JFK/UMASS Station and free shuttle bus to Library.

Burial Site
Arlington National Cemetery
Arlington, Virginia

John F. Kennedy was shot to death by an assassin, Lee Harvey Oswald, on November 22, 1963, as he rode through the streets of Dallas, Texas. He was taken to Parkland Hospital where he died at 1:00 p.m.

Kennedy's body was brought back to the White House and placed in the East Room for 24 hours. On the Sunday after the assassination, the President's flag-draped coffin was carried to the Capitol Rotunda to lie in state.

Kennedy was buried with full military honors at Arlington National Cemetery across the Potomac River from Washington, D.C. At the end of the funeral service, the President's wife, Mrs. Jacqueline Kennedy, lighted an eternal flame to burn continually over the President's grave.

Visitor's Information

Open daily, 8:00 a.m.-7:00 p.m., April-September; 8:00 a.m.-5:00 p.m., rest of year. Telephone: (703) 697-2131.

Arlington National Cemetery in Arlington, Virginia, is adjacent to Washington and accessible from there via the Memorial Bridge.

John F. Kennedy Memorial Plaza
Main and Market Streets
Dallas, Texas

An open style monument, located in the Dallas County Historical Plaza, is a tribute to President Kennedy, who was assassinated nearby in 1963. Designed as a place of meditation by architect Phillip Johnson, it has walls to block noise for persons engaging in spiritual contemplation.

Visitor's Information

Admission to the monument, which can be seen at all times, is free. The memorial is in downtown Dallas near U.S. Route 77.

The Sixth Floor
Houston Street
Dallas, Texas

The sixth floor of the former Texas School Book Depository, now the Dallas County Administration Building, from where Lee Harvey Oswald fired the shots that killed President John F. Kennedy, has been turned into a permanent educational exhibition examining the life, death and legacy of Kennedy within the context of American history.

John F. Kennedy

Historic photographs, original interviews, artifacts, 40 minutes of specially commissioned documentary films, and interpretive displays examine the history and significance of an unforgettable chapter in American history.

An audio tour, including oral history interviews with many participants in the events of the era, gives an added dimension to the exhibition.

Visitor's Information

Open Sunday-Friday, 10:00 a.m.-6:00 p.m.; Saturday, 10:00 a.m.-7:00 p.m.; closed December 25. Telephone: (214) 653-6666

Admission: Exhibition and audio tour: adults, $6.00; seniors(65+), $5.00; ages 6-18, $4.00. Exhibition only: adults, $4.00; seniors(65+), $3.00; ages 6-18, $2.00.

The Sixth Floor Visitors Center is located directly behind the old Texas School Book Depository, now the Dallas County Administration Building, facing Dealey Plaza at the western edge of downtown Dallas. The entrance is on Houston Street between Elm and Pacific Streets. Public bus transportation is available.

Lyndon Baines Johnson, 36th President, 1963-1969

Birthplace of Lyndon B. Johnson

Lyndon B. Johnson Library and Museum

Lyndon B. Johnson Memorial Grove

Lyndon Baines Johnson

Thirty-Sixth President
1963 - 1969
Democrat

Lyndon Johnson was born near Stonewall, Texas on August 27, 1908. His grandfather, a Confederate Army veteran, founded nearby Johnson City. In 1913 Lyndon's family moved there, and except for a brief return to the farm in Stonewall, remained there during his youth.

Lyndon attended local schools, working part time jobs and participating in the debate and baseball teams. After graduation in 1924 he headed west for California, where he worked as an elevator operator, carwasher, field hand, and cafe worker. A year later he returned home and again drifted from job to job. In 1927 Johnson entered Southwest Texas State Teachers College at San Marcos, continuing to work various part time jobs to pay for his schooling. After attaining his teaching certificate, he became a principal and teacher in Cotulla, Texas.

He returned to Southwest and got his B.S. in 1930, and then moved to Houston where he taught public speaking and debating at a high school. Around this time he began to take part in state Democratic politics, and in 1931 began a four year stint as secretary to a Texas congressman.

In 1934 Lyndon Johnson married Claudia (Lady Bird) Taylor, the daughter of a well-to-do planter from Marshall, Texas. A strong supporter of Franklin Roosevelt and the New Deal, the following year he became director of the National Youth Organization in Texas.

Lyndon Johnson was elected to fill a vacant seat in the House of Representatives in 1937, and was returned by the voters five more times. Under the guidance of Sam Rayburn, who was then the Speaker of the House, Johnson learned the intricacies of Congress. During the 1940 elections he chaired the Democratic Congressional Campaign Committee. He joined the Navy after the attack on Pearl Harbor and served for seven months until President Roosevelt recalled all Congressmen from active duty.

In 1948 Johnson won election to the Senate. Once there, he proved to have a remarkable flair for the job. Within three years he was chosen as the Majority Whip, and in 1953, at the age of 44, he became the youngest Minority Leader in the Senate's history.

In 1955, after the Democrats regained control of the Senate, Johnson became the Majority Leader. He developed a reputation as a skillful player in Washington, cooperating several times with the Eisenhower Administration to gain passage of national security measures and the Civil Rights Acts of 1957 and 1960.

A strong contender for the top spot on the Democratic ticket in 1960, Johnson accepted the Vice-Presidential nomination. After the Democrats' victory, he participated in the Kennedy Administration as chairman of the National Aeronautics and Space Council, the Peace Corps Advisory Council, and the President's Committee on Equal Employment Opportunity, among other duties. On November 22, 1963, he was riding several cars behind the President when Kennedy was killed by gunfire. Several hours later he was sworn in as President aboard Air Force One by Federal Judge Sarah Hughes, a Kennedy appointee. He was thus the first Vice-President to be present at his President's assassination, the first to be sworn in on an airplane, and the first to be sworn in by a woman.

Though active in the passage of a great deal of liberal legislation, Johnson was not perceived as a man greatly committed to the causes of civil rights or the poor. But the new President proved to be a surprise. He saw to the immediate passage of some of Kennedy's most cherished programs. The Revenue Act of 1964 reduced taxes, trimmed the federal budget, and led to the longest economic boom in the country's history. The Civil Rights Act of 1964, passed after a bitter and divisive fight in the Senate, assured the country's black population of voting rights, integrated schools, fair trials, and required that any program required federal aid be integrated.

In Johnson's first State of the Union Address, he called for a "war on poverty." To that end, The Economic Opportunity Act of 1964 created VISTA, a domestic Peace Corps, which recruited Americans to work in poverty stricken areas to help reduce illiteracy and unemployment and improve social services. This act also created the Head Start program, which provided pre-school education for disadvantaged children. Johnson also saw to the passage of a wilderness conservation act and federal money for urban mass transit.

In 1964 Lyndon Johnson won the Democrats' nomination for his own term in the White House. His victory over conservative Republican Barry Goldwater of Arizona was the biggest plurality up to that time.

With his election victory and a Democratic Congress, Johnson was able to pass more legislation. The Elementary and Secondary Education Act of 1965 sent billions into heretofore neglected school systems. The Civil Rights Act of 1965, passed after violence befell a civil rights march in Alabama (left unprotected by Governor George Wallace), abolished literacy and other tests for voting and authorized the federal government to register voters in certain areas.

Lyndon Baines Johnson

The Appalachian Regional Development Act, which had been voted down in 1964, was approved in 1965, sending over a billion dollars to the more depressed parts of that region. Public works projects, job retraining programs, and youth camps were part of the bill's provisions. The Housing and Urban Development Act of 1965 sent billions more into the cities for urban renewal and low income housing. A new Cabinet post, the Department of Housing and Urban Development, was created and Johnson appointed the first black cabinet member, Robert Weaver, as its head.

A dream of many former New Dealers was for health insurance coverage for America's elderly. In 1965 the Medicare program became law, providing, among other things, for hospital and nursing home care for people over the age of 65. The first environmental laws were passed during this time, among them a water pollution control law and a highway beautification program.

These "Great Society" programs were passed during a period of economic prosperity and low unemployment. But the costs of the war in Vietnam were beginning to rise midway through Johnson's term of office, and as military spending increased there was less money for social programs at home. The Great Society became another victim of Vietnam.

Johnson faced two hemispheric crises during his administration. In 1967 a new agreement over Panama's sovereignty and defense of the canal was rejected by the Panamanians, causing friction between the two nations. More serious was the situation in the Dominican Republic, where a civil war was breaking out between right and left wing factions vying for power. Fearing a communist takeover, Johnson ordered 22,000 American troops onto the island to help keep the peace. After complaints by Latin American nations, who feared the return of the American "Big Stick," Johnson asked for, and got, a peace force made up of OAS (Organization of American States) troops to keep order.

Despite his anti-Communist stance, Johnson met with Soviet Premier Aleksi Kosygin in Glassboro, New Jersey in 1968 to discuss foreign affairs and U.S.- Soviet relations.

American involvement in Southeast Asia had begun a long time before Johnson was in the White House, and by the time he became president, there were several thousand troops stationed in South Vietnam. On August 2, 1964, the administration announced to the world that two American ships patrolling off the coast of North Vietnam had been attacked. A few days later Congress passed the Bay of Tonkin Resolution which gave the president a great deal of power to act militarily. Thus began the escalation of American involvement in Vietnam. Air strikes in North Vietnam were increased and more ground troops were sent to help the South Vietnamese. Johnson believed in the domino theory, which claimed that the fall of South Vietnam to Communism would lead to the submission of other nations in the region.

By 1966 the war had been reduced to a stalemate and Johnson was unable to bring North Vietnam to the peace table. He unilaterally stopped the bombing of North Vietnam several times as an incentive for talks. By 1968 many Americans had grown weary of the conflict and protests against the war were growing. The Tet Offensive, which in January gave the North Vietnamese a temporary hold on much of South Vietnam, further eroded support for U.S. involvement. In an early Democratic primary, Minnesota Senator Eugene McCarthy, an anti-war candidate, won a sizable portion of the vote. On March 31, 1968, Lyndon Johnson appeared on national television to announce that he would not seek or accept his party's nomination for another term. During that speech he also announced a de-escalation of the war and a moratorium on bombing above the 20th parallel. This last point eventually led to the beginning of peace talks in Paris in May.

Lyndon Johnson retired from the presidency to the LBJ Ranch in Texas, where he spent some of his time writing his memoirs. He died on January 22, 1973.

Historical Landmarks

Birthplace of Lyndon Baines Johnson
LBJ Ranch Unit
Lyndon B. Johnson National Historical Park
Stonewall, Texas

The first child of Rebekah Baines and Sam Ealy Johnson, Jr., Lyndon was born on August 27, 1908, at a farm on the banks of the Pedernales River near Stonewall, about a mile east of the present LBJ Ranch site, in Gillespie County, Texas. Two of his sisters, Rebekah Luruth and Josefa Hermine, were also born in this home, a modest two-story structure that was the smaller of two on their grandparents' farm. In 1913, when Lyndon was five years old, the family moved to Johnson City, about 13 miles to the east, in Blanco County. In 1922, the birthplace home which had been built by Lyndon's grandfather about 1899, was sold by Sam Johnson and after passing through the hands of various owners, it was torn down in the 1930's.

In 1964, Johnson family interests repurchased the site and commissioned a reconstruction. The house is a typical Texas farmhouse of the late 19th century. An open central hallway, or "dogtrot," runs between two large rooms on the east and west sides. In the outer wall of each room is a stone fireplace with a wooden mantel. An ell to the rear of the western room contains a dining room, old kitchen, and a modern kitchen that did not exist in the original house. Furnishings include Johnson family items or period pieces.

Visitor's Information

See following information on the LBJ Ranch Unit in the Lyndon B. Johnson National Historical Park which includes his birthplace.

Lyndon B. Johnson National Historical Park
Stonewall, Texas and Johnson City, Texas

The National Historical Park, administered by the National Park Service, covers 717 acres of land and consists of the LBJ Ranch Unit near Stonewall and, 15 miles east, the Johnson City Unit.

The LBJ Ranch Unit contains the Birthplace House; Junction School; Texas White House and associated structures; the operating ranch with fields and pastures, show barn, cattle pens, and registered Hereford cattle; and the Johnson Family cemetery.

Junction School
Stonewall, Texas

This is the one-room country school where young Lyndon began his formal education in 1912 at the age of four. Fifty-three years later in 1965, Johnson returned to the Junction School to sign into law the highly significant Elementary and Secondary Education Act. To witness this special occasion, the President invited his first teacher, Miss Katy Deadrich, whom he flew to the site from her home in California. Later he purchased the one-room school through the National Park Foundation for donation to the National Park Service.

LBJ Ranch
Stonewall, Texas

In 1951, Johnson purchased the LBJ Ranch which had been owned by an aunt and uncle for four decades. It was located about a mile west of the site of his birthplace and became his permanent home until his death in 1973. The low, spacious ranch house of limestone and timber on the Pedernales River served as the "Texas White House" during Johnson's presidency, 1963-1969. Associated with the presidency were the elaborate communications and security systems and a private airstrip that permits all but the largest jets to land virtually at the back door. Near the main house are other historic buildings including a hanger, a communications building, and garages. The hanger provided a place where the President, his family and friends could view motion pictures, and it frequently served as an impromptu press conference room. Between the main house and the river is "The Grove," an outdoor area sheltered by live oaks that was the site of many presidential barbecue parties.

The ranch is still a working Hereford cattle operation and the show barn and cattle pens are away from the main house.

Burial Site
Johnson Family Cemetery
Stonewall, Texas

The Johnson Family Cemetery is located only a short distance from Lyndon's birthplace and close to the Pedernales River. This is the final resting place of the President and of four generations of his family. Lyndon B. Johnson died on January 22, 1973 of a heart attack at his ranch. His body was flown to Washington, D.C. on the same plane in which he had been sworn in as president nine years earlier after President John F. Kennedy's assassination. Following services in Washington, his body was flown back to Dallas and, after a simple ceremony, buried in the Johnson Family Cemetery.

Visitor's Information

The LBJ Ranch Unit is reached only by a free bus tour from Lyndon B. Johnson State Historical Park (see below). The tour conducted by the National Park Service includes

Johnson's birthplace, the Junction School he attended, a drive through LBJ ranch with views of the Texas White House, LBJ Ranch lands, registered Hereford cattle, and his burial site in the Johnson Family Cemetery.

The Johnson City Unit includes a Visitor Center; Johnson's boyhood home; and the Johnson Settlement, the restored home of LBJ's grandparents; and the City itself, a pleasant agricultural town where Lyndon lived during his formative years.

Visitor Center
9th and G Streets
Johnson City, Texas

Located immediately west of Johnson's Boyhood Home is the LBJ National Historical Park Visitor Center. In addition to information on the various areas of the park, there is a special multi-media slide program on LBJ and Johnson City. Using historic and modern photographs it presents an overview of Lyndon Johnson's Hill Country with scenes of historic places and people including young Lyndon.

Boyhood Home
9th Street between F & G Streets
Johnson City, Texas

When Lyndon was five, the Johnson family moved into a one-story frame house, a block off Main Street, in Johnson City, where Lyndon lived for the next 22 years. When built in 1901, the house contained a front parlor, east bedroom, hall, dining room, and kitchen, In 1907, the owner added a west wing to provide two additional bedrooms. Two L-shaped porches flanked the front, a screened porch was situated to the rear of the eastern bedroom and hall, and an open porch and bath were behind the west wing. The home is situated on a 1 3/4 acre block surrounded by city streets with live oaks and hackberry trees.

With assistance from the Johnson family, the National Park Service has restored and refurnished the Boyhood Home, with some family heirlooms and period pieces, to its condition in the 1920's when Lyndon lived there as a boy and young man.

Lyndon Baines Johnson

Johnson Settlement
Johnson City, Texas

From the Boyhood Home there is a walking trail to the Johnson Settlement. This complex of restored historic structures traces the evolution of the Texas Hill Country from the open-range cattle kingdom days of Lyndon Johnson's grandfather, Sam Ealy Johnson, Sr., whose original log house still stands, to the local ranching and farming of more recent times. An Exhibit Center introduces visitors to the history of the Settlement and the area with photographs, text, artifacts, graphics, and audiovisuals.

Visitor's Information

Open daily 9:00 a.m.-5:00 p.m.; closed January 1 and December 25. Telephone: (512) 868-7128.

Admission: Free.

The Visitor Center for the Johnson City Unit is one block south of U.S. 290 (Main Street) and G Street. Johnson City is about 50 miles west of Austin and 60 miles north of San Antonio.

Lyndon B. Johnson State Historical Park
U.S. 290
Stonewall, Texas

The park was created in honor of a native Texan who achieved the nation's highest office. It is unique among the state's parks in the manner in which it was acquired. Friends of the then President Johnson raised money to purchase property directly across the Pedernales River from the President's LBJ Ranch. In 1967, the Texas Parks and Wildlife Commission accepted the land and created the park in recognition of President Johnson as a "national and world leader."

The Visitor Center is the focal point of Lyndon B. Johnson State Historical Park. Programs introduce visitors to the land and environment of the Hill Country so closely associated with Johnson. Exhibits display memorabilia from President Johnson's boyhood and a wide variety of materials representative of Hill Country ethnic groups. There are also pictures from the presidential years and photos of famous guests at the nearby LBJ Ranch.

Bus tours of the LBJ Ranch conducted by the National Park Service start from this State Park Visitor Center

Visitor's Information

Open daily 8:00 a.m.-5:00 p.m. Bus tours of LBJ Ranch (tour takes 1 1/2 hours), daily, 10:00 a.m.-4:00 p.m.; closed December 25. Telephone for Park information, (512) 644-2252; for bus tour information, (512) 868-7128.

Admission: Park and bus tours are free.

Main entrance to Lyndon B. Johnson State Historical Park is on U.S. 290, one mile east of Stonewall, Texas.

Alumni House
Southwest Texas State University
400 North LBJ Drive
San Marcos, Texas

Lyndon B. Johnson is Southwest Texas State University's most famous alumnus, having graduated in 1930. His connection with the university is obvious with an LBJ Student Center, LBJ Presidential Scholars, LBJ Outstanding Senior Award at commencement, and a major street leading to campus is LBJ Drive.

During part of his time at SWT, he was a boarder in the house now serving as the Alumni House. The house, built in 1896, contains a portrait of Johnson and numerous photographs of him, some sent by Johnson to the school, and others taken of him on his visits to campus. There is also a collection of Johnson memorabilia including the desk, chair and pen he used in 1965 when he signed the Higher Education Act on campus, plus other photographs and books.

Lyndon Baines Johnson

Visitor's Information

Open Monday-Friday, 8:00 a.m.-5:00 p.m., closed holidays. Telephone: (512) 245-2371.

Admission: Free.

To reach the university, take the Highway 12 exit west from I-35 (between Austin and San Antonio), turn right onto LBJ Drive at the City Square.

The Lyndon Baines Johnson Library and Museum
2313 Red River Street
Austin, Texas

The Library and Museum, on the campus of the University of Texas at Austin, occupies three floors of an eight-story building. The Library contains over 35 million pages of historical documents of the Johnson era used primarily by scholars.

The Museum, which mounts at least two major exhibitions per year based on subjects of American history, also provides year-round exhibits, displays and audiovisual programs depicting Johnson's life and career. There are gifts given to the President of the United States by leaders of other countries, American political memorabilia, a 1910 Model "T" Ford similar to the Johnson family car when Lyndon was a boy, a replica of the White House's Oval Office used by the President, significant accomplishments of the Johnson presidency, and a motion picture and displays on the life and work of Lady Bird Johnson.

Visitor's Information

Open 9:00 a.m.-5:00 p.m. every day except December 25.   Telephone: (512) 482-5279.

Admission: Free.

The University of Texas campus where the Lyndon Baines Library and Museum is located is just west of I-35.

Lyndon Baines Johnson Memorial Grove on the Potomac
Lady Bird Johnson Park
George Washington Memorial Parkway
Arlington, Virginia

The 17-acre Grove, memorializing the thirty-sixth president, lies within Lady Bird Johnson Park, across the Potomac River from Washington, D.C. Built by public contributions, the grove of hundreds of white pine and dogwood trees stands near the Pentagon on what was formerly called Columbia Point, and is administered by the National Park Service.

Focal point of the grove is a tall rugged block of granite, selected to symbolize the energy of a dynamic man often described as larger than life. The giant rock, which stands 19 feet high and weighs 43 tons, was discovered in a Texas quarry and transported to Virginia.

Spaced along the walkway surrounding the stone, four granite markers bear quotations from speeches of Lyndon Johnson that express his philosophy on the quality of the environment, on education, civil rights, and the Presidency.

Visitor's Information

Open during daylight hours year-round. Telephone: (202) 285-2598.

Admission: Free.

The Grove is in Lady Bird Johnson Park on George Washington Memorial Parkway, west of I-95 and the 14th Street bridge. On the Virginia side there is a foot bridge across the Boundary Channel.

Richard Milhous Nixon, 37th President, 1969-1974

Richard Nixon Birthplace

Richard Nixon Library

Hall of World Leaders at the Richard Nixon Library & Birthplace

Richard M. Nixon

Thirty-Seventh President
1969 - 1974
Republican

Richard Milhous Nixon was born to a devout Quaker family on January 9, 1913, in a simple farm house in Yorba Linda, California, a village 30 miles southeast of Los Angeles. He was the second of the five sons of Frank Nixon and Hannah Milhous Nixon. When Richard was nine his family moved to Whittier, California where his father operated a gas station and country store. Young Nixon later attended Whittier College, a small Quaker institution, and won a scholarship to Duke University Law School. He graduated in 1937, third in his class.

He returned to Whittier and joined the town's oldest law firm, gaining experience as a small town police prosecutor. He was also involved in community activities, and it was at a play tryout that he met schoolteacher Thelma Patricia Ryan, whom he married in 1940.

Richard Nixon went to Washington in 1942 to work for the tire rationing section of the Office of Price Administration, and in August joined the Navy as a lieutenant. He served in New Caledonia for most of the war.

When he returned to California he ran for and beat nationally known New Deal Democrat Jerry Voorhis for his Congressional seat. Though Nixon was a new member of the House, he was given a seat on the House Committee on Education and Labor, where he participated in drafting the Taft-Hartley Act. He also became a member of the House Un-American Activities Committee, assuming a prominent role in the investigation of Alger Hiss. Hiss was accused by Whittaker Chambers, an editor at Time Magazine, of Communist activities. Thanks in great part to Nixon's work, Hiss was indicted and convicted of perjury for his testimony.

After two terms in the House, Nixon parlayed his national exposure from the Hiss investigation and won a seat in the United States Senate in 1950. He impressed the Republican Party (especially its 1944 and 1948 standard bearer Thomas Dewey) so much that he was asked to run with Dwight Eisenhower as Vice-President in 1952. During the campaign questions arose about a special fund that had been raised to underwrite his Senate expenses. Several Republican leaders suggested he be replaced on the ticket. But in a brilliant televised speech Nixon successfully defended himself, at one point discussing the one gift he *did* accept; his daughter's cocker spaniel named Checkers. The so-called "Checkers Speech" was so adroitly written and performed that Nixon remained on the ticket which went on to win handily in November.

As Vice-President, Nixon served Eisenhower as a foreign emissary, traveling to 56 countries in eight years. In 1958 he and his wife were the targets of such hostile demonstrations in South America that Eisenhower had to send troops to protect his Vice-President. While on a 1959 trip to Moscow, at a display of kitchen appliances at the American National Exhibit, he engaged Soviet Premier Khrushchev in a lively discussion which became known as the "kitchen debate."

Richard Nixon was the overwhelming choice of Republicans to face off against John Kennedy in the 1960 election. He lost by one of the narrowest margins ever, no doubt due in part to his performance before the cameras in four televised debates with his opponent.

Nixon returned to California to practice law and write his memoirs, which he titled *Six Crises*. In 1962 he ran for governor of California, but lost. In a bitter news conference the following morning he told reporters that "you won't have Richard Nixon to kick around anymore, because, gentlemen, this is my last press conference." He then moved to New York and became a partner in a law firm on Wall Street. But California would hardly be Nixon's last press conference, for he was slowly building a base of support which would lead him to the White House.

The political comeback of Richard Nixon from his defeat at the hands of the California electorate to his whisker thin victory in the Presidential Election of 1968 is one of the most remarkable in American politics. Nixon faced not only the Democratic candidate, Vice President Hubert Humphrey, but a strong third party challenge from Alabama Governor George Wallace, who ended up with a stronger showing than any third party candidate in our nation's history (five states and 46 electoral votes). Nixon won a decisive electoral victory, but his plurality was less than one percent.

The war in Vietnam was slowly drawn to a close during Nixon's administration, as U.S. troop involvement dropped from over half a million in 1969 to about 30,000 in late 1972. But his approval of an attack on Cambodia in 1970 created an even greater backlash against the war, especially after it was learned that bombing of that country had been going on in secret since 1969.

North Vietnam began to accept more terms at the peace talks in 1972 after the United States increased its military activity, which included the mining of Haiphong Harbor and the bombing of North Vietnam. After several breakdowns in the talks, a cease fire was finally signed on January 28, 1973. Along with a cease fire, Nixon was also able to secure the release of hundreds of American prisoners of war.

Relations with mainland China improved dramatically during Nixon's administration. In 1972 he became the first U.S. President to visit that country, holding talks which led to the opening of diplomatic relations. That same year he travelled to Russia, where he signed an agreement to limit strategic arms. The following year, when Soviet leader Leonid Brezhnev visited the United States, Nixon signed a nuclear nonaggression pact as well as several agreements on science and cultural exchanges.

When a Middle East cease fire that had been arranged by Nixon's first Secretary of State was disrupted by a war between Israel and several Arab neighbors in 1973, the new Secretary of State, Henry Kissinger, negotiated an end to the conflict.

Nixon's domestic programs, which he collectively called the "New Federalism," called for local government to take a more active role in providing services, and so his revenue sharing system allocated a greater share of Federal funds to the states and cities. Yet while domestic spending was cut, military spending was increased.

Unemployment and inflation created problems that forced him to abandon his hands-off policy towards the economy. At one point interest rates were higher than they had been since the Civil War, forcing Nixon, in August of 1971, to adopt an economic policy which called for wage, price, and rent freezes. This part of the plan was labeled Phase I. In Phase II, Nixon appealed to American's sense of volunteerism by lifting many of those controls. When he lifted all mandatory controls in January of 1973, a sudden spiraling of prices forced him to re-assert federal control with a 60 day price freeze.

Not helping matters was that the country suffered its first peace time energy crisis in 1973 when oil producing nations placed an embargo on oil. Nixon called for greater exploitation of United States energy reserves.

Though the Supreme Court had, in 1971, upheld busing as a means for promoting integration in the schools, Nixon stated that he wanted implementation to be kept at the minimum allowed by the law. This issue became an extremely divisive one, especially after the President, in an attempt to appease Southern conservatives, tried to appoint a Southerner to the Supreme Court. Two of his appointees were turned down by the Senate. The third, Virginia attorney Lewis Powell, was confirmed.

Nixon and his Vice-President, Spiro Agnew of Maryland, were re-elected in 1972 by one of the largest margins ever in a presidential race. But the arrest in June of several men employed by the Committee to Re-Elect the President at the offices of the Democratic National Committee in the Watergate Hotel in Washington, though little noticed during the campaign, would eventually lead to the collapse of the Nixon Presidency. An attempt to deny Nixon's involvement in the "Watergate" affair ultimately failed, as several aides to the President linked him directly to the cover-up. (Another investigation led to an Internal Revenue Service review of Nixon's tax returns, after which he was assessed $300,000 in back taxes.) In 1974 the President was named by a grand jury as an unindicted co-conspirator in the case, and the House Judiciary Committee recommended that he be impeached for his participation in the affair.

On August 8, 1974, in a nationwide televised address, Richard Nixon became the first President to resign from office. He then went into seclusion at his San Clemente, California home. On September 8th, President Gerald Ford, who had been appointed Vice-President after the resignation in 1973 of Spiro Agnew, granted Nixon a pardon for any federal crimes he might have committed while in office. In 1976 a New York State court, finding that he had obstructed justice in connection with the Watergate and Pentagon Papers affairs, disbarred him from practicing law in that state.

In recent years the former president has written several books. He has also granted a few in-depth interviews about his years in the White House, and opened a presidential library.

Historical Landmarks

Birthplace of Richard M. Nixon
18061 Yorba Linda Boulevard
Yorba Linda, California

Frank Nixon had come to California from Ohio in 1907 and worked at a variety of jobs before moving five years later to Yorba Linda. There, he constructed a house and began raising citrus fruits for a living. His son Richard Milhous was born on January 9, 1913.

The residence stands in a small grove of trees at the top of a hill above Yorba Linda Boulevard. The main section of the structure is 1 1/2 stories in height; a shed dormer is located on the north side of the gable roof, which is low pitched and covered with asphalt shingles. The front elevation features overhanging eaves and a shallow gabled vestibule. The rear of the house, probably created by enclosing a porch, is one story high with a flat roof.

Richard M. Nixon

When Richard Nixon was nine years old, the family moved to nearby Whittier. After the family departed, the birthplace home changed hands several times before being acquired around 1948 by the Yorba Linda School District, which owned the adjacent property. Subsequently, the house faced destruction several times. In 1959, however, the school board and the citizens of Yorba Linda officially designated the house as a historic site.

Still on the same site, the house has been restored and filled with original family furniture including the piano Richard learned to play as a boy. In an audio narration, the president speaks of his early musical aptitude and describes life in the modest farmhouse.

Visitor's Information

See information below.

Richard Nixon Library & Birthplace
18001 Yorba Linda Boulevard
Yorba Linda, California

The Richard Nixon Library & Birthplace, built with private funds at a cost of more than $21 million, covers nine acres. It includes the 52,000 square foot, Spanish-style library structure and the house in which Richard Nixon was born. It is the first Presidential center to be built and operated without federal funds.

The Library's archives is the most complete record available for students and scholars of Nixon's life and career. The collection includes extensive audiovisual material, papers from his vice presidential, senatorial, congressional, and out-of-office years, his private diaries, book manuscripts, a complete collection of key presidential documents, and papers donated by other members of the Nixon administration.

The highlight of the library is its large number of museum quality exhibits and displays on the life and career of Richard Nixon. They include his early years, the campaign for Congress, the Hiss-Chambers affair, his Senate years, the Vice Presidency, the first televised Presidential debates, highlights of Nixon's presidency such as Vietnam, relations with Russia, dealings with the People's Republic of China, and other significant events including Watergate. In a room devoted to World Leaders, unique display cases rise twenty five feet to the ceiling showcasing priceless gifts from countries around the world. The center of the room features bronze-tone, life-size statues of ten of the century's greatest leaders: Charles de Gaulle of France, Konrad Adenauer of West Germany, Winston Churchill of Great Britain, Yoshida Shigeru of Japan, Anwar Sadat of Egypt, Golda Meir of Israel, Chou En-Lai and Mao Tse-tung of China, and Nikita Khrushchev and Leonid Brezhnev of the Soviet Union.

There is a historically accurate re-creation of one of Nixon's favorite places in the White House, the Lincoln Sitting Room. It has the brown armchair and ottoman used by the President during his years in the White House, as well as several period antiques.

Throughout the exhibits are interactive video displays to provide added information on a variety of subjects. The theater shows a 27-minute motion picture, "Never Give Up: Richard Nixon in the Arena," which focuses on the theme of "comeback."

Visitor's Information

Open daily, Monday-Saturday, 10:00 a.m.-5:00 p.m.; Sunday, 11:00 a.m.-5:00 p.m.; closed January 1, Thanksgiving, December 25. Telephone: (714) 993-3393.

Admission: adults, age 12 and above, $3.95; children, 11 and under, free; seniors, age 62 and above, $2.00.

To reach the Library from Los Angeles, go south on I-5 to Highway 91, exit east on Highway 91 and continue to Highway 57. Exit north on Highway 57 and proceed to Yorba Linda Boulevard, exit east and proceed to Library in the City of Yorba Linda.

From San Diego, go north on I-5 to Highway 57. Exit north on Highway 57 and proceed to Yorba Linda Boulevard. Exit east and proceed to Library in the City of Yorba Linda.

Richard M. Nixon

Richard Nixon's Florida White House
500 & 516 Bay Lane
Key Biscayne, Florida

After his election as President, Nixon sold the co-operative apartment that he and Mrs. Nixon owned in New York City and purchased two adjoining bay front residences near Miami for $250,000.

The Key Biscayne compound was one of his favorite vacation homes and served as the Florida White House when he was there. The Nixons later sold the homes.

Visitor's Information

The property is privately owned and visiting is not permitted.

Richard Nixon's California White House
Del Presidente Avenue
San Clemente, California

Situated on a 75-foot bluff overlooking the Pacific Ocean, the Western White House is a Spanish-style house built in the 1920s of white adobe, with a red tile roof. There are ten rooms and five bathrooms on a five-acre estate containing lawns, gardens and palm and eucalyptus trees. The house is built around a patio with tile walkways and a decorative fountain.

Known as the Cotton Estate, it was purchased by Nixon from the widow of Henry Hamilton Cotton for $349,000 and renamed La Casa Pacifica. It was a favorite vacation place for Nixon but it was sold after he left the Pesidency.

Visitor's Information

The house is privately owned and visiting is not permitted.

Gerald R. Ford, 38th President, 1974-1977

Gerald R. Ford Birthsite

Gerald R. Ford Library

Gerald R. Ford Museum

Gerald R. Ford

Richard M. Nixon
Thirty-Eighth President
1974 - 1977
Republican

Gerald R. Ford was born Leslie King, Jr. on July 14, 1913 in Omaha, Nebraska. His parents divorced when he was two, and his mother remarried a man named Gerald R. Ford. Young Leslie took his stepfather's name.

Young Gerald Ford then moved with his family to Grand Rapids, Michigan. There, among other community activities, he became a Boy Scout, ultimately achieving the highest rank possible, Eagle Scout. After graduating from high school in 1931, he entered the University of Michigan. While studying political science and economics, he played center on two national championship football teams, was named most valuable player in 1934, and was offered a professional contract by two teams in his senior year. Forgoing professional sports, he went to Yale, where before being accepted for the law program, coached football and boxing. To earn tuition money he became a partner in a modeling agency, and modeled sport clothes for an article in Look magazine. After graduation in 1941 he returned to Grand Rapids and was admitted to the bar.

Ford served four years in the Navy as an aviation operations officer. After the war he returned to his law practice, and in 1948, with the support of Michigan Senator Arthur Vandenburg, ran for and won a seat in Congress. It was during that campaign that he married Elizabeth Bloomer, a model and dancer with Martha Graham's company.

Michigan voters continually returned Ford to the House for a quarter of a century. In 1963 he was elected chairman of the House Republican Conference. In December of that year he was named to the Warren Commission which investigated the assassination of John Kennedy. He was a staunch defender of the Commission's findings, and in 1965 wrote *Portrait of the Assassin*, which described some of his observations of the case. In 1965 he won the position of House Minority Leader, which he held until his appointment to the Vice-Presidency.

As a Congressman, Ford was known as a party loyalist. He voted for the Civil Rights Acts of 1964 and 1965, flexible price supports for farmers, greater defense appropriations, and supported the troop withdrawal from Vietnam. He opposed federal aid for education, higher minimum wages, and instigated impeachment proceedings against Supreme Court Justice William Douglas on charges of conflict of interest.

On August 10, 1973, Vice-President Spiro Agnew resigned after pleading no contest to charges of accepting a bribe. Two days later Ford was nominated by Richard Nixon to serve the rest of Agnew's term under provisions spelled out in the 25th Amendment. Ford was approved by both houses and sworn in on December 6, 1973. He spent a great deal of time as Vice-President speaking on behalf of the beleaguered President. But facing impeachment, Nixon chose to resign on August 9, 1974. Gerald Ford was sworn in as the country's 38th president at noon that day in the East Room of the White House.

Ford's biggest task was to restore confidence in a nation battered from two years of the Watergate crisis. He ultimately changed all but three members of the Nixon cabinet as well as the CIA director, whom he replaced with the United States Ambassador to China, George Bush. On September 8, he granted a full pardon to Nixon for any offenses he might have committed while in office. Although he gave the pardon because he felt it would end the country's preoccupation with Watergate, the public outcry was overwhelmingly negative.

Attempting to place the Vietnam War behind the country, Ford also announced an amnesty program for draft dodgers and deserters which required they perform public service work as compensation. About one out of five of those eligible took the President's offer.

The country was experiencing severe inflation and recession during Ford's first year in office. In early 1975, he asked Congress to cut personal and corporate taxes by $16 billion and for drastic cuts in spending. He also initiated steps to wean America off foreign oil. A recovery had begun by late 1976.

In February of 1976, Ford, through several executive orders, began a reform of the nation's intelligence gathering services which restructured several organizations and limited their domestic activities.

When South Vietnam fell to the North Vietnamese in early 1975, Ford ordered the evacuation of thousands of American citizens and South Vietnamese sympathizers from that country. In April, Cambodia also fell to the Communists, and when the new Cambodian government seized an American cargo ship, the Mayaguez, Ford, after diplomatic measures failed, ordered the Marines into action to retrieve the ship and its crew.

In 1975 Israel and Egypt signed a pact which kept the two armies apart and called for U.S. civilians to man truce-observation posts in the region. This treaty was negotiated by Henry Kissinger, one of the few Nixon cabinet members Ford retained.

Gerald R. Ford

Gerald Ford faced a tough fight for the Republican nomination in 1976, barely beating Ronald Reagan at the convention that year. While campaigning he survived not one but two assassination attempts, both by women. In the general election he faced a heretofore unknown Georgia politician named Jimmy Carter. Ford's performance in several televised debates, as well as the country's desire, after Watergate, for new faces in Washington, cost him the election. He was the first sitting President in 44 years to be rejected by the electorate.

Since leaving office Ford has served on the board of directors of several corporations, wrote his autobiography, and opened a presidential library in Grand Rapids, Michigan. In 1982 his wife Betty, whose courage after breast cancer helped thousands of women face their own cancer ordeal, helped found a center for the treatment of alcoholism and drug abuse.

Historical Landmarks

Birthplace of Gerald R. Ford
3202 Woolworth Ave.
Omaha, Nebraska

The ornate Victorian house on Woolworth Avenue was one of the finest homes in Omaha. The 3-story house reflected the status of its wealthy occupants, the King family. The King's only son, Leslie, married Dorothy Gardner. In the summer of 1913, the young couple lived in this house with the senior Kings, awaiting Dorothy's first child, who was born on July 14, 1913.

Shortly after his birth the new mother took her son to live with her parents in Grand Rapids, Michigan. The King marriage ended in divorce and in 1916, Dorothy remarried. The 3-year old boy was adopted by his stepfather and became Gerald Rudolph Ford, Jr.

In 1971, the birthplace home was razed following a fire. In 1974, following Ford's succession to the presidency, an Omaha businessman, James M. Paxson purchased the property, intending to build a memorial. Based on the winning plan in a design competition, a garden scene of walkways and shrubbery mark the original elements of the former home. An architectural firm added a colonnade modeled after the south portico of the White House, thereby linking the President's birthplace to his home in Washington, D.C. A kiosk, representing the stately turret of the original home, contains birthsite information as well as presidential mementoes.

Mr. Paxson donated the birthsite and gardens to the City of Omaha in 1977. The following year a Betty Ford Memorial Rose Garden containing 400 rose bushes of many varieties was added on an adjacent lot to honor the former First Lady and represent another link to the White House.

Visitor's Information

Open daily during daylight hours.

Admission: Free.

To reach the Birthsite, take I-480 to Woolworth Avenue exit west.

Gerald R. Ford Boyhood Home
649 Union Avenue S.E.
Grand Rapids, Michigan

Ford lived in this 3-story frame house from 1923 to 1930, through his junior year in high school, with his mother, adoptive father, and three step-brothers. The house was built around 1910 in a prosperous middle class residential neighborhood. The house exemplifies middle-class housing of its time in the United States and reflects the economic and social context of Ford's formative years in a Middle Western city.

Visitor's Information

The house is privately owned and visiting is not permitted.

Gerald R. Ford

Ford Family Home
514 Crown View Drive
Alexandria, Virginia

This 2-story brick and clapboard house was built for the Fords in 1955 in what was then a new development. They moved in during March of that year and remained until August 19, 1974, when he and Mrs. Ford moved into the White House. He lived here during his Congressional career and his service as Vice President. The house was sold to a private owner in January 1977.

Visitor's Information

The house is privately owned and visiting is not permitted.

Gerald R. Ford Library
1000 Beal Avenue
Ann Arbor, Michigan

The Gerald Ford Library is located on the North Campus of the University of Michigan, Gerald Ford's alma mater (B.A. 1935). Unlike other presidential libraries, its Museum component is located in a different city. The Gerald Ford Museum is in Grand Rapids, Michigan, one hundred and thirty miles west of Ann Arbor, in the congressional district that Mr. Ford represented, 1949-73 (see below).

The Library is an archival repository of historically valuable memoranda, letters, photographs, and other textual documentation. Most of the material, nearly twenty million pages, consists of office files from the Ford White House regarding domestic and international affairs, as well as U.S. politics. In addition to Ford's own congressional, vice presidential, and presidential papers, there are files of more than 100 White House advisors and staff assistants, the President Ford Committee's 1976 campaign records, and the personal papers of Mrs. Ford and others associated with the President.

The audiovisual holdings contain more than 300,000 still photographs, 1265 hours of videotapes, 800,00 feet of film, and 2,100 hours of audiotape.

Visitor's Information

Open 8:30 a.m.-4:45 p.m., Monday-Friday; closed on Federal holidays. Telephone: (313) 668-2218.

Admission: Free.

To reach the Library take U.S. 23 to Plymouth Road Exit heading west. Proceed 1.3 miles to Beal Avenue, a small road on the left, and proceed on Beal for less than one mile to Library.

Gerald R. Ford Museum
303 Pearl Street N.W.
Grand Rapids, Michigan

The 44,000 square foot, sleek two-story triangular museum is the central attraction in a 20-acre park complex along the west bank of the Grand River in downtown Grand Rapids. The Museum has a 300-foot glass wall providing a panoramic view of the river and the skyline of Grand Rapids. There is a reflecting pool and fountain at the front entrance and a pedestrian bridge links the Museum with downtown hotels and shops.

The main exhibition floor is devoted to President Ford's life and career and to the nature of the presidency. Tours of the facility begin with an award winning film, "Gerald R. Ford: The Presidency Restored," which highlights many of the exhibit themes. These include the resignation of President Nixon, the confrontation with Cambodia, America's Bicentennial celebration, Mrs. Ford's role as First Lady, personal memorabilia from Ford's childhood, gifts from world leaders, and foreign affairs. An exhibit on his first election campaign for Congress in 1948 features a replica of his campaign headquarters; a red, white and blue military-style Quonset hut with the furnishings and flyers of a shoestring volunteer operation. One gallery away is a replica of his last political headquarters, a full scale model of the White House oval office in 1976.

Visitor's Information

Open Monday-Saturday, 9:00 a.m.-4:45 p.m.; Sunday, Noon-4:45 p.m.; closed January 1, Thanksgiving, December 25.
Telephone: (616) 456-2675.

Admission: 16 years and older, $2.00; senior citizens, $1.50; under 16, free.

The Museum is easily reached via Exit 85B off U.S. 131.

Gerald R. Ford Retirement Home
Thunderbird Country Club
40-471 Sand Dune Road
Rancho Mirage, California

After they left the White House, January 20, 1977, the Fords rented a home at 20775 Smoke Tree Lane, Thunderbird Heights, Rancho Mirage, California, until March 1978. Then, they built a permanent retirement home in the same area near the 13th green of the Thunderbird golf course, where they currently reside.

Visitor's Information

The entire area is private property and visiting is not permitted.

James Carter, 39th President, 1977-1981

Plains Nursing Center
Birthplace of James Earl Carter

Boyhood Home of Jimmy Carter

Jimmy Carter's 1976 Campaign Headquarters, now the Visitor's Center for the National Historic Site

Museum of the Jimmy Carter Library at the Carter Presidential Center

James Earl Carter

Thirty-Ninth President
1977 - 1981
Democrat

James Earl Carter was born on October 1, 1924 in Plains, Georgia. His father ran a farm and a store in the town of Archery, located near Plains. His mother Lillian was a nurse who later in life joined the Peace Corps. When Jimmy was four the family moved to the farm in Archery. Young Jimmy was only five when he started work, selling boiled peanuts on the streets of Plains.

An excellent student throughout his life, Jimmy also played on the high school basketball team. After high school he entered Georgia Southwestern, and in 1942 received an appointment to the United States Naval Academy in Annapolis, Maryland. (To fulfill a mathematics requirement he spent some time at the Georgia Institute of Technology.) He entered the Academy in 1943 and graduated three years later near the top of his class.

In 1946 Carter married Rosalyn Smith of Plains, whom he had been dating for a year.

After "getting his sealegs" on the U.S.S. Wyoming and U.S.S. Mississippi he volunteered for submarine duty, and graduated from submarine training school in 1948. In 1952 he became the engineering officer of the nuclear powered submarine Sea Wolf, which was commanded by Hyman Rickover, the man known as the father of the nuclear submarine.

When Jimmy's father died in 1953, he left the service, and with Rosalyn returned to Plains where he took over the family farm and peanut warehouse. While the business grew, Jimmy began to take part in the community, serving on his local board of education, hospital and library boards. In 1962 he ran for the Georgia Senate and won the first of two consecutive terms.

In 1966 Jimmy Carter ran for and lost the Democratic primary for governor. For the next four years he worked to gain the office and beat his Democratic primary and Republican opponents handily. As governor he consolidated hundreds of state agencies, pushed through laws to provide equal state aid to schools, set up community centers for handicapped children, passed laws to decrease secrecy in government, protect the environment, and preserve historic sites. He also opened job opportunities for black Georgians in state government.

James Earl Carter

Georgia law prohibited a governor from succeeding himself, but Carter already had other plans. In December of 1974 he announced his candidacy for the Democratic presidential nomination. Though he was so unknown outside his state that, while serving as Governor, he could appear as a contestant on the television show "To Tell The Truth" without a single panelist guessing his profession, Carter was able to win the Iowa caucus in January of 1976. By August, when the Democrats met in New York City, he had sewn the nomination up, and won on the first ballot. In the general election, facing incumbent Gerald Ford, Carter won a close popular and electoral victory.

From the outset, Carter's administration provoked controversy. His first major decision after inauguration in 1977 was to pardon draft evaders of the Vietnam War. Later, he approved a plan to upgrade the less-than-honorable discharges of deserters.

As he did as governor, Carter set out to cut or consolidate government agencies, and won approval from Congress to begin that process at the Federal level. That same year, 1977, Congress passed, at Carter's request, a reduction in the income tax and the establishment of a new Cabinet level office, the Department of Energy. Later, he would create another Cabinet level office when the Department of Education was created and the Department of Health, Education, and Welfare was renamed the Department of Health and Human Resources. In another controversial move, he canceled construction of the B-1 bomber, supporting instead development of the Cruise missile.

By 1978 Carter's administration was forced to deal with increased inflation. The President attempted to seek voluntary cooperation from businesses and organized labor to help the problem, but that approach had little effect. Carter did win Congressional approval of a national energy program designed to reduce American dependance on foreign oil, but imports remained high. In 1979 the country suffered another oil and gas shortage. In July of 1979, hoping to find answers to the problems besetting the country, Carter replaced six of his Cabinet members.

Carter announced a new program to fight inflation in March of 1980, which included a reduction in the federal budget and a tax on imported oil. But inflation rose to 15 per cent per year by mid-1980, compared to 6 per cent the year he took office.

Jimmy Carter came into office a strong supporter of human rights around the world. He banned trade with and withheld aid to any country suspected of violating people's human rights. He achieved one of his administration's goals when he signed a treaty with Panama in 1978 which will turn control of the canal over the Panamanians at the end of 1999. The following year America established full diplomatic relations with mainland China.

The Carter administration also signed a treaty with the Soviet Union, known as SALT II, which limits the use of nuclear weapons. In late 1979, while the country and the

Senate (which by law must approve all treaties) debated the treaty, Russia invaded Afghanistan, and Carter asked the Senate to postpone considering the treaty. He also instigated a boycott by several nations of the 1980 Olympics, which were being held in Moscow that year.

Perhaps the greatest moment in Carter's tumultuous term of office came when, after much work on the President's part, the leaders of Egypt and Israel signed a peace treaty.

The worst moments began on November 4, 1979, when Iranian revolutionaries, with the consent and support of the Iranian government, stormed the United States Embassy in Teheran and held U.S citizens there hostage. They demanded that the United States return the deposed Shah of Iran, who had a month earlier been allowed to enter the country for medical treatment. Carter refused, and after diplomatic attempts at release failed, he cut ties with the Iranian government and began a series of economic sanctions. But the government of Iran refused to release the hostages, and the situation dragged on. A frustrated Carter approved an armed rescue attempt in April of 1980 which failed, leaving eight servicemen dead. Carter's Secretary of State, Cyrus Vance, resigned over the mission.

Skyrocketing inflation, higher fuel costs, and the hostage crisis dogged Carter in his last year in office. His popularity was so low that Massachusetts Senator Edward Kennedy was able to launch a near-successful bid to take the nomination away from him in 1980. Carter faced former California governor Ronald Reagan in the general election as well as a strong third party candidate, Illinois Representative John Anderson. Carter was badly beaten by Reagan in November, and thus became the first sitting elected President since Hoover to be turned out of office. Ironically, only minutes after Carter left office, all the hostages in Iran were freed.

Jimmy Carter returned to Plains where, after publishing his memoirs in 1982, began involving himself in activities which represent his commitment to the people of the world. He founded the Carter Center of Emory University, which is a forum for discussing national and international issues. He has worked as a volunteer carpenter on projects for Habitat for Humanity, a non-profit organization that builds homes for the poor. The Jimmy Carter Presidential Center in Atlanta was completed in 1986. The former president has been sent to Panama and Nicaragua by his successors, Ronald Reagan and George Bush, to monitor elections in those countries, and he is still a spokesman on the cause of human rights.

Historical Landmarks

Birthplace of James Earl Carter
Plains Nursing Center, Inc.
225 Hospital Street
Plains, Georgia

Jimmy Carter was the first president to be born in a hospital. His birth took place on October 1, 1924, in the Wise Hospital, a one-story building completed in 1921, with attractive open columned porches and a Spanish tile roof. Significant changes have occurred over the years. Grey-black fiberglass shingles have replaced the red tile roof, the open porches and columns have been removed to provide a weatherproof area but giving the building a box look, and the Wise Hospital is now used as a nursing home.

Before she died, "Miss Lillian," President Carter's mother, visited the nursing home to show the staff which room was the "birthing room." She pointed out a room on the northwest wing which was left in its original condition after that visit. It is the first room on the left where the hall narrows to its original width. No plaque designates the location and the room is kept locked.

Visitor's Information

Visitors are allowed in the nursing home but not in the birthplace room.

Jimmy Carter National Historic Site
Plains, Georgia

The Jimmy Carter National Historic Site, which is operated by the National Park Service, has been set aside to commemorate the life of the 39th President and to preserve the town of Plains, Georgia. The rural southern culture of Plains that revolves around farming, church and school had a large influence in molding the character of Jimmy Carter which in turn shaped his political policies.

The railroad depot at Hudson and Main Streets, which served as Carter's campaign headquarters during the 1976 election and has a small museum with original furniture, photographs and memorabilia, is now the Visitor Center for the National Historic Site. Self-guided tours begin at the depot and include Carter's boyhood home, the school he attended, the hospital where he was born, the softball field where he and his brother, Billy, played on rival teams during Jimmy's Presidency, the cemetery where generations of his family are buried, and the Carter residence, which is under the protection of the United States Secret Service, and where no visiting is permitted.

Visitor's Information

Open daily, 9:00 a.m.-5:00 p.m.; closed December 25. Telephone: (912) 824-3413.

Admission: Free.

Plains, Georgia is 10 miles west of Americus on U.S. 280.

The Carter Center and The Jimmy Carter Library
One Copenhill Avenue
Atlanta, Georgia

When he left the White House, Jimmy Carter wanted to pursue many of the interests he had developed during his presidency and earlier. Since those activities would not be appropriate within the setting of a presidential library, Carter conceived a complex which would include a traditional presidential library with its associated museum supported by the federal government and a privately supported Center dedicated to various humanitarian programs.

Initial occupants of the Carter Center include the Carter Center of Emory University, the offices of Carter Center, Inc., and offices for two philanthropic organizations, the Task Force for Child Survival and Global 2000. Contributed by a Japanese businessman-friend of President Carter, there is also a Japanese garden imitating the landscape of deep mountains and secluded valleys with two waterfalls, which has many symbolic meanings for the Carter Center.

The Jimmy Carter Library contains over 27 million pages of material from the Carter White House along with more than 1 1/2 million photographs, and hundreds of hours each of audiotape and videotape. The documents range from exchanges between President Carter and heads of state and diplomatic treaties to records of what was served for dinner and how many paperclips were used by the White House staff. The audio and videotapes and photographs document a wide variety of activities, ranging from the visit of world dignitaries to a foot race between the President and his daughter.

The Museum of the Carter Library was planned as a museum about the American Presidency, and the introductory film and many of the exhibits focus on the office itself and what the thirty-eight previous occupants had done there. Exhibits include a full scale replica of the Oval Office as it existed when Jimmy Carter was president, a formal place setting for a state dinner at the White House, a "campaign room" which traced the 1976 presidential campaign, and elegant gifts given to President Carter by heads of state, as well as handcrafted gifts from the American people.

Specific events in the Carter administration covered in the museum include the Panama Canal Treaty, the Camp David Accords and the Egyptian-Israeli Peace Treaty, normalization of relations with the People's Republic of China, and the Iranian hostage crisis. Centerpiece of the exhibits is a "Town Hall Meeting" where visitors using interactive video displays can ask questions of President Carter and see him respond much as he had during various campaigns.

Visitor's Information

Open Monday-Saturday, 9:00 a.m.-4:45 p.m.; Sunday, noon-4:45 p.m.; closed January 1, Thanksgiving, December 25.   Telephone: (404) 331-3942.

Admission: adults, $2.50; senior citizens, $1.50; under 16, free.

To get to the Jimmy Carter Library from the south, take I-75/85 north to Exit 96A (Boulevard/Glen Iris) and turn left at dead end; turn right at Highland Ave.; continue 1/2 mile to Cleburne Ave. and turn left into the Carter Center parking lot.

From the north, take I-75/85 south to Exit 100 (North Ave.) and turn left; at North Highland Ave. turn right; continue one block to Cleburne Ave. and turn right into Carter Center parking lot.

Ronald Wilson Reagan, 40th President, 1981-1989

Birthplace of Ronald Reagan

Ronald Reagan's Boyhood Home

Ronald Reagan Presidential Library and Center for Public Affairs

Ronald Reagan
Fortieth President
Republican
1981 - 1989

Ronald Reagan was born on February 6, 1911 to a shoe salesman and his wife in Tampico, Illinois. The young Reagan, nicknamed Dutch by his father, took an early interest in acting. When he was nine years old his family, which had moved frequently while his father searched for work, settled in Dixon, Illinois. In high school Dutch was active on the football, basketball, track, and swimming teams.

In 1928 Reagan entered Eureka College in Eureka, Illinois. Although he had earned a partial scholarship, he also worked as a lifeguard and dishwasher to meet expenses. He also played football, ran on the track team, and was captain of the swimming team. In addition, he won roles in many college plays. He was popular enough to win the presidency of his student body one year.

In 1932, following graduation, Reagan became a sports announcer for several radio stations in Iowa. In 1937, while in California to cover the Chicago Cubs spring training camp he was asked to take a screen test for Warner Brothers. The studio signed him to a contract and gave him his first film role in *Love is On the Air*, in which he played a sports announcer. For the next 27 years Reagan would appear in some fifty films. His best known roles were as football star George (the Gipper) Gipp in the 1940 film, *Knute Rockne — All American*, and as a man whose legs were cruelly amputated, in the 1942 film *Kings Row*.

During World War Two, Reagan, who was disqualified from active military service because of poor eyesight, worked in Hollywood making training films. He was discharged at the rank of captain in 1945.

In 1947 Ronald Reagan became President of the Screen Actors Guild for the first of five terms. In 1952, four years after his divorce from actress Jane Wyman, (whom he had married in 1940), he married actress Nancy Davis. From 1954 to 1962 Reagan was host of the television series "The General Electric Theater," starring in several episodes, too. He also spent time touring the country as a representative of G.E. It was in these speeches in which Reagan, a former Democrat who had supported F.D.R. and Harry Truman, began to enunciate a conservative philosophy. He turned his support to Republican candidates such as Dwight Eisenhower.

Ronald Reagan

Ronald Reagan was asked to give a fundraising speech for presidential candidate Barry Goldwater in 1964. The conservative speech drew record numbers of contributions for the campaign. Encouraged to enter the political arena, in 1966 Reagan ran for and won the Governor's office in California. His belief was in less government, and he set out to accomplish that by freezing the hiring of state workers and reforming the welfare system. A tax hike produced a surplus in the California treasury which he turned around and redistributed to taxpayers. He was re-elected in 1970 and remained in office until early 1975.

After attempts in 1968 and 1976 to win the Republican nomination for the presidency, Reagan was able to take the 1980 nomination on the first ballot. The country, dissatisfied with President Carter's handling of inflation and the Iranian hostage crisis, gave Reagan a wide margin in the November election. At the age of 68, Ronald Reagan became our oldest elected president.

One of Ronald Reagan's first acts as President was to propose an economic plan which provided tax cuts, large reductions in welfare and unemployment, and the reduction of federal agencies that were deemed to be wasting money. The plan also called for large increases in defense spending. The Economic Recovery Act of 1981 was passed which contained the largest income tax reduction in America's history.

Reagan had inherited an inflationary economy which in the summer of 1981 went into recession. As more and more Americans lost their jobs, the tax revenue dropped and the deficit began to grow. Congress then adopted what was the largest tax increase in United States history. The recession began to abate by 1983, but the deficit had already reached record levels.

Just as Reagan's term of office began, he nearly lost his life when shot in the chest by a deranged gunman who was stalking him outside a Washington, D.C. hotel. Also shot in the March 30, 1981 attack were three others, including James Brady, the president's press secretary. While a Secret Serviceman (who had blocked a bullet intended for the president) recovered, Brady suffered massive head wounds which affected his ability to perform most daily functions. The President recovered fully from his wound.

In 1981 Ronald Reagan appointed the first woman to the Supreme Court, Sandra Day O'Connor. He was also the first President to have three women serving in cabinet-level positions at once. An early casualty in Reagan's Cabinet was his Secretary of Interior, James Watt, whose embarrassing public statements ultimately forced his resignation.

Other legislation passed during Reagan's first term were the Garn-St. Germain Depository Institutions Act, which created more competition for money market funds by banks and savings and loans. The Job Training Partnership Act of 1982 provided job training for unskilled youths and needy adults. Several changes to the Social Security law were made in 1983 to help with a shortfall of funds.

Ronald Reagan enjoyed an immense popularity with the American people, and was easily re-elected in 1984 over Jimmy Carter's former Vice-President, Walter Mondale of Minnesota.

A Reagan inspired tax reform bill passed by Congress in 1986 helped reduce the federal deficit, but a stock market crash in October of 1987 forced a new round of tax increases as the economy staggered.

As President, Ronald Reagan saw to the largest peacetime military buildup in the country's history. He also pushed for money to support the Strategic Defense Initiative, a research program (dubbed "Star Wars" by the press), whose goal was to eliminate the fear of nuclear attack. As the buildup continued, U.S.- Soviet relations worsened.

Yet, despite his pro-military and at time virulent anti-Communist stance, Ronald Reagan met several times with Soviet leader Mikhail Gorbachev, eventually signing an historic treaty which called for the destruction of medium range ground launched U.S. and Russian nuclear missiles.

In Latin America, the United States and the Soviet Union had each staked out a side in conflicts in both Nicaragua and El Salvador. Although Congress forbade the sending of military aid, large sums of money for other support was sent. In an unrelated incident, the island of Grenada was invaded by the United States in 1983 after rebels overthrew the island's government and U.S. citizens were placed in danger.

The Middle East was another source of much activity by the Reagan administration. In August of 1982, Marines were sent into Lebanon as part of a peacekeeping force during a U.S.- sponsored withdrawal of PLO units from that country. In August of 1983, over 240 of them were killed when a terrorist bomb destroyed their headquarters.

Terrorism, most of it sponsored by Middle East countries, was rampant in the Eighties. In October of 1985 Reagan ordered Navy jets to intercept an Egyptian airliner carrying Palestinian terrorists who had hijacked an Italian cruise ship, the Achille Lauro, and killed an American citizen. The airliner landed in Sicily, and the terrorists were brought to trial. In 1986, after a bomb killed a U.S. serviceman in a nightclub in Germany, Reagan ordered an air strike on suspected terrorist centers in Libya.

The Iran-Contra affair grabbed headlines during the last two years of Reagan's second term, when it was learned that profits from sales of U.S. weapons to Iran were being used to support Nicaraguan rebels. Though the stated policy was not to sell weapons to Iran, Reagan had approved the sales in the hopes it would help speed the release of several Americans being held hostage in Lebanon by terrorists with close ties to Iran. The shifting of funds to the Nicaraguan rebels, or Contras, was made by a group of men apparently acting without the knowledge of the President. Eventually, NSC aide Oliver North and national security advisor John Poindexter were convicted for their roles in the scheme. These convictions were later reversed by the U.S. Supreme Court.

In 1989, following the election of his Vice-President, George Bush, to the presidency, Ronald Reagan retired to his home in Bel Air, California. He continues to speak on various issues, and is an occasional spokesman for foreign companies. In March of 1991, ten years after he was shot by a handgun, Reagan made a dramatic appeal for the passage of the Brady Bill (named after his press secretary), requiring a seven day waiting period for the purchase of a handgun.

Historical Landmarks

Birthplace of Ronald Wilson Reagan
111 Main Street
Tampico, Illinois

In 1906, John Edward Reagan and Nelle Clyde Wilson moved 26 miles from Fulton, Illinois to Tampico, Illinois, a small town in the rural northwestern part of the state. They lived in a five-room apartment, without toilet facilities, above a bakery in a two-story brick building. There were two bedrooms and one was used by Nelle as a sewing room. Ronald W. Reagan, the youngest of their two sons was born here on February 6, 1911.

A few months after Ronald's birth, the family moved to a white-frame residence, called Burden House after its owner, in another part of town. The structure had been built in the 1870's but it had modern plumbing and an indoor toilet. Burden House is privately owned and visiting is not permitted.

Visitor's Information

The birthplace apartment has been restored with furnishings of the period.

Open daily, Memorial Day-Labor Day, 10:00 a.m.-Noon and 1:00 p.m.-4:00 p.m. Telephone: (815) 438-2815.

Admission: adults, $1.00, under 16, $.50.

Tampico is about 125 miles west of Chicago and approximately 50 miles east of Davenport, Iowa, near State Route 172.

Ronald Reagan's Boyhood Home
816 South Hennepin Avenue
Dixon, Illinois

On December 6, 1920, when Ronald was 9 and his brother Neil was 11, the Reagan family moved to Dixon, Illinois. Ronald and his older brother shared one of the three upstairs bedrooms. Their parents shared another room, and the third was used as a sewing room by Nelle Reagan who supplemented the family income by doing alterations and mending. In addition to the kitchen, the downstairs of the house had a sitting room, a parlor, and a dining room.

The house was conveniently located for the family as the boys attended school just 3 1/2 blocks north on Hennepin Avenue. Reagan remained in Dixon for the next eleven years until he was 21.

Visitor's Information

From 1920-1923, Ronald Reagan attended the South Side School, later known as South Central School. Currently under renovation, the school will be the home of the Dixon Historical Center, which is scheduled to open in 1992. It will show the way classrooms appeared in the 1920's, when Ronald Reagan attended there, and contain a museum with displays on the life of Ronald Reagan.

Reagan's Boyhood Home has been restored to its 1920 condition and contains furniture typical of the period.

Open December-February, Sunday, 1:00 p.m.-4:00 p.m.; Monday and Saturday, 10:00 a.m.-5:00 p.m.; March-November, Sunday, 1:00 p.m.-4:00 p.m.; Monday, Wednesday-Saturday, 10:00 a.m.-5:00 p.m.

Ronald Reagan

Closed January 1, Thanksgiving, December 25; all other holidays, 1:00 p.m.-4:00 p.m. Telephone: (815) 288-3404.

Admission: Free.

U.S. 52 passes within a few blocks of Reagan's Boyhood Home on Hennepin Avenue between 8th and 9th Streets in Dixon, Illinois.

Ronald Reagan Presidential Library and Center for Public Affairs
40 Presidential Drive
Simi Valley, California

The Library opened in November, 1991. The building projects Western-style ambiance, with extensive use of redwood, Spanish tile, adobe tile, functional patios, roof overhangs, and frequent and easy access to the out-of-doors and the sound of moving water.

The Library contains extensive archives including the personal and White House papers of the President and his associates, as well as photographs, motion pictures and audio and video tapes.

Museum exhibits feature original presidential documents, photographs, video tapes and document the themes and significant events of the Reagan presidency. There is an exact replica of the Oval Office as it appeared during the Reagan Presidency.

The Center for Public Affairs will focus attention on significant policy issues, both national and international in dimension, facing our country in the years ahead.

Visitor's Information

Opem dayly, Monday-Saturday, 10:00 a.m. — 5 p.m.; Sunday, noon — 5 p.m.; closed January 1, Thanksgiving, December 25. Telephone: (805) 522-8444.

Admission: Adults 16-61, $2.00; 62+, $1.00; Children under 16, free.

To reach the Library from I-101, take exit to Olson Road, proceed on Olson which becomes Madera Road; near Simi Valley it intersects with Presidential Drive. From I-118, take Madera Road exit south to intersection with Presidential Drive.

Ronald Reagan Ranch
Rancho del Cielo
Refugio Canyon
Santa Barbara, California

The 688-acre ranch, originally called the Tip Top Ranch, was purchased in 1974 for $574,000 and is located in the secluded Santa Ynez Mountains, 22 miles from downtown Santa Barbara. During Reagan's presidency, the Rancho del Cielo (Ranch in the Sky), was where President Reagan relaxed by horseback riding and chopping wood. When he was at the ranch, it served as the California White House.

Visitor's Information

The ranch is private property and visiting is strictly forbidden.

Reagan Home
668 St. Cloud Road
Bel Air, California

The one-acre, $2.5 million estate, with a 6,500-square foot house containing three bedrooms, a library, dining room, barbecue room, pantry room, two servants' rooms, a heated swimming pool and a three-car garage, is modest by local standards. Located in Bel Air, a high-priced residential section in west Los Angeles, there are a number of movie/show business celebrities living in the area.

Visitor's Information

The house is private property and visiting is strictly forbidden.

George Herbert Walker Bush, 41st President, 1989-

George Bush's Birthplace

Bush Family Summer Home

George Herbert Walker Bush

Forty-First President
1989 - Present
Republican

America's current President was born on June 12, 1924, in Milton, Massachusetts. George Bush's father, Prescott Bush, was a successful businessman who represented Connecticut in the United States Senate from 1952 to 1963. The family had moved to Connecticut before George was one year old, and spent their summers at the home of George's maternal grandfather in Kennebunkport, Maine.

George Bush attended a private day school when he was very young, and later entered the prep school Phillips Exeter Academy in Andover, Massachusetts, where he was captain of the baseball and soccer teams, as well as class president. He graduated in 1942, but instead of pursuing a college education, joined the Naval Reserves. After flight training he was commissioned an ensign - and became America's youngest Navy pilot.

On September 2, 1944 his plane was shot down while on a mission over an enemy-held island. Though his two crew members were killed and his plane was damaged, Bush managed to complete his mission before bailing out. After his rescue by a submarine, he was awarded the Distinguished Flying Cross. He later returned to active duty, remaining in the service until the end of the war.

His last months in the service were spent at the Oceana Naval Air Station in Virginia. In January of 1945 he married Barbara Pierce, whom he had met just before the war began.

Bush began his belated college education at Yale in 1945, earning a place in the Phi Beta Kappa honor society while playing for (and captaining one year) the Yale baseball team. To this day, the President still bristles when confronted with a coach's assessment of the former first baseman as "good field, no hit."

After graduation in 1948 George Bush decided to enter the oil business in Texas, taking a job as an equipment clerk with a firm in Odessa. He was soon transferred to California to work as a salesman of drilling bits. After another transfer back to Texas, the Bushes settled in Midland. That was 1950, the year that George and a friend decided to start their own oil company. Three years later he and his partner merged with two friends to form Zapata Petroleum Corporation. When the company formed a separate branch to drill for oil in the Gulf of Mexico, Bush became its president. He and Barbara then moved to Houston, where the company's headquarters was located.

George Bush's interest in politics grew in the 1950s, and in 1962 he was elected chairman of the Republican Party of Harris County, where Houston is located. After failing to win a U.S. Senate seat in 1964, he ran for and was elected to the U.S. House of Representatives in 1966. Though a conservative voice in the House, Bush voted for a bill which guaranteed open housing to minorities and elimination of the draft. He also supported the establishment of a code of ethics for members of Congress. He was re-elected without opposition in 1968.

In 1970 Bush gave up his seat in the House to make another run for the Senate, losing this time to Lloyd Bentsen. (Bush would later defeat Bentsen and his presidential running mate, Michael Dukakis, in 1988). President Nixon, who had encouraged Bush to take a stab at the Senate, appointed him ambassador to the United Nations in December of 1970. There he advocated, on behalf of the Nixon administration, for continued representation of Nationalist China, while accepting Communist China's entry into the U.N.. Eventually Taiwan was expelled by the U.N. in favor of mainland China.

In 1973, near the height of the Watergate scandal, Bush took over as chairman of the Republican National Committee. It was a difficult time for Bush, who at first defended the president until tape recorded evidence proved the Chief Executive's complicity in the cover-up. On August 7, 1974 Bush requested Nixon's resignation on behalf of the Republican party, which took place two days later.

Gerald Ford, Nixon's successor, appointed George Bush to head the United States Liaison Office in Beijing, China. In 1975 Ford asked him to return to the Washington area to become Director of the CIA. After his confirmation by the Senate, Bush set out to restore the morale of an agency badly shaken by revelations stemming from Watergate, Vietnam, and other affairs. He succeeded in bringing the agency's self respect back, while at the same time improving its management structure. After Democrat Jimmy Carter's inauguration in 1977, Bush resigned the post.

In May of 1977 George Bush announced his candidacy for the presidency in 1980, but while the head start gave him an early advantage, he eventually lost the nomination to Ronald Reagan, who asked him to run as his Vice-President. The two men beat the incumbent Carter-Mondale ticket in November.

As vice-president Bush took an active role in the administration. He was appointed chairman of the National Security Council's crisis management team and of a task force dealing with drug smuggling in Florida. He was praised for his performance after Reagan was shot.

George Herbert Walker Bush

The 1988 presidential nomination was not handed to the Vice President, and only after some early, bruising primary losses was Bush able to gather the momentum he needed to secure the nomination. He chose as his running mate Indiana Senator Daniel Quayle. The two faced off against Massachusetts governor Michael Dukakis and former Bush political foe Lloyd Bentsen. The Bush/Quayle ticket won easily, and for the first time since Martin Van Buren succeeded Andrew Jackson in 1837, a Vice-President followed his former running mate into the White House through the ballot box.

A financial crisis greeted the Bush administration at the outset, as the savings and loan industry went through its worst period since the Great Depression of the 1930s. Bush proposed legislation to restructure the industry, which included roughly $50 billion in aid. Later, more money would need to be infused into the system as the true scope of the crisis became apparent.

As the Eighties drew to a close the environment became a dominant issue in the country. The largest oil spill in America's history occurred in Alaska in March of 1989, and two weeks later Bush ordered the U.S. military and other federal agencies to Prince William Sound to help clean up the oil spill.

The use of illegal drugs in America was also a big issue. Bush responded with a proposal for legislation which called for better enforcement of drug laws and expanded programs to help addicts. In February of 1990 he met in Columbia, (one of the major suppliers of illegal drugs to the United States,) with the presidents of several drug producing nations in an attempt to fight the drug trade.

Changes in the Soviet Union, which included the reduction of its armed forces, were met warmly by the Bush Administration, which responded with cuts of its own in the European theater. Later, the two countries agreed to destroy a large portion of their nuclear and chemical weapons. Bush developed a strong working relationship with Soviet leader Mikhail Gorbachev. In late 1991 Gorbachev resigned after an upheaval which changed the USSR to a Commonwealth of Independent States headed by Boris Yeltsin.

In 1989 George Bush ordered United States troops into Panama, stating that American lives in the Latin American country were in jeopardy after a U.S. serviceman was killed by Panamanian soldiers. The troops were also under orders to help overthrow the dictatorship of Manual Noriega. The Panamanian president, who had earlier that year refused to acknowledge election results which clearly indicated he had lost, was also refusing to answer charges that he was involved in drug smuggling. Noriega surrendered to the United States in January of 1990, and the rightful winner of the Panamanian election was installed as President. U.S. troops left shortly thereafter.

In August of 1990, Iraqi president Saddam Hussein ordered his troops to occupy the Persian Gulf nation of Kuwait. Almost immediately, Bush ordered U.S. troops into the region to protect other nations in danger of attack. President Bush, using his experience as a diplomat, put together a multi-national force of nations, backed by U.N. resolutions which called for Iraq's withdrawal from Kuwait. A deadline for withdrawal on January 15th, 1991 passed without any indication the Iraqis would comply with the U.N. resolutions.

The subsequent military engagement was brief, but extremely destructive. After an air campaign of seven weeks, ground forces were sent in to evict Iraqi troops from Kuwait. In only 100 hours the war was over and Kuwait was free. For George Bush, who had promised his country that the Gulf War would not "be another Vietnam," the victory brought a national unity not seen since the end of World War Two. But by the end of 1991 Bush was being accused of spending too much time on foreign affairs and not enough time on domestic problems.

Historical Landmarks

Birthplace of George Herbert Walker Bush
173 Adams Street
Milton, Massachusetts

George Bush's parents, Prescott S. Bush, a rubber products executive, and Dorothy Walker Bush, rented the house in Milton, Massachusetts, in 1923 when Prescott's employer moved from Columbus, Ohio, to Braintree, Massachusetts.

George H.W. Bush was born on June 12, 1924, in a makeshift delivery room on the second floor of the 15-room, three-story Queen Anne Victorian house. When George was less than a year old, the family moved to Connecticut where Prescott Bush became a United States Senator.

Visitor's Information

The house is privately owned and visiting is not permitted.

Boyhood Home
Grove Lane
Greenwich, Connecticut

When the family first moved to Greenwich in 1925, they lived in a house on Stanwich Road for six years. In 1931, the family moved to an eight-room house on Grove Lane. This was George's primary boyhood home and he lived here until he left to attend prep school in Andover, Massachusetts.

Visitor's Information

The houses are privately owned and visiting is not permitted.

Bush Family Summer Home
Walker's Point
Kennebunkport, Maine

President Bush's summer home, which has six bedrooms and six bathrooms, is situated on 11.3 acres of land on Walker's Point, a rocky peninsula off Kennebunkport's Ocean Avenue. It was the President's grandfather, George Herbert Walker Bush, a New York Stockbroker, who built Walker's Point in 1903. It later became President Bush's childhood summer home. President Bush purchased the home from his mother in 1981. It is a private family home and is the place where the President and Mrs. Bush feel most "at peace." It also serves as the summer White House when the President vacations at Walker's Point.

Visitor's Information

The President's home is under the protection of the United States Secret Service and visiting is not permitted.

The White House (South Entrance)

United States Capitol

Mount Rushmore National Memorial

Presidents' Cottage Museum

George Washington's Folding Camp Bed, ca.1775-1780

Bust of Abraham Lincoln in the Hall of Fame for Great Americans

MULTI-PRESIDENTIAL SITES

In addition to landmarks and other sites that memorialize individual Presidents, there are a variety of historic structures and other places that are devoted to more than one President or to all Presidents. This chapter presents information on the significant multi-Presidential sites available to the public.

The White House
1600 Pennsylvania Avenue
Washington, District of Columbia

One of the most popular tourist attractions in America is the combination home and office of the President of the United States.

It was 1790 when Congress voted to move the nation's capital from New York City to the newly created District of Columbia on land ceded by Virginia and Maryland. In July 1792, Irish-born architect James Hoban won the architectural competition to design the President's home, beating several other entrants, including future President Thomas Jefferson.

Hoban's design was based on the country houses of the British isles and the main facade is said to resemble the Duke of Leinster's house in Dublin.

Like so many Federal projects to follow, the construction of the President's home took a long time, so long, in fact, that it was not completed until after George Washington left office. Our second President, John Adams, moved in to the still incomplete home on November 1, 1800, a few days before he was voted out of office.

Though his own plans for the President's home were rejected, once in office the third President, Thomas Jefferson, working with architect Benjamin Latrobe, carried out several of his ideas for the mansion, including a terrace at each end of the building.

These would be the first of many additions and changes to be made to the Executive Mansion over the years. Some, however, would not be out of choice.

On August 24, 1814, during the War of 1812, the mansion was burned by invading British troops. Only a violent rainstorm prevented the fire from completely destroying the building. President and First Lady Dolley Madison, who had made the home into a beautiful and splendid national showplace, were forced to flee the city. Mrs. Madison barely had time to save the Gilbert Stuart portrait of George Washington that hung in the house. The Madison's lived in several private homes while renovations continued on the house, and it wasn't until September 1817 that James Monroe, who succeeded Madison, was able to move back.
Additions to the mansion continued. The South Portico was completed in 1824, the North Portico in 1829.

Many of the Presidents and their wives, in their own ways, each added something to the Executive Mansion. Andrew Jackson, despite his rural and "western" ways, was the first President, in 1833, to have an indoor bathroom. Mrs. Millard Fillmore, a former teacher, made the Oval Room on the second floor into the mansion's first library. James Polk had gas lights installed. Franklin Pierce had the first central heating system installed. James Buchanan refurnished the Blue Room. During the Grant administration, the East Room, which had been used to quarter troops during the Civil War, was refurbished.

In the late 1800's many plans were proposed to restore the mansion, but it wasn't until the administration of Theodore Roosevelt that the building was repaired. Roosevelt also had a separate wing built expressly for office functions. He also made official the name White House, which the mansion had been popularly called almost since its beginning. In 1927, a third story was added to provide more living space in the residence. Franklin Roosevelt had an air raid shelter and a movie theater built in the east terrace.

After Harry Truman took office in 1945, there was a growing fear that the White House would collapse under its own weight. The Trumans moved to Blair House, across Pennsylvania Avenue, for four years, while extensive reconstruction was undertaken. The entire interior of the White House was removed after careful cataloging and numbering. Then workers set about the task of fortifying the structure of the building. A new basement and foundation were constructed, and a new steel framework was erected within the mansion. By 1952, the old interior had been reinstalled and the job complete.

Those original interiors later underwent restoration under the guidance of First Lady Jacqueline Kennedy beginning in 1961 and continued by First Lady Patricia Nixon in 1970.

The White House has 132 rooms but only a few are seen during public tours. These include: the East Room, which is the largest in the White House. It is used for receptions, ceremonies, press conferences, and other events. The bodies of seven Presidents have lain in state there, and it has been the scene of several weddings, including those of Nellie Grant, Alice Roosevelt, and Lynda Johnson. The Green Room, which once served as Thomas Jefferson's dining room, is now furnished as a parlor and is used for receptions. Most of the furniture was made in New York by Duncan Phyfe about 1810. The Blue Room is usually considered the most beautiful room in the White House and is often used by the President to receive guests. It is furnished to represent the period of James Monroe, who purchased pieces for the room after the fire of 1814. The Red Room, used for small receptions, has long been a favorite of the First Ladies. John Adams used this as a breakfast room, and Rutherford B. Hayes took the oath of office here on March 3, 1877. The room is decorated as an American Empire parlor of 1810-30. The State Dining Room, which can seat 140 guests at dinners and luncheons has painted English oak paneling dating from the 1902 renovation.

In addition to being the President's home, the more than one and a half million visitors annually almost make the White House America's home.

Visitor's information

Open Tuesday-Saturday, 10:00 a.m.-noon; closed Sunday, Monday, and some holidays, and for official functions. Guided tours given from 8:00 a.m.-10:00 a.m. with special tickets available only from members of Congress. The White House garden is open for tours on selected weekends in April and October and for candlelight tours during the Christmas season. On Easter Monday the traditional Easter Egg Roll takes place on the south lawn. For more information about events and times, call (202) 456-7041 or (202) 472-3669.

Admission: Free.

The White House is located in downtown Washington at 1600 Pennsylvania Avenue N.W. between the Old Executive Office Building and the Treasury Building. The Metro (subway) stops at Farragut Square, McPherson Square, and Metro Center (13th Street) are all within a five minute walk.

United States Capitol
Capitol Hill
Washington, District of Columbia

An architectural masterpiece reminiscent of an ancient Roman temple, the Capitol sits on the crest of a knoll dominating the Capitol City. It is not only a national shrine, but also a worldwide symbol of liberty. Since 1800, except for short periods, it has been the seat of Congress; the flag flies over it day and night.

The Capitol and Congress are closely associated with the selection of the Presidents, the ceremonial aspects of their office, and their role in the government. The Chief Executives are officially elected in the Capitol. They take their oaths of office and deliver their inaugural addresses in public ceremonies at the east front of the Capitol. Most of them held Congressional seats prior to reaching the higher office; and two, John Quincy Adams and Andrew Johnson, even returned after their presidency for further service. In death, the Presidents are mourned in the rotunda.

Thomas Jefferson, in 1801, was the first Chief Executive to be inaugurated at the Capitol. He took his oath of office in the Senate Chamber. Other early Presidents who followed also took their vows there or in the House Chamber. Beginning with Andrew Jackson, in 1829, they have usually been sworn in during outdoor ceremonies at the east front.

John Adams, in 1800, was the first President to address a joint session of Congress in the Capitol. Woodrow Wilson, in 1913, broke the custom initiated by Adams' successor, Jefferson, that the President should not appear there in person. Frequently, since Wilson's time others have personally delivered State of the Union speeches and other communications to the Congress.

The original Capitol was designed by Dr. William Thornton, and the cornerstone was laid by President George Washington on September 18, 1793. In 1800, when the Government moved from Philadelphia to Washington, only the Senate wing was finished. The south wing for the House of Representatives was completed in 1807. Construction continued and as more states were admitted to the Union more space was needed; new wings were added to the building in the mid-1850's. Today the Capitol is 766 feet long, 350 feet wide and contains about 540 rooms on five main levels. It includes a President's Room, an office for the Vice President, and various staff facilities, besides the House and Senate Chambers. The President's Room, near the Senate Chamber, has been used occasionally by Chief Executives to sign Congressional bills.

The famed dome of the Capitol, modeled after European examples, springs from a drum-like base, which is surrounded by a peristyle colonnade of 36 fluted Corinthian columns. Inside the colonnade is a group of long semicircular windows; atop it is an exterior gallery. Above the peristyle, a clerestory features additional semicircular windows. A row of console brackets separates the clerestory from the ribbed surface of the cap of the dome. A lantern decorated with a colonnade of 12 fluted Corinthian columns surmounts the cap, which is crowned by the Statue of Freedom.

Visitor's Information

Open daily, 9;00 a.m.-4:30 p.m.; closed January 1, Thanksgiving, December 25. Guided tours begin in the rotunda from 9:00 a.m.-3:45 p.m. House and Senate gallery passes are available from your Representative and Senator respectively. Telephone: (202) 224-3121.

Admission: Free

The Capitol is in downtown Washington at 1st Street between Independence and Constitution Avenues. The Metro (subway) stop is Capitol South.

Mount Rushmore National Memorial
Keystone, South Dakota

This stunning tribute to four United States Presidents was originally conceived by South Dakota historian Doane Robinson in 1923 as a monument to western heroes Jim Bridger, John Colter, and Kit Carson.
When noted sculptor Gutzon Borglum was given the job, his first act was to select Mount Rushmore as the site for the memorial. His reasons were the smooth faced granite, its

5,000 foot height which dominated the terrain, and the fact that it faced the sun most of the day. Borglum also thought the project should be of national significance rather than regional and the monument became Presidential.

The four Presidents chosen reflect the first 150 years of American history in four of her leaders. George Washington symbolizes the struggle for independence; Thomas Jefferson the idea of a representative government; Abraham Lincoln the permanence of the Union and equality for her citizens; and Theodore Roosevelt the 20th century role of the United States in world affairs.

On August 10, 1927, President Calvin Coolidge officially dedicated Mount Rushmore as a national memorial. It took fourteen years of blasting and chiseling with jackhammers, nine design changes necessitated by deep cracks and fissures discovered in the rock, and almost a million dollars to complete. Borglum died in March 1941 but his son, Lincoln, continued for another seven months spending whatever funds remained to work on Washington's coat, Lincoln's head, and Roosevelt's face, which was never completed.

Visitor's Information

The visitor center near the base of the memorial has a 15-minute audiovisual presentation on the history of the site. From mid-May to mid-September, the sculptor's studio is open daily and evening lighting programs are presented in the amphitheater.

Open daily 8:00 a.m.-10:00 p.m., mid-May to mid-September; rest of year, 8:00-5:00 p.m.
Telephone: (605) 574-2523.
Admission: free.
Mount Rushmore is 25 miles southwest of Rapid City and three miles from Keystone, South Dakota, on State Route 244.

Presidents' Cottage Museum
The Greenbrier
White Sulphur Springs, West Virginia

The story that in 1778, a woman helpless with rheumatism was cured after being immersed in a pool of sulphur water near The Greenbrier, brought hordes of ailing people to the "magic fountain." Soon rustic shelters and log cabins were built to be rented to eager visitors.

In 1834, a wealthy New Orleans plantation owner, Stephen Henderson, built a two-story colonnaded home overlooking the spring. It later became known as the Presidents' Cottage because of the many United States Presidents who spent their summers there. These included Martin Van Buren, Millard Fillmore, Franklin Pierce, and James Buchanan. John Tyler was the most frequent visitor and spent his honeymoon here in 1844 following his marriage to Julia Gardner of New York. Van Buren, Fillmore, and Tyler used the Cottage as a summer White House.

The Greenbrier, which owns the President's Cottage, is a famous world class resort which has also been host to at least twelve other Presidents from Andrew Jackson to Lyndon Johnson. For unknown reasons, the Presidents who visited after the Civil War did not stay in this cottage, but in other cottages or, in this century, in The Greenbrier Hotel.

The house originally consisted of just four rooms, two downstairs and two upstairs; two back rooms were added later. There is no kitchen as guests took their meals in a separate dining room that stood in the middle of the grounds, or after it opened, in the hotel's main dining room.

In 1931 the cottage was renovated to create The Presidents' Cottage Museum which contains 19th century artifacts, documents, books, photographs and a scale model of White Sulphur Springs in 1859.

Visitor's Information

The Museum is available to guests of The Greenbrier. Telephone: (304) 536-1110.

The Greenbrier is easily accessible by car via I-64.

St. John's Episcopal Church
Corner of 16th and H Streets NW
Washington, District of Columbia

The "Church of Presidents," across from Lafayette Square, is an excellent example of Federal-style architecture and was one of the first buildings, after the White House, built around the square. It was designed by Benjamin Latrobe and constructed in 1815-16 in the form of a Greek cross. A lantern cupola sitting above a flat dome dominates the gabled roofline, which towers above the high sidewalls. At the intersections of the transepts are four massive pillars.

When the church opened, a pew was reserved for President Madison. He chose Number 28, later redesignated Number 54, and the next five Presidents, Monroe, John Quincy Adams, Jackson, Van Buren, and William Henry Harrison occupied the pew. Since then, by tradition, pew 54 has been set aside for the President. Recent Presidents who have attended include Franklin D. Roosevelt, Truman, Eisenhower, Kennedy, Lyndon B. Johnson, and Bush.

Visitor's Information

Open daily, 8:00 a.m.-4:00 p.m. Telephone: (202) 347-8766.

Admission: Free.

St. John's Episcopal Church is in downtown Washington near the McPherson Square Metro station.

The Museum of the Presidents
Lincoln College
300 Keokuk
Lincoln, Illinois

The Museum is located in the same facility as the Lincoln Museum; the McKinstry Memorial Library in Lincoln College. On display are documents signed by every President and, in some instances, entirely in the President's own handwriting, together with their pictures and commemorative medals.

Visitor's Information

Open Monday-Friday, 10:00 a.m.-noon, 1:00 p.m.-4:30 p.m.; Saturday-Sunday, 1:00 p.m.-4:30 p.m.

Admission: Free.

Lincoln College is located at the intersection of State Routes 10 and 121.

Henry Ford Museum & Greenfield Village
20900 Oakwood Boulevard
Dearborn, Michigan

This sprawling museum complex covers ninety-three indoor and outdoor acres and spans more than 300 years, exploring the sweeping technological changes that transformed America from a rural, agrarian society to an urban, industrial nation. There are exhibits dealing with transportation, agriculture, communications, entertainment, domestic life, and power and industry.

The Henry Ford Museum contains several Presidential items. Its Transportation Collection features four Presidential vehicles: the 1961 Lincoln that President Kennedy was riding in when he was assassinated, the 1939 "Sunshine Special" Lincoln used by Presidents Franklin Roosevelt and Harry Truman, the 1950 Lincoln Cosmopolitan "Bubble-top" which was used by Presidents Truman, Eisenhower, and Kennedy, as well as a 1902 Brougham used by President Theodore Roosevelt.

The museum also displays a leather trunk containing a folding camp bed used by George Washington during the American Revolution, and a Victorian Rocking chair in which Abraham Lincoln was sitting during the performance of "Our American Cousin" at Ford's Theater in Washington, D.C. when he was shot. In addition to the chair, his playbill, and the shawl brought to him on that fateful evening are exhibited.

Greenfield Village is famous for its historic sites and homes that have been moved here and restored to their original condition. The courthouse used by Abraham Lincoln when he traveled the Illinois "mud circuit" as a young attorney is part of its collection.

Visitor's Information

Open daily 9:00 a.m.-5:00 p.m.; closed Thanksgiving and December 25. Greenfield Village building interiors are closed January 2 to mid-March. Telephone: (313) 271-1620.

Admission to either Henry Ford Museum or Greenfield Village: adults, $11.50; 62+, $10.50; ages 5-12, $5.75. Combination tickets to both Museum and Village: adults, $20.00; ages 5-12, $10.00.

Entrances to the Museum and Village are located on Village Drive at Oakwood Boulevard, just west of the Southfield Freeway (M-39) and just south of Michigan Avenue (US 12). Interstate routes I-75 and I-94 also provide access from all directions.

Hall of the Presidents Living Wax Studio
1050 S. 21 Street
Colorado Springs, Colorado

More than one hundred life-size wax figures crafted at the London Studios of Madame Josephine Tussaud include all United States Presidents and many First Ladies. The figures are placed in related settings such as Thomas Jefferson making finishing touches on the final draft of the Declaration of Independence and Teddy Roosevelt charging up San Juan Hill.

Visitor's Information

Open daily, 9:00 a.m.-9:00 p.m., June-September; 10:00 a.m.-5:00 p.m., rest of year. Telephone: (719) 635-3553.

Admission: adults, $3.50; ages 6-11, $1.75.

From I-25 take Exit 141 West, 2 miles on U.S. 24 to 21st Street.

Parade of Presidents Wax Museum
Highway 16A South
Keystone, South Dakota

This Wax Museum, just two and a half miles from Mount Rushmore, features the Presidents of the United States and many other figures of historical significance. Each President is in a setting that displays one of his more memorable deeds. For example, John Adams and Thomas Jefferson are shown signing the Declaration of Independence, Franklin Roosevelt is meeting with Joseph Stalin and Winston Churchill at Yalta in 1945, and Abraham Lincoln is debating Stephen Douglas.

Visitor's Information

Open mid-April to October 1; 8:30 a.m.-7:30 p.m., Memorial Day-Labor Day; 9:00 a.m.-5:00 p.m., remainder of season. Telephone: (605) 666-4455.

Admission: adults, $5.00; children, $2.50; under 6, free.

To reach the Museum take Route 16A south from Mount Rushmore.

United States Army Quartermaster Museum
Fort Lee, Virginia

The Quartermaster Corps was founded only two days after the Army itself in 1775, and is the oldest service corps in the U.S. Army. The Museum is devoted to the history of the Quartermaster Corps. Among the displays are military uniforms, weapons and equipment dating from 1775. Presidential-related items include saddles used by Franklin Pierce and Ulysses S. Grant, and Presidential flags used by Presidents Theodore Roosevelt, Taft, Wilson, Harding, Truman, and Eisenhower. The Museum also has President Eisenhower's

Mess Uniform Jacket, olive drab uniform coat, and the catafalque on which his casket rested during his funeral ceremony.

Visitor's Information

Open Tuesday-Friday, 10:00 a.m.-5:00 p.m.; Saturday & Sunday, 11:00 a.m.-5:00 p.m.; closed Mondays, Thanksgiving, December 25 and January 1. Telephone: (804) 734-1854.

Admission: Free.

The entrance to Fort Lee is on State Route 36, two miles east of Petersburg.

The Hall of Fame for Great Americans
University Avenue and West 181st Street
Bronx, New York

Designed by renowned architect Stanford White in 1901, this 630 foot sweeping granite colonnade houses the bronze portrait busts of 97 great Americans. Of these, twelve are United States Presidents.

The Hall of Fame was founded in 1900 by New York University to encourage deeper appreciation of the illustrious individuals who have contributed to the American experience. Modeled after the Parthenon in Rome, the rotunda is adorned by 16 Corinthian columns of Connemara green marble and crowned by a coffered dome. Here, along with authors, artists, educators, theologians, and scientists, are the busts of George Washington, John Adams, Thomas Jefferson, Abraham Lincoln, James Madison, John Quincy Adams, Andrew Jackson, James Monroe, Grover Cleveland, Theodore Roosevelt, Woodrow Wilson, and Ulysses S. Grant. Also elected is Franklin D. Roosevelt, whose bust has not yet been created.

Visitor's Information

Open daily, 10:00 a.m.-5:00 p.m. Telephone: (212) 220-6312.
Admission: Free.

The Hall of Fame is located on the campus of Bronx Community College. The main entrance is at Hall of Fame Drive, which is west of University Avenue between 180th and 181st Streets. By subway from Manhattan, take the number 4 train on the Lexington Avenue line in the direction of Woodlawn. Get off at Burnside Avenue and walk west (up the hill) three blocks to University Avenue, turn right and proceed to the campus entrance.

National Portrait Gallery
Smithsonian Institution
8th and F Streets NW
Washington, District of Columbia

The National Portrait Gallery is located in the Old Patent Office Building, one of the oldest government buildings in Washington. During the Civil War it served as a hospital and was the scene of Lincoln's second inaugural ball. The beautiful restored building has a courtyard with twin-cast fountains and a sculpture garden.

The Gallery is devoted exclusively to portraiture, and displays paintings, drawings, prints, sculptures and photographs of Americans who have contributed significantly to the history, development and culture of the nation. With the exception of Presidential portraits and special exhibitions, works are not displayed or admitted to the permanent collection until ten years after the subject's death.

The Hall of Presidents, located on the second floor of the Gallery, is decorated in the grand style of the mid-nineteenth century, and features portraits and associative items which describe the interplay of public and private events in the lives of our chief executives. There are Presidential paintings by Gilbert Stuart and John Trumbull, collections of Time magazine covers, Matthew Brady photographs, and the last photograph ever taken of Abraham Lincoln.

Visitor's Information

Open daily, 10:00 a.m.-5:30 p.m.; closed December 25. Telephone: (202) 357-2700.

Admission: Free.

The Gallery can be reached with the Metro system, Yellow and red lines, to Gallery Place station; use 9th Street exit.

Independence National Historical Park
Third and Chestnut Streets
Philadelphia, Pennsylvania

In this park, at Congress Hall, during the period that Philadelphia served as the Nation's Capital (1790-1800), occurred the inaugurations of George Washington, for his second Presidential term, and John Adams. Other structures in the complex also have association with the Presidents. The park, in the old portion of the city, was also the scene of many aspects of the Nation's founding and initial growth and several momentous national events. These include meetings of the First and Second Continental Congresses; adoption and signing of the Declaration of Independence, which marked the creation of the United States; and the labors of the Constitutional Convention of 1787, which perpetuated it.

The nucleus of the park and its outstanding historical buildings is Independence Hall. Built between 1732 and 1756 as the State House for the Province of Pennsylvania, both the Second Continental Congress and Constitutional Convention convened there. Serving in those bodies were future Presidents Washington, John Adams, Jefferson, and Madison. The carefully restored, stately, and symmetrical hall, a 2 1/2-story red brick structure, is the most beautiful 18th-century public building of Georgian style surviving in the United States.

The interior focus of interest is the Assembly Room, the east one on the first floor, where the Declaration of Independence and the Constitution were formulated and signed. It has been restored to its appearance at the time of the Continental Congress.

The First Continental Congress, which included George Washington and John Adams, met in Carpenters' Hall, two blocks east of Independence Hall, on Chestnut Street between Third and Fourth Streets. It has a small collection of Windsor chairs used by the delegates and other memorabilia.

In connection with the U.S. Bicentennial celebration, the National Park Service had reconstructed the Jacob Graff, Jr. House and City Tavern. Two blocks west of Independence Hall, on the southwest corner of Seventh and Market Streets, the 3 1/2-story brick Graff House, is where Jefferson, a roomer, wrote the Declaration of Independence. The first floor contains displays; the parlor and bedroom that Jefferson lived in on the second floor have been restored and are furnished with period pieces. City Tavern, at the northwest corner of Walnut and Second Streets, where members of the Constitutional Convention and Continental Congress and Government officials, including some future Presidents, stayed while in Philadelphia, is furnished and operated as an 18th-century tavern

Visitor's Information

The Park Visitor Center at Third and Chestnut Streets shows a 28-minute film, "Independence" and Rangers there can provide helpful information about the site.

Open daily, 9:00 a.m.-5:00 p.m.; Independence Hall and some other buildings remain open into the evening during the summer. Visitor Center closed January 1 and December 25. Carpenters' Hall open Tuesday-Sunday, 10:00 a.m.-4:00 p.m.; closed January 1, Easter, Thanksgiving, December 25, and Tuesdays during January and February. Telephone: (215) 597-8974.

Admission: Free

The following directions lead to a parking garage on 2nd Street between Chestnut and Walnut Streets. *Eastbound* via I-76 (Schuykill Expressway): Exit at Vine Street (I-676 and US 30) and follow to 6th Street. Turn right on 6th and follow to Chestnut. Turn left on Chestnut and follow to 2nd and turn right on 2nd Street. *Westbound* via Benjamin Franklin Bridge (US 30): From the bridge follow signs to 6th Street (south). From there follow Eastbound directions. *Southbound* via I-95: Take the Center Street exit to 2nd Street. *Northbound* via I-95: Use exit marked "Historic Area." Continue straight ahead to Reed Street. Turn right and follow to Delaware Avenue. Turn left on Delaware and follow to exit for Market Street (on right). At Market, make an immediate left onto 2nd Street.

The Presidential Museum
622 North Lee Avenue
Odessa, Texas

Immediately after the assassination of John F. Kennedy, a group of Odessa citizens met to discuss a memorial to the slain President. The idea was expanded into a museum and memorial to the presidency and those who have held the office.

The Presidential Room opened in the basement of the Ector County Library in 1965. Over the years it expanded, first taking over the entire basement and changing its name to The Presidential Museum and then, when the library moved to another building in 1981, it expanded into the entire building.

The Museum is the only one in the country devoted to the Office of the President. It features collections related to the Presidents, Vice-Presidents, First Ladies, also-ran candidates, and Presidents of the Republic of Texas. The bulk of the collection is campaign material, but also includes portraits, signatures, documents, commemorative items, and original cartoons. The Hall of Presidents gallery features the Dishong collection of First Lady inaugural gown replicas.

There is also a 3,500 volume library on subjects related to the Presidents and the Office of the Presidency.

Visitor's Information

Open 10:00 a.m.-5:00 p.m., Tuesday-Saturday; closed Sunday, Monday, and most major holidays. Telephone: (915) 332-7123.

Admission: Free.

The Museum is located on the corner of 7th Street and Lee Avenue, one block west of Grant Avenue (US Highway 385).

GEOGRAPHICAL INDEX

District of Columbia

Geographical Index

Mississippi

Missouri

Nebraska

Geographical Index

Geographical Index

Geographical Index

Geographical Index

INDEX OF ILLUSTRATIONS

James Knox Polk

Zachary Taylor

Millard Fillmore

Franklin Pierce

James Buchanan

Abraham Lincoln

Andrew Johnson

William Howard Taft

Woodrow Wilson

Warren Gamaliel Harding

James Carter

Ronald Wilson Reagan

George Herbert Walker Bush

Multi-Presidential Sites